CABINET-MAKING
IN EASY STAGES

CABINET-MAKING IN EASY STAGES

Dr. J. J. SHENKMAN

ARGUS BOOKS LIMITED

ARGUS BOOKS LIMITED
Model & Allied Publications
Wolsey House
Wolsey Road
Hemel Hempstead
Herts HP2 4SS

© Argus Books Ltd 1984

First published 1984

ISNB 0 85242 833 2

Phototypesetting by Grange Filmsetting Ltd, Birmingham
Printed by R. J. Acford, Chichester

Contents

INTRODUCTION   7

1. THE SMALL WORKBENCH   9
How to make a simple multi-purpose small workbench with only a saw, hammer, drill and screwdriver.

2. THE UPHOLSTERED BOX STOOL   12
A solidly constructed useful upholstered stool with storage for magazines, toys or clothes, made on the small workbench and introducing some basic cabinet-making techniques.

3. THE WORKSHED AND WORK CABINET   20
If making the stool was enjoyable, how to go about setting up a workshop and making a custom-built work cabinet.

4. SHARPENING SAWS, CHISELS AND PLANES   24
Why tools dull, compositions of steel, tempering. Grindstones and sharpening stones, protecting chisels, sharpening scrapers. Saw setting and sharpening, including making a saw anvil.

5. SAWING, CHISELLING AND PLANING   30
Types of tools and how to use them.

6. GLUEING   36
Jointing or glueing, how glue works, structure of wood, preparation of surfaces, demonstration by repair and cannibalisation of cricket bats.

7. THE SMALL HARDWOOD BOOKCASE   39
A small, attractive bookcase in solid oak with two shelves, a drawer and a secret drawer. Further cabinet-making joints and methods, including various dovetails and inlay work.

8. FINDING, GETTING AND SEASONING CABINET-MAKING WOODS   49
Likely sources, tree cutting and log sawing, preservation. What happens during seasoning and how to treat individual timbers.

9. VENEER CUTTING AND VENEERING   55
Reasons for veneers. A home-made veneer saw of remarkable accuracy and flexibility. Preparation of groundwork and veneers, edge finishing, curved work, cauls and veneering frames.

10. THE DOVETAIL SEWING BOX   64
An exercise in using sawcut veneers, the small bandsaw, piano hinges, inlaying with hardwood stringing, etc.

11. BRASS CASTING   74
Freedom in furniture design, methods of melting brass, pattern-making, sand or plaster moulds, pouring, finishing and polishing.

12. THE ROTATING BOOKCASE 79
An intricate exercise covering additional orthodox methods with consideration of design and visual arrangement, templates, curved legs, bending timbers and curved veneers.

13. FINISHING AND POLISHING 89
Traditional oil/wax/French polish and associated considerations.

14. THE JOINTLESS UPHOLSTERED STOOL 93
A stool without rails or stretchers or mortise and tenon joints, using gusseted joints, jigs and pressure glueing.

15. A SMALL TABLE WITHOUT MORTISE AND TENON JOINTS 100
Using fillets and bent stripwood with jigs and decorative veneer to make a lightweight but strong and attractive table.

16. THE JOINTLESS UPHOLSTERED CHAIR 106
An exercise in complex jig work, lamination and steam-bent gussets to produce a strong but nice-looking chair.

17. THE SEWING BOX AND MATCHING TRIPOD TABLE 116
An elegant elliptical sewing box with drawer made from pressure-glued laminates, with a part solid, part laminated tripod table of 'stressed skin' construction.

18. DESIGN AND THE AMATEUR CABINET-MAKER 127
The theory behind workmanship, functional beauty and aesthetics discussed and illustrated with examples from fine art pottery, silverware and paintings. Principles of furniture design with reference to classic ideas of art, with examples of classic design explained, and sources of information on aspects of design suggested.

INDEX 142

Introduction

About twelve years ago, as the duties of raising a family were lessening, I began to look around for a hobby to occupy the hours spent at home waiting for the telephone to ring. I had the usual set of spanners and other tools to service the family car and woodworking tools to put up wardrobes and shelves and carry out repairs around the house.

We never had enough of the right quality furniture, and particularly needed a small metal tripod stool, which I decided to make. It was never finished as it proved too noisy, too dirty and too strenuous a job. Instead, I decided to try to make one in wood, but had to opt for an upholstered box stool. It took twelve years to solve the problem of the tripod stool made in wood— it is discussed in the very last project in this book.

The box stool started me into cabinet-making and this book is written by an amateur for amateurs who want to take up fine woodworking as a hobby. It is a pursuit which involves gentle physical work, is not too noisy and upsetting for the neighbours, can be taken up and put down at will, does not mean long hours away from home, is not dirty, and involves the use of the mind, hand and eye.

Wood is the most amenable yet toughest material nature has invented. Everybody loves wood, its feel, look, texture, smell and colour. Indeed wood is a part of our collective sub-conscious. It is present in most myths and fairy stories. It seems natural that we should want to involve it in our leisure time. This book describes how to progress from the simpler projects in wood to the most complex laminated structures needing the use of jigs for assembly.

All the tools needed can be bought at a D.I.Y. hardware shop, the most expensive being a small bandsaw. However, the first few projects need only the simplest tools and if for one reason or another you decide cabinet-making is not for you, then there would have been no great expense in time or money. If, after making the first few pieces of furniture, you decide that a whole new world of skills is opening up, then the acquisition of knowledge takes place as it is needed rather than as a formal course of training.

A couple of hours each day need to be set aside. Patience is needed to put some of the furniture together as some may take a year or so. Tools are acquired as they are needed and the total outlay will be much less than joining a local golf club. Some are best made yourself, for example the work cabinet, which should be exactly the right height to suit your build. This is the most important piece of equipment which you will need.

Many techniques are described, not often met in woodworking books. Brass casting is an exciting art well within the enterprising amateur's capability. It is not without its risks and gets the brow perspiring and the pulse racing. Veneer and laminate cutting is described in detail using a special home-made saw. This should be of great interest to many professionals as it would free them from the whims of the veneer manufacturers. Any old rotten piece of wood, from Grandma's apple tree to walnut off-cuts at the local sawmill, can be converted into veneers using this home-made saw, and sawcut veneers give the comfortable feel of working with solid wood, when glued to stable modern groundwork. Alternatively,

7

accurately cut sheets of wood can be glued into laminated shapes, and combined with more traditional cabinet-making techniques to produce a whole new range of furniture shapes.

There is a chapter on how to acquire trees, how to cut them down and saw them up, together with how to season wood. There is a section on individual English timbers. For those who play cricket, there is an account of how to repair cricket bats and at the same time learn about the excellence of modern glues. Because of its importance to the furniture maker, the structure of wood and glueing is described in detail. The technique of gusseting pieces of wood is borrowed from the wartime methods of wooden aeroplane manufacture to show how lighter, stronger stools, chairs and tables can be made.

There is an extensive chapter on design for those who want to make their very own furniture. Workmanship, functional beauty and aesthetics are carefully defined and explained. Aesthetics in cabinet-making is discussed in detail and its function in our homes is described. Design is a huge topic, and guidance is given how to build up an 'information bank', with particular reference to woodwork books, photography, nature, scrapbooks, notebooks, woodwork museums, aircraft museums, art galleries and the major British museums and collections.

Don't expect to make a living or much of a profit from cabinet-making. It is very labour intensive and the price you could charge for a piece of furniture will be minuscule compared with the time you would wish to spend making it. You will easily cover the cost of your tools and materials, but little else. At first be content with using your hand, eye and mind at the same time; later you will achieve mastery of your tools and materials and eventually, if you become interested in design, you will want to investigate the relations between structure, symmetry, balance, line, shade and texture using wood and furniture as a medium. It is then that cabinet-making becomes an art and you do indeed drink the nectar of the Gods.

1. The Small Workbench

Most of us enjoy working with our hands, but we indulge this pleasure in many different ways. Some of us perfect our gardens, producing immaculate lawns and neat rows of vegetables. Others tinker with our cars or undertake ambitious building or D.I.Y. projects. A few have very specialised hobbies. But when we have established our gardens and have raised our children to an age when they don't need us every five minutes, we perhaps dream in our new-found idle moments of creating things which will be treasured and used for the rest of time. Then we sigh at our lack of skill and ignorance about how to design such objects.

So it was twelve years ago, as I nodded off after lunch one Sunday afternoon. I was woken by a familiar voice complaining bitterly about the piles of books in the corner, and, as I roused myself, knocking over the empty teacup on the carpet, 'Oh, for a coffee table and a bookcase', I sighed. For months we had been looking around in the local shops. The modern ones were cheap and nasty, the antiques too expensive.

As I sat up, I kicked over the teacup again, and was by now totally irritated at my incoordinate behaviour and being nagged on a Sunday afternoon. I was fed up and angry at not having a bookcase and a coffee table. I wished I could 'cock a snook' at those profit-seeking furniture shops and antique hypermarkets.

Our house was full of do-it-yourself wardrobes, and the garage was lined with sagging 'self erect' shelves, but the fine work of furniture-making and cabinet-making was quite beyond me. I left school having produced a lap joint, a dovetail joint and a broomholder whose arms slowly sank under the combined destructive effects of a heavy besom broom and the English weather.

At the end of my garage were a power drill, a few assorted screwdrivers, a blunt plane, a hammer with a loose head, a few chisels which had been used as levers for paint tin lids, a rusty saw with a loose handle and a wobbly chair on which I worked. I mused about my equipment and, in my nagged, roused and disturbed state, wondered which piece I hated the most. It was that wretched chair on which I spent 90% of my effort, wobbling instead of sawing and chiselling.

In the garden my son and his friends were playing cricket against a small workbench, which I had made for him. However, he used it for everything except working on. I had never thought of using it as a workbench myself, but it certainly looked stable and solid enough—and so it was.

Fig. 1

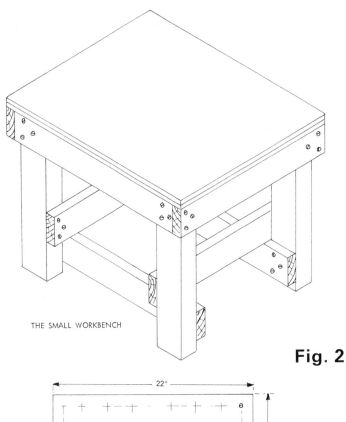

THE SMALL WORKBENCH

Fig. 2

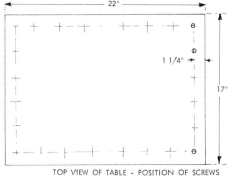

TOP VIEW OF TABLE - POSITION OF SCREWS

22"

1 1/4"

17"

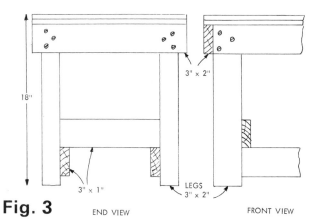

Fig. 3

18"

3" × 2"

3" × 1"

LEGS
3" × 2"

END VIEW

FRONT VIEW

Thus it was twelve years ago I decided to use that small workbench as a means to start furniture and cabinet-making. Since then time has suggested a number of improvements. This first chapter is how to make one

THE WORKBENCH

It has a double layered top, independently screwed, held by rows of screws attached to the top rails. When the top layer becomes too damaged it is easily replaced. One layer of ply is too flimsy to act as a solid surface.

It is 17 in. wide, 22 in. long and 18 in. high. The legs and rails are screwed together, avoiding the weakening effect of

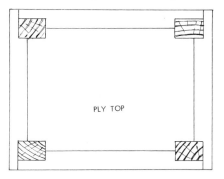

PLY TOP

TOP SEEN FROM UNDERNEATH TO
SHOW ARRANGEMENT OF RAILS **Fig. 4**

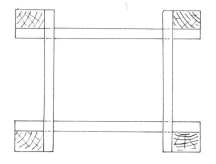

ARRANGEMENT OF BOTTOM RAILS

mortise and tenon joints. If any of the rails are damaged they are easily replaced without having to dismantle the table totally. The 3 in. × 2 in. legs appear over-heavy, but not so when it will have to last over ten years.

All corners are rounded or chamfered, including the bottoms of the legs. This avoids splinters and larger pieces being split off during use. The upper rails are 2 in. thick so clamps can be used on them to hold jobs to be drilled and planed. A 1 in.

Fig. 5

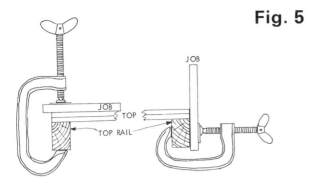

JOB

JOB
TOP
TOP RAIL

HOW THE RUGGED TOP RAIL IS USED
FOR CLAMPING ON PIECES OF WOOD

softwood rail would be quite inadequate to hold a clamp.

All screws holding the top on should be at least $1\frac{1}{4}$ in. in from the edge to avoid snagging the saw teeth. They should be countersunk $\frac{1}{16}$ in. for the same reason. The proper way to put a screw in is shown in Fig. 6.

THE CUTTING LIST:

Legs	3 in × 2 in. × 17 in.	(4)
Top rails	3 in. × 2 in. × 17 in	(2)
	3 in. × 2 in. × 20 in.	(2)
Bottom rails	3 in. × 1 in. × 15 in.	(2)
	3 in. × 1 in. × 20 in.	(2)

2 pieces of $\frac{1}{2}$ in. ply, external grade, 22 in. × 17 in.

1 in. × 10 Screws (50)
2 in. × 10 Screws (50)

The original small workbench was repaired, but a second was made with various modifications. The two are some-times used together as a pair of sawhorses. Their uses are numerous. In the early days, the original one was used as a platform on which a drill stand was mounted, to 'rough drill' out mortises. It is invaluable as a table on which a small bandsaw is placed and used to saw up large pieces of timber which will not fit into the workshed. Turned upside-down, the worktables act as trestles to saw up logs for the fire. The children chop firewood on their tops. A heavy metalwork vice can be clamped to the top. They act as a support for drilling pieces of timber. Children learning wood-work choose these tables to saw on, rather than the orthodox sawhorses so beloved of carpenters and joiners since time immemorial; they complain of feeling insecure on the sawhorses.

Over the years, the original table was used for many other purposes other than woodworking. It acts as a platform for spanners while working under the bonnet of the car. The laundry basket rests on it while washing is being hung out on the washing line. It is the right height for standing on while cleaning the windows. In the summer it becomes a tea table for the hammock and a wicket for the child-ren's cricket. In the winter it becomes a goal-post and a backing for the air rifle targets.

After 12 years the original table began to disintegrate. The ply layers began to crumble and peel and the upper rails came away revealing dry rot at the top of one leg. The top was riddled with drill holes, embedded air rifle pellets and blobs of glue. There were splashes of red, black and silver paint. The edges were charred from soldering and scarred with sawcuts. The bottoms of the legs were rounded with use and the rails were grossly cut with the log saw. A spider's nest had been snugly hidden under the top in the corners between the top and legs.

Time had been a hard taskmaster for that small workbench. The whole family had used it, but more than anything, it has been the original stepping off stage for a start to cabinet-making.

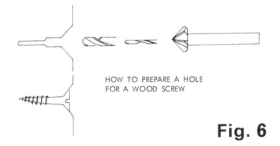

HOW TO PREPARE A HOLE
FOR A WOOD SCREW

Fig. 6

2. The Upholstered Box Stool

Having made the small worktable, find out if you could enjoy furniture and cabinet-making by using it to make an upholstered box stool.

Because the time expended seems out of proportion to what is produced, furniture-making can appear very frustrating. To start with, it is as well to make something simple, although using many of the cabinet-making techniques, before spending money on expensive tools and undertaking more complex projects which might be left unfinished.

Buy a simple book on cabinet-making and have it at hand to help solve problems as soon as they arise. Even so, the most exciting way to learn is by 'doing', and sorting out difficulties as you meet them.

The box stool is 18 in. high, 18 in. long and 1 ft. deep. The corners are held by rows of secret mitred dovetails. There are ogee legs and a floor in the bottom provides useful storage space. The top is button upholstered and opens by means of chest or cranked hinges. It is made of $\frac{3}{4}$ in. hardwood and should provide rugged use over many years.

The aims of this chapter are to show:
(1) How to make a secret dovetail joint, which is a cabinet-maker's joint 'par excellence'.
(2) Some lessons in designing.
    (a) Versatility of the basic shape.
    (b) Sources of ideas.
    (c) Model making.
    (d) Mock-ups.
    (e) How to look at a piece of wood and use it to its best advantage.
(3) Use of the small workbench.
(4) Use of templates to repeat shapes.
(5) D.I.Y. mitring.
(6) D.I.Y. finishes.
(7) Home-made sash-cramps.
(8) D.I.Y. upholstery.

The following tools will be needed:
Power drill
Orbital sanding disc
2 × 6 in. G-cramps
Trysquare
Steel rule
Blowlamp
Carving gouges
Mallet
Use of metal working vice
Panel saw
Mortise chisels, $\frac{1}{2}$ in., $\frac{1}{4}$ in.
Adjustable bevel
Tenon saw
Padsaw (to fit Stanley knife)
Drill bits and countersink

Its construction depends on using the small workbench and, if possible, an old table or chest of drawers at the end of a garage or in a garden shed.

Fig. 7

Fig. 8

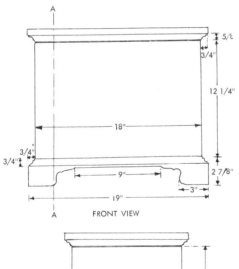

Fig. 9

THE BOX STOOL

The stool can be modified into a piano stool (which is taller) or a double piano stool (which is longer), or a blanket chest (which is broader). All these would provide much needed storage space.

The secret dovetails may appear complicated but are not difficult to make. Present taste dictates that dovetails are exposed, the pattern they make being used as a decorative feature. The designer assumes that the maker has complete mastery over cutting dovetails, but these are not for the beginner. In contrast, the secret dovetails make very strong joints and conceal the small slips and errors of the novice.

Don't feel obliged to follow the designs exactly as shown. Design is a matter of

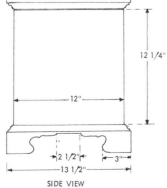

FRONT VIEW

SIDE VIEW

Fig. 10

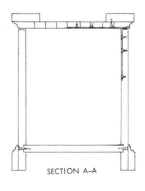

SECTION A-A

Fig. 11

Fig. 12

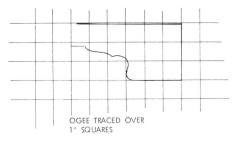

OGEE TRACED OVER
1" SQUARES

After planing, the boards may warp a little as the weather changes. Don't worry too much because with the aid of secret dovetails, the boards can be forced into flatness again as the box is assembled.

When the surface of the board has been cleaned up and the grain clearly seen, take note of the knots, fungal stains, shades and wavy grain. Select the pieces with the most vivid and interesting markings as the front of the stool and try to arrange cutting so

Fig. 13

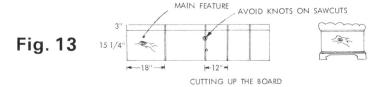

MAIN FEATURE   AVOID KNOTS ON SAWCUTS

3"

15 1/4"

←—18"—→   ←—12"—→

CUTTING UP THE BOARD

personal taste. Some people do not like ogee legs. If you are unhappy, look through home fashion magazines, antique books and visit local furniture shops. Then make a small balsa-wood model and look at it from all angles over several days. There is nothing more restful in the dark evenings than carving away at bits of balsa, glueing them together with balsa cement and then reshaping. The cement dries quickly so the model can be remade several times in an evening.

If you are still unsure, make a full-sized mockup in cardboard and masking tape, colouring with car spray touch-up. Glue and pin on some upholstery material. When you find it 'livable-with' take its dimensions and give it to the children to play with.

THE TIMBER

A piece of hardwood $6\frac{1}{2}$ ft. long and $18\frac{1}{2}$ in. wide and $\frac{3}{4}$ in. thick is needed; an elm coffinboard should be perfect. Most joinery works will plane such a board for a small sum. The small ridges left by the planer can be removed with an orbital sander and a smoothing plane, but this will be difficult without a proper work cabinet. Oak can be obtained in wide boards, but avoid its sapwood as it is useless for furniture making.

that these features are in the middle. Avoid having knots at the edges of the four sides of the box. They will interfere with the dovetails.

Mark out the plank with double lines set $\frac{1}{8}$ in. apart. Saw between the lines, supporting both pieces in order to avoid a large splinter coming away with one piece. Put the offcuts to one side, as they will be used for the lid and the thickeners.

The hardwood should be easy to saw provided it is dry, that is to say seasoned. If it is heavy going, you could be using the wrong saw. A crosscut saw should have 8-11 teeth/inch and a ripsaw 6 teeth/inch. The number of teeth per inch is stamped on the blade next to the handle. If it is a well-used saw, it could be blunt or have lost its 'set'. A beginner may not realise how blunt a saw is until he uses a sharp one; they have to be sharpened fairly frequently, especially when used on hard dry wood.

Few people know how to sharpen and set a saw or realise that sawing becomes a pleasure when using a keen saw. I must confess that in my early days I often wondered why it was such hard work and why the saw used to 'bind' so often in the sawcut. Saw sharpening and setting is described in a later chapter. When you have mastered the art you will even be able to 'hear' the difference between when a blunt and sharp saw is being used.

AVOID SPLINTERING THE END OF A PLANK WHEN SAWING IN HALF

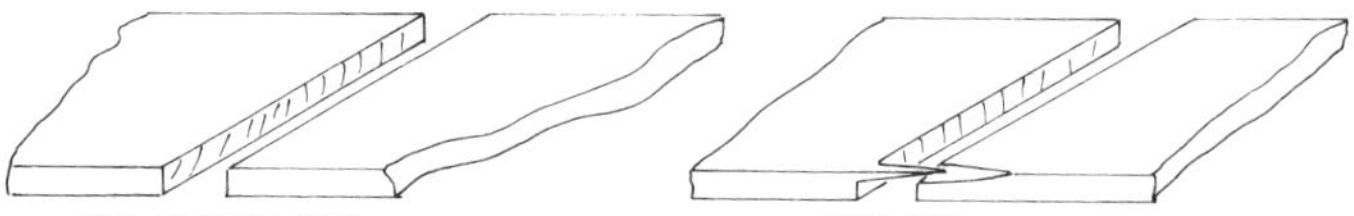

Fig. 14

END UP WITH THIS   NOT THIS

Before beginning to make the box a brief explanation of 'how and why' is appropriate. The four corners are joined by secret dovetails. The lower part of the box is pulled together by screwing the sides on to the outer edges of the shelf:

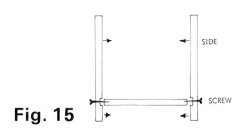

Fig. 15

The screwheads are hidden by 'thickeners' on the lower part of the box, which are themselves held by screws put in from the inside of the legs:

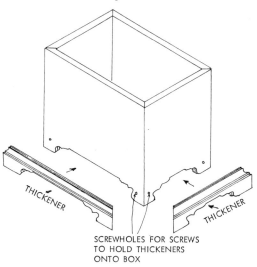

SCREWHOLES FOR SCREWS
TO HOLD THICKENERS
ONTO BOX

'MENT OF THICKENERS AND BOX

Fig. 16

THE BOX

Square a.. 'lane the four sides. For those without a full-size workbench this will be

WALL

PLANE
JOB
CLAMP
WORKTABLE

WOODEN
BOX

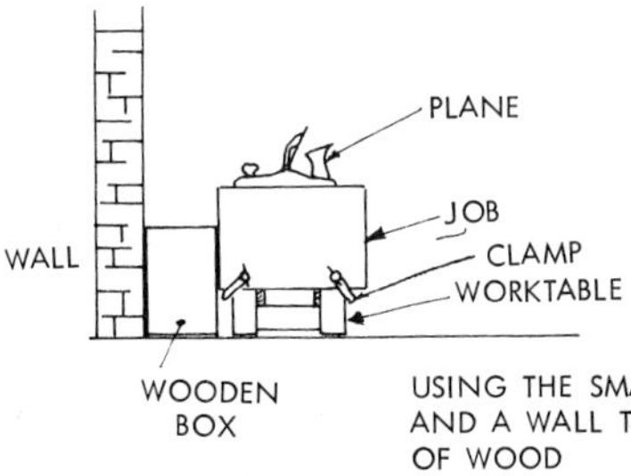

USING THE SMALL WORK TABLE
AND A WALL TO PLANE A PIECE
OF WOOD

Fig. 17

difficult, but can be managed on the worktable. A combination of metal smoothing plane, orbital sander and G-cramps can be used. The end is trued up using a block plane, if you have one, or a metal smoothing plane used at an angle.

PLANING THE
END GRAIN

Fig. 18

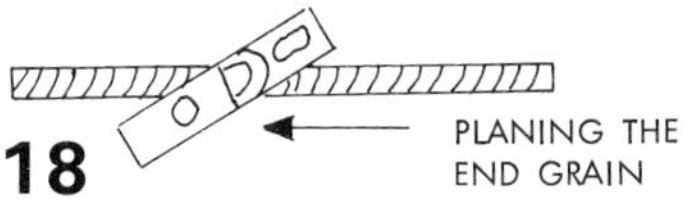

Avoid splitting the corners by bevelling them or by planing from each edge, towards the centre. When all the four sides are smooth cut the dovetails. This may seem a tall order to the beginner, so if you are unfamiliar with the technique start by practising on scrap hardwood before attempting the secret dovetails.

Make these three practice joints in order – (1) Simple lap dovetail, (2) Through-dovetail, (3) Secret dovetail. First make a simple lap dovetail. Mark out as shown using a marking gauge to get the same thickness of pin and tail.

Fig. 19

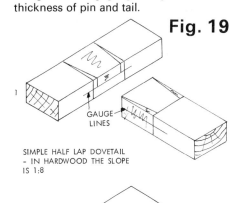

GAUGE
LINES

SIMPLE HALF LAP DOVETAIL
– IN HARDWOOD THE SLOPE
IS 1:8

Fig. 20

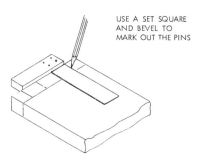

USE A SET SQUARE AND BEVEL TO MARK OUT THE PINS

The Through Dovetail: Use the same slope of dovetail (1:8) to make the through-dovetail. First square the ends of the boards and then gauge around the ends equal to the thickness of the boards. Using a trysquare, mark off at each squared end the thickness of a 'pin' on the outer side of the board (Fig. 20). Then divide up the space between into as many pins as are appropriate. Turn the board end up and use a bevel to mark across to make the slope of the dovetail (Fig. 21).

Fig. 21

Mark the waste wood with a thick pencil squiggle so you can cut into the waste wood with your tenon saw. Chisel out the waste, starting a little way from the gauge mark to allow for the wedge shape of the chisel end being driven inwards across pencil and gauge lines.

Clean up the pins. Lay the board for the tails on the worktable and stand the ends of the pins vertically on it. Mark around (Fig. 22).

The ends of the markings for the tails are squared across the end of the board. The

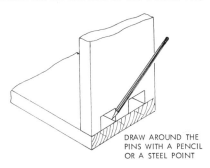

DRAW AROUND THE PINS WITH A PENCIL OR A STEEL POINT

Fig. 22

flat side cannot be marked so care has to be taken to keep the tenon saw square. Don't forget to squiggle in the waste wood!

This is how your practice through-dovetail should look when it is finished.

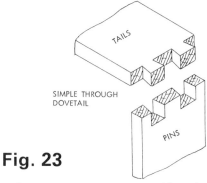

TAILS

SIMPLE THROUGH DOVETAIL

PINS

Fig. 23

As a next stage you could make a through-dovetail with mitred ends.

The secret mitred dovetail. This is a similar joint to the through-dovetail with mitred ends, but is as if two thin sheets of wood mitred at the ends have been glued on the outside of both pins and tails.

Fig. 24

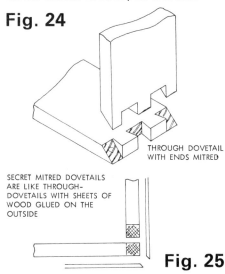

THROUGH DOVETAIL WITH ENDS MITRED

SECRET MITRED DOVETAILS ARE LIKE THROUGH-DOVETAILS WITH SHEETS OF WOOD GLUED ON THE OUTSIDE

Fig. 25

The pins are marked out first leaving (in the case of the stool) $\frac{5}{32}$ in. at the outer edge, to be mitred later. The ends are mitred at 45° as shown (Fig. 26). The

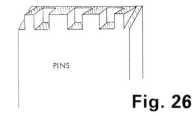

PINS

Fig. 26

ends of the pins are rebated $\frac{5}{32}$ in. to leave a ridge $\frac{5}{32}$ in. square.

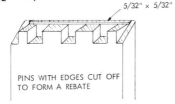

PINS WITH EDGES CUT OFF TO FORM A REBATE

Fig. 27

The end of the 'tails' board is rebated $\frac{5}{32}$ in. and the pins are placed on it and drawn around.

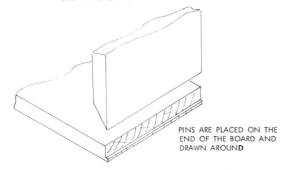

PINS ARE PLACED ON THE END OF THE BOARD AND DRAWN AROUND

Fig. 28

Remove the waste—test fit as far as the projecting laps will allow. Now comes the tricky part. Carefully pare each lap to 45° holding the board against the side of the workbench with the two G-cramps. Mitre the ends. Hidden high spots will prevent a perfect fit. Coat pins or tails liberally with blue chalk and test fit. Pare off any bumps left covered with blue chalk.

This technique is seldom mentioned in woodwork textbooks. For the beginner it is a great help, for with patience and perseverance he will produce a secret dovetail every bit as good, judged by external appearance, as that produced by an expert.

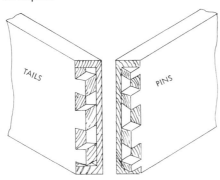

TAILS   PINS

Fig. 29

THE SECRET MITRED DOVETAIL JOINT

When you are confident about making the joint, start on the four rows of mitred dovetails at each corner of the stool. Mark out the pins on the four corners of the front and rear boards and the tails on the ends. If pins and tails are on the same board, the box is very difficult to assemble.

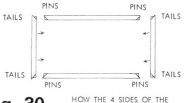

TAILS   PINS   PINS   TAILS

TAILS   PINS   PINS   TAILS

Fig. 30

HOW THE 4 SIDES OF THE BOX ARE ASSEMBLED

Congratulations if the four rows of dovetails fit. If you were pleased with your success you will enjoy cabinet-making.

Fit the four sides together and around the inside mark two parallel lines. Between these a rebate will be cut to take the hardwood or blockboard floor. The bottom of the floor should be 2 in. from the bottom of the legs. Cut along each line with a Stanley knife guided by a steel rule. Chisel out the waste.

Cut the floor to size leaving a $\frac{1}{32}$ in. gap each side between the floor and bottom of rebate. The action of tightening the screws into the floor from the outside of the box will force the four sides together. The upper part of the box can be clamped together by making a frame out of softwood and tapping down wedges.

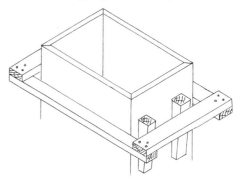

Fig. 31

THE BOX IS GLUED AND ASSEMBLED USING A FRAME AND WEDGES

Assemble the box using slow setting resin glue such as Cascamite. Wipe off excess from inside and out.

Cut out a cardboard template of the ogee and use the area to the left of the dotted line to mark out on the box. (The distance between dotted line and right hand edge depends on the thickness of the thickeners. See Fig. 12). Drill a series of holes around the curves and saw along the straight part with a padsaw blade fitted in a Stanley knife handle. Carefully save the offcut for the top.

Fig. 32

DRILL OUT THE CURVES

It is easier to cut out the ogees after the box has been assembled. Also there is less chance of the legs splitting off.

Next make the thickeners to go around the base.

2 pieces 20 in. × 3 in. × $\frac{3}{4}$ in. are needed.
2 pieces 13 in. × 3 in. × $\frac{3}{4}$ in.

The method of making and assembly is:
(1) Cut the moulding around the top.
(2) Mitre the ends.
(3) Cut out the ogees after screwing and glueing.

Fig. 33

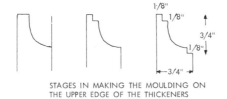

STAGES IN MAKING THE MOULDING ON THE UPPER EDGE OF THE THICKENERS

(1) Shape the moulding by clamping to the small workbench and use gauge, Stanley knife, mortise chisel and carving gouge. Finish off with rounded and square blocks covered in glasspaper.
(2) The thickeners are mitred around the box, screwed and left in place.

Fig. 34

ATTACH THICKENERS BY GLUEING AND SCREWING FROM INSIDE OF BOX

Again, the difficulties of mitring are eased by the liberal use of blue chalk. The last thickener is particularly difficult to fit, as both ends have to be mitred at the same time. Glue and screw.

(3) Use the ogee template, this time using its full width. Remove and save the offcut. Leave the final finishing until the lid has been made.

THE LID

The lid consists of a sheet of blockboard on to which are screwed four pieces of hardwood to act as a support for the upholstery and moulded insets to rebate the lid to the box.

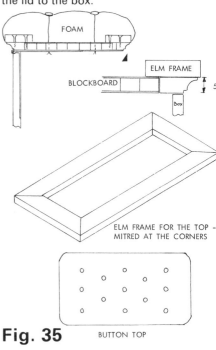

ELM FRAME FOR THE TOP – MITRED AT THE CORNERS

Fig. 35

BUTTON TOP

The elm insets are carved in the same way as the thickeners, fitted, mitred, glued and screwed.

A chest hinge is made from a double ended flap hinge (Fig. 36). You will need

Fig. 36

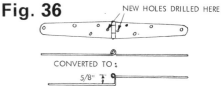

NEW HOLES DRILLED HERE

CONVERTED TO:

BEND TO 5/8" FROM THE CENTRE OF HINGE

to use a metal working vice (which could be clamped to the worktable) and a blowlamp. A new hole is drilled near the hinge joint itself for an extra screw. The hinge is inset into the box and lid as shown. Make sure the centre of the hinge is exactly above the edge of the box.

18

FINISHING

–is most time-consuming and frustrating, but very important.

All the plane marks, bruises, orbital sander marks, scratches and chisel marks have to be removed. The aim is to display the grain to its best advantage and seal the grain to keep out the dirt and dust. As the surfaces of most hardwoods are durable, they do not need protection against scratches, so oiling and/or waxing may be all that is needed. The surface must be as flat and smooth as possible. Use aluminium oxide paper and finally, grades of wet and dry.

Brush off all the dust and wash down with turps. Coat liberally with a mixture of Cuprinol $\frac{1}{3}$rd and boiled linseed oil $\frac{2}{3}$rds or several coats of teak oil. Allow to dry and wax liberally. The gloss is brought up by hard work.

The top is upholstered with polyurethane foam, then calico and finally dralon. Buttons in the same material as the dralon can be made at most shops where upholstery materials are sold.

Use 3 in. thick foam and pull tight with calico, tacking on the upper edge of the elm frame. $\frac{3}{32}$ in. holes to correspond with the buttons are drilled through the foam and blockboard lid. The dralon is placed on the calico and the buttons are attached starting at the centre one and working outwards. Use a 4 in. sharp needle with thick twine. Thread from the inside of the blockboard, through the foam, calico and dralon covering, attach the button and return the needle back to the inside of the lid. Knot and secure, pulling the buttons well down into the foam. Arrange the buttons so the attractive diamond shaping creases appear between the buttons. Turn in the edges of the dralon and tack to the edge of the elm frame. Cover this with suitable braid and gimp pins.

Next, screw on the hinges and line the lid with a rectangle of dralon to hide the joint between hardwood insets and blockboard, the hinge ends and the twine knots holding on the buttons. Make sure the tacks do not interfere with the box as the lid is closed. Cover them with braid.

A stay can be fitted to the lid to prevent it opening too wide, but this will already be helped by the moulding on the lid inset.

The stool is finished and should give many years of hard use. If you enjoyed making it then the next major projects should be somewhere to work and something on which to work.

3. The Workshed and Work Cabinet

By now you are fed up with bending over the small worktable. It should have done its job by allowing you to prove to yourself that cabinet-making is your hobby.

Next, (1) Find a place devoted only to woodworking. (2) Make a work cabinet with a woodworking vice.

A workshed at the end of the garden is an ideal situation. The end of a garage is second best, as it always has other jobs to perform, such as storing bicycles, garden tools, mowers and of course, the family car.

The bigger the shed, the better; the smallest possible is 8ft. × 6ft. There should be as much light as possible coming on to the work cabinet. Let the windows stretch the whole length of one side and try to arrange that one half of the roof is Perspex. Remember that in this country the mid-winter light is very poor indeed, daytime lasting only eight hours. A wooden floor is most comfortable, and should be raised at least 9in. off the ground on concrete piers. A concrete floor is hard wearing, but it is cold on the feet and always attracts the damp, if not through it then by condensation.

Grow shrubs or a hedge near it to soften its outline and make it inconspicuous. Perhaps drill a hole beneath its eaves to let robins roost and nest. They provide company while you work! Have an electric point fitted, but consult the local Electricity Board about it, otherwise you will need a heavy duty waterproofed three-core cable. Put up plenty of shelves and hooks for tools and screws etc.

The lightest side of the shed will be taken up by the most important piece of cabinet-making equipment—the work cabinet. It will make working with tools an immense pleasure. It provides a level immovable surface at the right height. It is designed to hold your work still while you shape it. It leaves your hands free to manipulate your tools, your body relaxed to provide the force necessary to drive them and the poise and steadiness of aim to move them accurately.

I emphasise it should be a work cabinet rather than a work bench because it contains a cupboard and drawers for storage. The more you stow away in it the better, as the weight assists its immobility. They can be bought ready-made for around £500. Remember that it will have to fit your shed and its height will have to suit you as an individual. People vary from 5ft.–6ft. 6in. and their arm

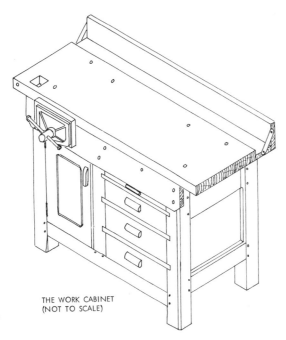

THE WORK CABINET
(NOT TO SCALE)

Fig. 37

20

Fig. 38 (part)

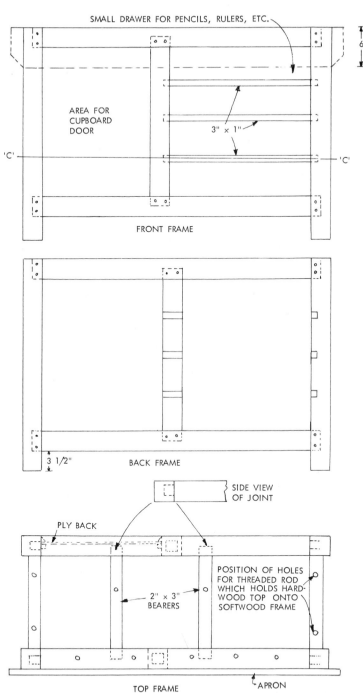

SMALL DRAWER FOR PENCILS, RULERS, ETC.

AREA FOR CUPBOARD DOOR

3" x 1"

6"

'C' ——— 'C'

FRONT FRAME

BACK FRAME

3 1/2"

SIDE VIEW OF JOINT

PLY BACK

2" x 3" BEARERS

POSITION OF HOLES FOR THREADED ROD WHICH HOLDS HARD-WOOD TOP ONTO SOFTWOOD FRAME

TOP FRAME

APRON

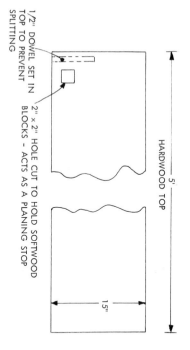

STEEL STAY HELD BY WING-NUTS - CAN BE FLAPPED FORWARD TO GIVE A LARGER WORK SURFACE

SOFTWOOD BACK

HARDWOOD TOP

7" x 2"

SIDE VIEW

1/2" DOWEL SET IN 2" x 2" HOLE CUT TO HOLD SOFTWOOD TOP TO PREVENT SPLITTING

BLOCKS - ACTS AS A PLANING STOP

HARDWOOD TOP

5'

1.5'

lengths are equally variable, so it is best to make your own.

It is difficult to give exact dimensions for the one described here. Its height will be between 32in-36in. Too low will cause backache, too high will make your arms ache. Make a mock-up out of planks and tables to find your optimum working height.

The base is made of softwood and plywood, the top of 2in. thick hardwood. It should be a minimum 4ft. 6in. long (the

Fig. 38 (part)

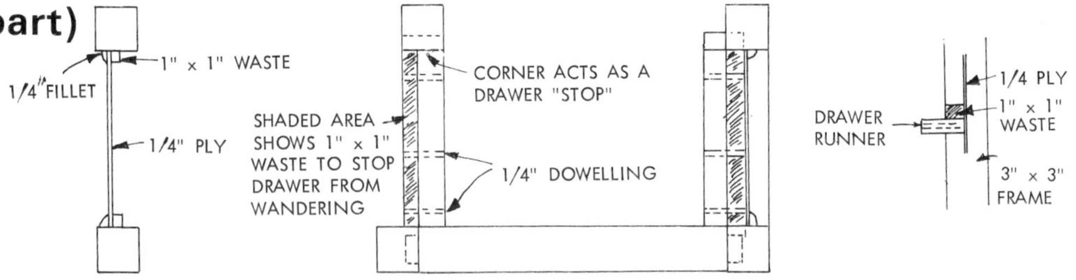

1/4" FILLET

1" x 1" WASTE

1/4" PLY

SHADED AREA SHOWS 1" x 1" WASTE TO STOP DRAWER FROM WANDERING

CORNER ACTS AS A DRAWER "STOP"

1/4" DOWELLING

DRAWER RUNNER

1/4 PLY

1" x 1" WASTE

3" x 3" FRAME

SECTION THRO' WORK CABINET at 'C-C'

longer the better.) The hardwood top will overlap 8 in. at each end to allow wood or a metal work vice to be temporarily clamped to it.

The frame is 3 in. × 3 in. softwood. Commercial work cabinets have their frames made of hardwood, but this is unnecessary as this frame is also boxed with plywood. The joints are dowelled mortise and tenon.

Rigidity and immobility must be total! If not, then your effort is going into moving the work cabinet, not into cabinet making.

There is a 6 in. wide hardwood apron along the front to protect the softwood frame; it also gives additional stiffness to the front three vertical members of the frame. The back and front frames are slightly different, as the central pillar of the rear frame is offset to act as a drawer stop. These are assembled first.

Before starting the frame, mount the power drill in a drill stand and screw it to the top of the small work bench. Use it to drill out the tenons. Mortise and tenons in softwood are great fun after the secret mitred dovetails. It's a chance to let off steam with a chisel and mallet.

Mark out the frame and double check the measurements. The main mortise and

tenons are straightforward and can be taken off the plan. Runners for the drawers are let into the frames as they are 3 in. × 1 in. softwood; they are $\frac{1}{4}$ in. dowelled to prevent splitting under the weight of the drawers. 1 in. × 1 in. waste is glued and nailed on them to act as drawer guides. The top drawer is only 2 in. high, but is a useful receptacle for pencils, rulers and other easily losable items.

Cut a square hole in the hardwood top about 7 in. from the end for a planing stop. This can be 'blind' over the softwood frame if you cannot have a long overhang. If you have a long overhang an orthodox planing stop held by a wingnut can be used. The hardwood top is held on with threaded rod, the top nuts being buried with pieces of dowelling. The positions are shown in the plan.

A vice is mounted, so that the wooden check is above the movable metal plate, but flush with the upper surface hardwood top. It is difficult to give precise instructions as to how to fit as one vice differs from another. Leave the top to settle and later plane true and coat liberally with linseed oil.

The sides and back are boxed with $\frac{1}{4}$ in.

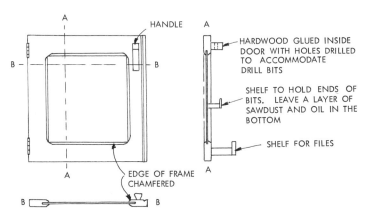

A

HANDLE

A

B

B

A

A

B

B

EDGE OF FRAME CHAMFERED

HARDWOOD GLUED INSIDE DOOR WITH HOLES DRILLED TO ACCOMMODATE DRILL BITS

SHELF TO HOLD ENDS OF BITS. LEAVE A LAYER OF SAWDUST AND OIL IN THE BOTTOM

SHELF FOR FILES

Fig. 39

Fig. 40

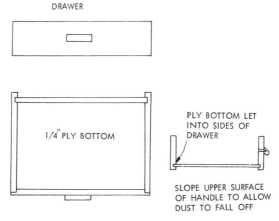

DRAWER

1/4" PLY BOTTOM

PLY BOTTOM LET
INTO SIDES OF
DRAWER

SLOPE UPPER SURFACE
OF HANDLE TO ALLOW
DUST TO FALL OFF

ply as shown and ply can be used to make the drawers and door to the cupboard. The drawers are made as shown, the rebates for the $\frac{1}{4}$ in. ply bottoms being made with a marking gauge, Stanley knife and $\frac{1}{4}$ in. mortise chisel. The edges of the drawer sides are glued and pinned. Candlewax on the drawer bottoms will ensure easy running for many years. Handles are made from hardwood with sloping tops to allow dust to fall off.

The door is made as shown in the plan, the rebates completed as before. Shelves and a tray are added as shown. The grooving and chamfering at the edges of the $\frac{1}{4}$ in. ply panel provides a nice finish, as does the rounding of the external corners

of the legs. A tool well is provided at the rear of the top, the back of which can flop forward to provide a larger work surface.

The drawers and frame are sanded and finished with three coats of polyurethane. Make sure the top is flat and level and occasionally give it another coat of linseed oil. Like the skin of a cricket bat it is very durable. Its oiliness helps to prevent adhesion of gobs of glue.

Finally, place it in position, fill it with tools and now you have the most important cabinet:making tool. Look after it and never saw directly on it. Protect it from chisels and nails. It should last generations.

4. Sharpening Saws, Chisels and Planes

Having made a workshed and work cabinet life becomes more comfortable for the do-it-yourself cabinet-maker. He can enter his own little world and use a custom-built work surface. His tools, screws and nails are neatly stowed away on shelves and in the cupboard and drawers of his work cabinet.

However, his tools won't seem to cut properly. Chisels refuse to pare, saws stick in the sawcuts and planes become tiring to use and tear up the wood fibres. The time has come to learn how to care for and sharpen his tools.

Examination of the blunt tools with a hand lens will show a fine white line across the tips of the saw teeth and along the cutting edges of the chisels and plane blades. They may be chipped where they have hit a nail or been accidentally knocked against another tool.

Running a hand along the teeth of a sawblade, backwards from tip towards handle, will reveal a difference in the feel of the teeth of the central part of the blade to those beneath the handle. The latter are hardly ever used and remain forever sharp. Pass a thumb across a blunt plane blade from flat side to bevel. A sharp edge feels lively and rough, a blunt edge feels smooth and dead.

Woodworking tools are sharpened every few hours, depending on how hard is the wood being worked on. Some English hardwoods such as elm and acacia are very abrasive. knots of walnut and oak may blunt or even chip the best steel. Just because your tools seem to get blunt quickly, don't feel cheated by the manufacturer. It is worth pausing to understand what steel is and how it is prepared. The techniques of tool sharpening will be understood better and there will be less likelihood of them sustaining damage or overheating.

Steel is iron which contains around 1 % carbon. Different tools have different compositions.

Saws	0.9 %
Chisels and Planes	0.7 %
Razors and Knives	1.4 %
Files	1.3 %

These minute differences are sufficient to alter the characteristics of the steel when it is subject to the heat processes known as TEMPERING, QUENCHING and ANNEALING.

To understand how these alter the nature of steel it helps to be able to visualise the structure. Surprisingly, steel is a crystalline compound composed of a jigsaw of three different kinds of substance:

CEMENTITE–A chemical combination of iron and carbon called iron carbide which is very hard and brittle.

FERRITE–Grains of pure iron, which are tough, resilient and ductile.

PEARLITE–A loose combination of iron and carbon atoms which is tough and hard yet more brittle than ferrite.

The characteristics of individual steels depend on the relative constitution of these three, which can be altered by tempering, quenching or annealing. The wonderful thing about steel is that by these processes it can be made hard enough to cut other steels or tough enough to take the repeated blows necessary to cut concrete.

Steel is hardened by heating to a cherry-red heat then quenching by suddenly immersing in water or oil. This makes it brittle but extremely hard. It is then tempered by reheating it to around 250°C (pale to middle straw colour) and re-quenching. The exact temperature to which it is heated will determine its hardness or toughness. Annealing is softening of the steel by heating and allowing to cool slowly, and is advisable to relieve internal stresses before re-hardening.

To maintain planes and chisels, a variety of sharpening stones and grindstones are needed.

Normal practice is to grind the blades to 25° and hone to 30°; for those with

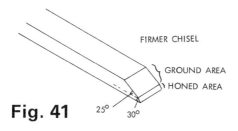

Fig. 41 25° 30°

access to a grindstone here are some simple guidelines.
(1) Sharpen with a wheel rotating away from the blade.

Fig. 42

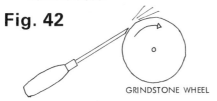

GRINDSTONE WHEEL

(2) Use as slow a rotation speed as possible to avoid overheating the blade.
(3) Cool the blade every two seconds in water so the heat built up by the grinding does not 'blue' the tip and destroy its temper.
(4) Check the squareness of the tip, if necessary sliding on a piece of masking tape at right angles a little way down the blade.
(5) Always wear goggles to prevent pieces of grit or iron damaging the eyes.
(6) Check the 25° using a plastic protractor or a bevel.

The grindstone will leave a coarse uneven end and the final edge has to be honed by an oil stone. This can be a double-faced carborundum or India, coarse followed by fine. For those who can afford an Arkansas stone, a superb cutting edge will be achieved. It is a natural quartz found only in certain parts of America, pale yellow white and opalescent, and is far superior to India or carborundum for achieving a final edge.

If you wish to be very particular about the edge, then complete it on a green Charnley Forest stone (still available in second-hand markets) or a leather strop. Whichever you choose, use a puddle of fine mineral oil to wash away the steel particles and cool the tip of the blade. Don't use vegetable or linseed oil as these will clog the pores of the stone. If the stone appears filled with debris, wash with paraffin or petrol. Use the whole surface of the stone to keep it as level as possible. If the centre is overused, this area will become concave. However, this can be corrected by grinding it flat on a paving stone with the help of sand and water.

Honing chisel and plane blades should *ALWAYS* be done on the bevelled side. There are many different ways, but always use the whole of the surface with small circular movements. Use your right hand beneath the blade to 'drag' it and your left hand above to apply downward pressure.

A wire edge will appear at the tip of the blade, and this should be removed by laying it flat on the oil stone, bevel upwards, and moving it side to side until it disappears. Many chisels are spoilt when

Fig. 43

WIRE EDGE

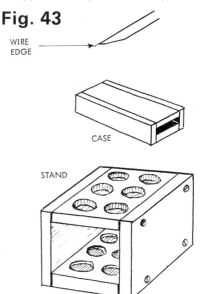

CASE

STAND

they are accidentally knocked against other tools, so make a small wooden case for each or a special stand to take them all.

Plane blades should be sharpened in a similar fashion, but remove their corners to avoid unsightly edges left on the wood after planing.

Wooden jack plane blades or large metal jack planes should have a more pro-

Fig. 44 PLANE BLADE SHAPES

SQUARED CORNERS OF A REBATE PLANE

ROUNDED CORNERS AND VERY SLIGHTLY ROUNDED BLADE OF A SMOOTHING PLANE

ROUNDED CORNERS AND MORE PRONOUNCED ROUNDING OF A JACK PLANE BLADE

nounced curve on their blades. This helps to prevent splitting at the edges. A smoothing plane should have less curve and a bullnose plane blade should have a level edge.

Gouges are sharpened by side-to-side rocking movements and the wire edge removed with a slipstone.

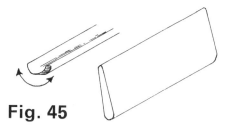

Fig. 45

Oil stones need care like any other tool. Make a box with a lid to protect them from becoming chipped or contaminated with dust.

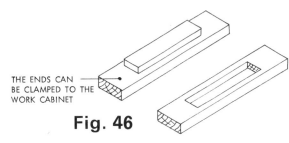

THE ENDS CAN BE CLAMPED TO THE WORK CABINET

Fig. 46

Another cabinet-maker's tool which needs frequent sharpening is the SCRAPER. Probably most D.I.Y. enthusiasts are unfamiliar with this flexible rectangular blade which is invaluable for finishing. It is used instead of coarse

90°

3/64"

5°

SHAVING

Fig. 47

THE HOOK ON THE SCRAPER

glasspaper to avoid scratches in the wood surface, and the one I use, made from an old saw blade, is 5 in. × 3 in. and $\frac{3}{64}$ in. thick.

The edges are best hooked over using the rounded side of a gouge, and the hooked edge is dragged across the surface to remove fine shavings.

The hook is hardly visible to the naked eye. Sharpen as follows:

(1) Lay the scraper on the work cabinet and flatten the edges with the rounded side of a gouge.

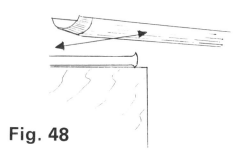

Fig. 48

(2) Place the scraper in a vice with edge uppermost and horizontal, and level with a flat file, removing the unevenness on the 'away' stroke.

(3) Square up the top, removing all file marks on an oilstone, coarse followed by smooth.

(4) Lay the scraper flat on the oilstone and with a few side-strokes remove all wire edge and burr.

(5) Set the cutting 'hook' by holding on the work cabinet with $\frac{1}{4}$ in. protruding and run a gouge along it at 85° to the blade with a slight upward motion. Do it twice.

Fig. 49

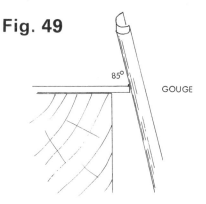

85°

GOUGE

The scraper produces dust instead of shavings when it is blunt and a white line appears along the edge in the same way as on a plane or chisel.

SAW SHARPENING AND SETTING

Mastery of this art is time well spent by the D.I.Y. cabinet maker. The amount of sweat and effort saved during sawing is quite out of proportion to that spent on sharpening and setting. Few people can do it, yet it is not a particularly difficult art to acquire.

On saws, the number of teeth to the inch varies from 4-20, depending on the purpose of the saw. A softwood ripsaw has 4, a hardwood ripsaw 6-7, a crosscut 8, a coarse tenon 8-12 and a fine tenon or dovetail up to 20. The number of teeth/inch is usually stamped on the blade, just beneath the handle.

Ripsaws are sharpened so their teeth act like chisels to plane out the slivers of wood along the grain. Crosscut have theirs sharpened like knives, as their tips are made to sever the wood fibres.

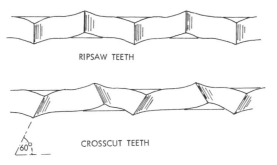

RIPSAW TEETH

CROSSCUT TEETH

Fig. 50

The teeth on all saws are slightly splayed to give them a 'set'. This makes the sawcut slightly wider than the blade and allows it to pass more easily through the wood. The best saws are tapered from the handle to the tip and from the teeth side of the blade towards the back. This both lightens the saw and allows it to slip more easily through the sawcut.

EQUIPMENT NEEDED TO SERVICE SAWS

(1) A good 6in. or 7in. triangular file made by Oberg or Nicholson.
(2) A lead-lined saw anvil (will be described in more detail, later).
(3) A hide hammer.
(4) Good quality flat file.
(5) A saw set
(6) A source of good bright daylight.

The steps in setting and sharpening a saw are taken in order:
1. Debuckling.
2. Topping.
3. Setting.
4. Dressing.
5. Sharpening.
Note that the actual sharpening is left until last.

If you are learning, go out and buy a cheap buckled misused saw and practise on that before trying the real thing.

1. Debuckling

Saws get buckled through the use of excessive force, because of inadequate 'set', bluntness or pushing the handle out of the line of direction of the sawcut. A badly buckled saw is a job for an expert, but simple bends in the saw can be removed by the amateur. Lay the saw, with the concave of the buckle downwards, on the hardwood surface of your work cabinet and hold the saw, bending it slightly, in such a way that the surface of the buckle is in contact with the hardwood. Beat the saw with a series of blows across the blade as shown, checking frequently that you haven't overdone it. (Fig. 52)

2. Topping

When a blade has been sharpened regularly, the line of the tips of the teeth

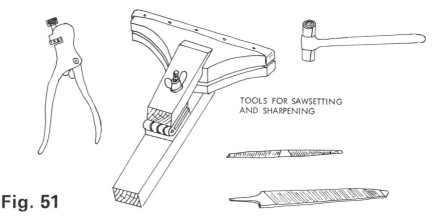

TOOLS FOR SAWSETTING AND SHARPENING

Fig. 51

Fig. 52

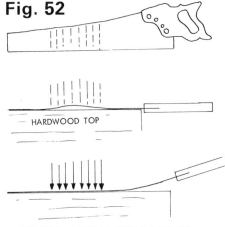

HARDWOOD TOP

REMOVING A BUCKLE FROM A SAWBLADE

becomes wavy and irregular, which can be seen by sighting along the blade. Fix a flat file in a piece of wood as shown and run it along the teeth until they are level. The holder shown is the preferred way of doing it and prevents your fingers from being caught between file and teeth.

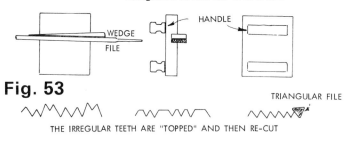

Fig. 53

THE IRREGULAR TEETH ARE "TOPPED" AND THEN RE-CUT

3. Setting

The teeth are set alternately to the left and right so the sawcut or kerf is just wide enough to allow the blade to clear it. Too much will make unnecessary work while

too little will cause the saw to bind. Only the tip of each tooth is set. If the tooth is bent at the root, it may snap off or the blade may crack.

Adjust the sawset until the number opposite the setting tooth corresponds with that on the blade, usually found beneath the handle.

Fig. 54 SET ONLY THE TIPS OF THE TEETH

4. Side Dressing

Inevitably, some teeth will be set more than others, so remove the projecting tips by laying the blade flat on a piece of wood and rub an oil stone gently along them to remove the high spots.

5. Sharpening

This is the last, but most important stage. Because of their different shapes crosscut and rip saws have to be treated differently. In both cases they are made very easy if you buy a saw anvil for £25 or make one for about £4. I cannot emphasise enough how simple it becomes when this infrequently described, rarely seen piece of equipment, is used.

The saw is held between the lead lined jaws, with $\frac{3}{8}$in. of the blade protruding. The bottom fits in the work cabinet vice, which brings the working area up to a comfortable height.

Rip saw teeth are sharpened so the cutting edge is at right angles to the blade. Place the file in the gullet and file the front of the tooth which is set away from you. Sharpen on the 'away' stroke. When one side is complete, turn the saw around and do the other side.

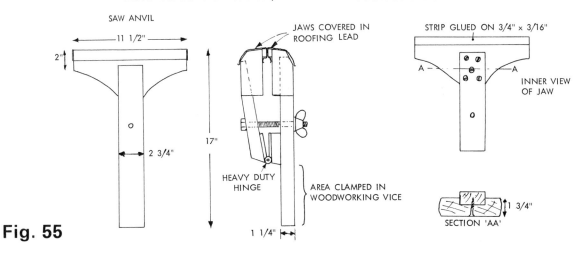

Fig. 55

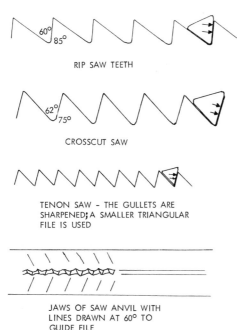

RIP SAW TEETH

CROSSCUT SAW

TENON SAW – THE GULLETS ARE
SHARPENED; A SMALLER TRIANGULAR
FILE IS USED

JAWS OF SAW ANVIL WITH
LINES DRAWN AT 60° TO
GUIDE FILE

Fig. 56

Crosscut and tenon teeth are shaped differently because they cut across the grain and sever the wood fibres. Guide-lines drawn on the lead jaws help to direct the file. File the front of the tooth on the away stroke. Because of the compound geometric effect, the gullet angle will be about 62°. Fine tenon and dovetail saws have their teeth set around 50° and are sharpened as with the crosscut.

After sharpening the teeth tighten the screws which hold on the handle. Make sure the teeth are adequately protected. Saw teeth are easily damaged by contact with other tools, so buy a plastic poster holder from your local gimmick shop, and slide it over the teeth. Polish any rust off with wire wool and if you have a damp workshed, smear the blade with grease or oil.

Although sawmakers control their means of manufacture very carefully some saws do seem better than others. The older saws which have survived bear this out and can be bought at secondhand shops for a few pounds. The covetous collectors do not seem to have decided yet to hoard them. Look for such names as Disston, Phila., Tyzack and Turner or the earlier Spear and Jackson. Wooden jack planes with blades by Sorby are also very good to use.

5. Sawing, Chiselling and Planing

Mastery of these with sharp tools is straightforward, but the behaviour of individual woods can only be learnt by experience. Much of what can be done with hand-tools is just as well performed by machines, but you owe it to the different timbers to learn about their properties through your own hands. Anyhow, it would be unwise to invest in woodworking machinery if subsequently you discover that cabinet-making was only a passing whim.

So what techniques is the D.I.Y. cabinet-maker trying to master?

1. Sawing.
(a) To saw down the grain with a ripsaw, keeping to within $\frac{1}{16}$ in. of a pencil line.
(c) To cut along the edge of pencil lines to make a good mortise and tenon joint.
(d) To cut with even finer tolerances with a gents saw, to make a snug dovetail.

2. Chiselling.
To use this unguarded cutting edge to:
(a) Learn to pare and cut, always being aware of the direction of the wood-grain.
(b) To learn that chisels are wedge-shaped and tend to move sideways as they are hammered through the wood.

Chiselling is more hazardous than sawing or planing. Adjacent teeth of a saw-blade prevent each tooth from cutting too deep, and in a similar way the sole of a plane prevents too thick a shaving from being removed.

3. Planing.
(a) To learn the function of the different kinds of plane.
(b) To gather knowledge of how different kinds of wood react to different blade settings.

Sawing

The golden rule of easy sawing is always have the saw sharp and correctly set. After this, support the timber being sawn, if necessary at both ends. Use the small workbench (or two if you have them) and saw on a lawn if you can. The four legs level themselves and the sawdust disappears amongst the grass. Mark both sides of the plank and, if possible, saw from both sides to keep the sawcut square. Start the saw off at a shallow angle using the knuckle of the left thumb to guide it for the first few cuts. After this raise the handle so the blade is inclined to 45° using long strokes without too much force. Don't press down on the blade otherwise the saw will bow and buckle and the sawcut wander. Keep about $\frac{1}{16}$ in. outside the line while ripping and a little closer while crosscutting. Extending the index finger gives much better saw control. Support both ends of the plank whilst crosscutting to prevent the two halves from snagging and nipping the blade, and support the wood as the sawcut ends, otherwise a large splinter will tear off and spoil the plank. If you can't keep the saw square to the plank stand a small set square by the blade. Avoid sawing damp timber as it jams the saw with the subsequent risk of buckling. 'Jamming' can occur with dry seasoned timber as the sawcut reveals internal tension and closes in on itself. A small wedge of wood will open the cut.

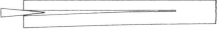

SAWCUT WEDGED OPEN TO PREVENT "BINDING"

Fig. 57

Ripping can be carried out with the timber upright in a vice.

Fig. 58

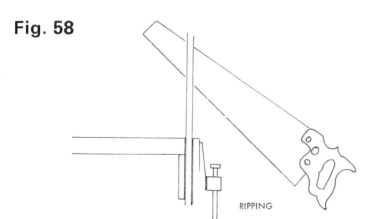

RIPPING

Tenon saw blades are much thinner and have a heavy steel or brass back to give rigidity and weight. A gents saw is very

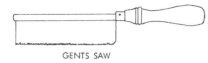

GENTS SAW

useful and inexpensive. It is really a miniature tenon saw.

While using a tenon saw, hold the wood in a vice or on a bench hook, which itself is held in a vice. Two bench hooks are very useful as they prevent the timber rocking as it is sawn.

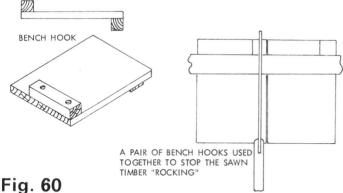

BENCH HOOK

A PAIR OF BENCH HOOKS USED TOGETHER TO STOP THE SAWN TIMBER "ROCKING"

Fig. 60

Chiselling

This is a skill acquired by painful experience, but it can be one of the most pleasurable jobs in cabinet making. Chisels have an unguarded cutting edge and can be lethal to both oneself and one's work. General advice is:

(1) Always keep the chisel sharp. A blunt chisel needs excessive force and causes accidents.
(2) Use a wooden mallet, never a steel headed hammer.

(3) Keep both hands behind the cutting edge.
(4) Buy a set of mortise chisels, $\frac{1}{8}$ in., $\frac{1}{4}$ in., $\frac{3}{8}$ in., $\frac{1}{2}$ in., $\frac{3}{4}$ in., 1 in.

Fig. 61

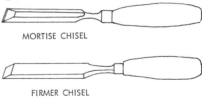

MORTISE CHISEL

FIRMER CHISEL

The edges of a mortise chisel are bevelled to allow reaching into inaccessible corners.

Use of the chisel depends on an intimate knowledge of the grain and how each

Fig. 62

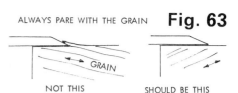

NOT THIS   SHOULD BE THIS

individual wood will react to the wedge shape of the tip. The commonest pitfall is splitting when it is not intended.

ALWAYS PARE WITH THE GRAIN **Fig. 63**

GRAIN

NOT THIS   SHOULD BE THIS

Fig. 64a

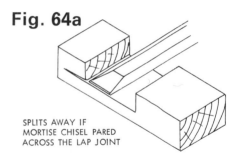

SPLITS AWAY IF MORTISE CHISEL PARED ACROSS THE LAP JOINT

Use multiple sawcuts when paring a lap joint.

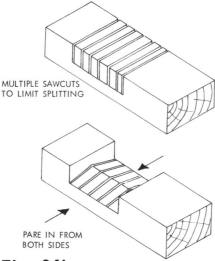

MULTIPLE SAWCUTS
TO LIMIT SPLITTING

PARE IN FROM
BOTH SIDES

Fig. 64b

The wedge shape of the chisel tends to drive it across the pencil line, so start a short distance into the wastewood.

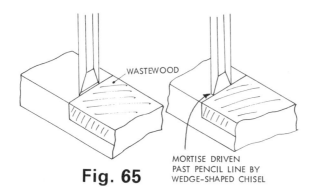

WASTEWOOD

Fig. 65

MORTISE DRIVEN
PAST PENCIL LINE BY
WEDGE-SHAPED CHISEL

Another common error is for mortices to end up wider at the bottom than the top because the chisel has been used away

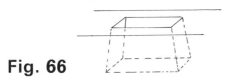

Fig. 66

from the vertical. Avoid this by using a small set square.

Use the chisel carefully along the side of a mortise, otherwise splitting occurs.

Fig. 67

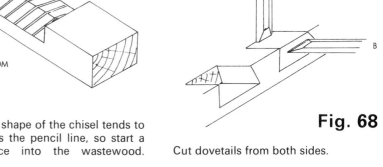

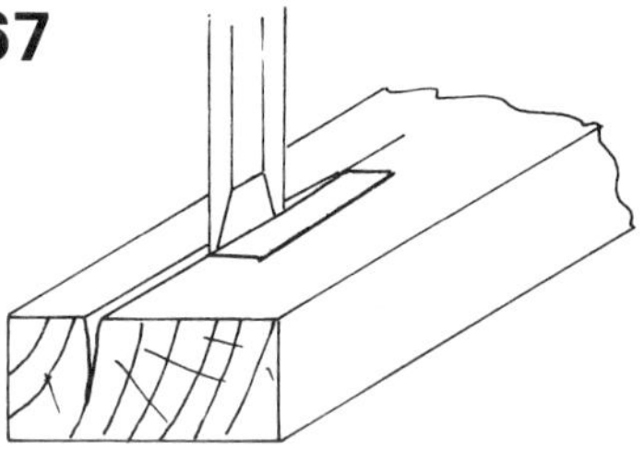

When chopping out dovetails make sure (a) goes deeper than (b), otherwise a chunk of wood will be split from the face of the plank.

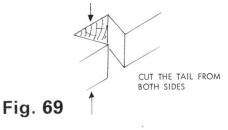

A

B

Fig. 68

Cut dovetails from both sides.

CUT THE TAIL FROM
BOTH SIDES

Fig. 69

Further hints on chiselling:

(1) Put wastewood beneath the work when chiselling downwards on the work cabinet.

(2) Drill as much wastewood as possible away, leaving the delicate mortise chisel to finish off.

(3) Exert pressure from the shoulder, leaving the hands to guide the cutting edge.

(4) Avoid using the palm of the hand to hit the handle. Over many years this will scar up the tendons of the hand.

(5) Always have a sharpening stone handy. A few strokes will restore the edge.

(6) You can split or pare with a chisel, but in cabinet-making most of the work is paring. Remember a split will always follow the grain and is a sight which forever haunts cabinet-makers.

Planing

There are many different kinds of plane and whole books have been written on the subject. The amateur cabinet-maker needs only five:

1.

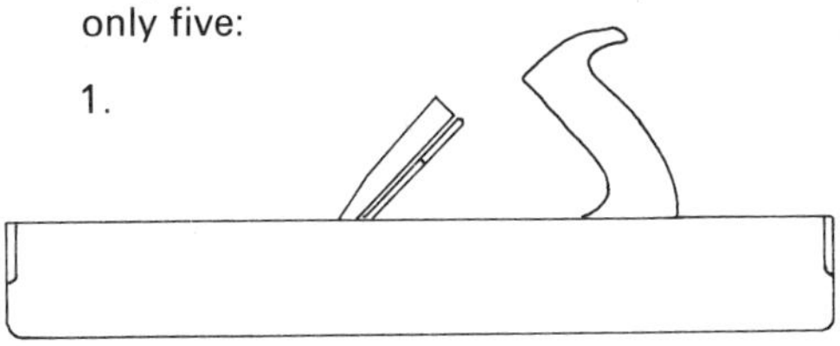

WOODEN JACK PLANE

Fig. 70

It is useful for producing a flat unfinished surface over large areas. Its length helps to true-up the surface.

2.

45°

STEEL SMOOTHING PLANE

Fig. 71

This tool has evolved over 2000 years and is similar in design to that used by the Romans. It is used for smoothing any roughness left by the jack plane.

3.

25°

BLOCK PLANE

Fig. 72

It is a smaller two-handed plane used for shaping and trueing around curves or across mitres. The blade is set at 25° and is the opposite way up to that of the jack or smoothing plane.

4.

20°

BULLNOSE PLANE

Fig. 73

A small but exceedingly useful one-handed plane for all sorts of jobs where the heavy smoothing plane is too big and clumsy. Its front can be removed to give the blade access into the tightest of corners.

5. Combination plane.
This is a rather expensive but useful plane, used for shaping rather than smoothing. It has 20 different kinds of blade used for rebating, grooving and making mouldings.

Most of these tasks can be performed with a chisel, knife and glasspaper, but are more elegantly carried out with this very useful time-saving plane.

Planing and smoothing are stages in shaping the rough initial-sawn plank, into a piece of cabinet-made furniture. Other tools are used in smoothing, including the drawknife, which is really a plane without

DRAWKNIFE

Fig. 74

a body. It is a deadly tool when used for removing the waney edge prior to using the jack plane.

It was used by Vikings to build their long boats. Using it provides the easiest means of achieving a rough level edge.

Using the Plane

A plane is a flat piece of metal or wood with a blade protruding through the bottom which shaves off a thin strip of wood. A 'step' will be produced which allows the plane to rock fore and aft, to cause the surface to be either convex or concave, so

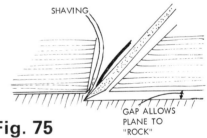

SHAVING

GAP ALLOWS PLANE TO "ROCK"

Fig. 75

a plane needs to be used with a 2 ft. steel cabinet-maker's rule to true the surface. A long board may tend to 'wind' with planing and drying and it is as well to check for this by looking along two squared battens.

EYE

CHECK FOR "WINDING"

Fig. 76

As mentioned, a plane can rock on its protruding blade, causing the front to point slightly up or down, so there has to

33

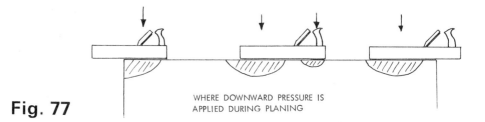

Fig. 77

WHERE DOWNWARD PRESSURE IS
APPLIED DURING PLANING

be adjustment of the points of pressure. At the beginning of the stroke, the plane is pressed on the front, at the end on the back and in the middle slightly more on the front than the back.

Jack and smoothing planes have their blades set at 45° with their back or

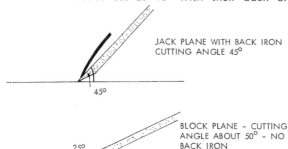

JACK PLANE WITH BACK IRON
CUTTING ANGLE 45°

45°

BLOCK PLANE - CUTTING
ANGLE ABOUT 50° - NO
BACK IRON

25° 25°

Fig. 78

breaking irons just above the cutting edge to make the shaving leave the wood without splitting forwards.

Block and bullnose planes have their blades set around 30°, with the blade reversed, so it acts itself as a shaving breaker.

The back iron is a very important part of the plane and its use needs a careful explanation. Its position relative to the tip of the blade will determine to what degree the shaving is split or broken as it leaves the wood. The further up the blade the back iron is set, the more splitting takes place. The nearer the tip, the earlier the wood fibres of the shaving are broken as they are turned back on themselves. Obviously, it is easier to split than to break and so it is hard work to plane with the back iron set nearer the tip.

However, where the grain is in all directions, the tendency of the plane to tear off chunks of wood can be diminished by setting the back iron close to the edge. Its optimum position has to be found by trial and error, but approximate settings are

SHAVING

SHAVING SPLITS OFF COARSELY AS THE BACK
IRON IS SET WELL BACK FROM THE CUTTING EDGE

SHAVING IS BROKEN IMMEDIATELY IT LEAVES
THE BOARD WHEN THE BACK IRON IS SET
CLOSE TO THE CUTTING EDGE. IT ALLOWS
THE PLANE TO BE USED AGAINST THE GRAIN.

Fig. 79

$\frac{1}{16}$ in. on coarse shavings for straight-grained softwoods and $\frac{1}{32}$ in. or less for fine shavings off wild grained hardwoods.

Before commencing to plane, check that the blade is set square by looking from the front of the plane to check the blade edge is parallel to the sole.

Planing is easiest with the grain, but this may change several times over the length of a plank. Where possible change the direction of planing, or, if not, reset the back iron.

Mention has been made of sharpening and shaping the plane blade to a slight curve and then rounding the corners. The jack plane is curved more than the smooth plane. It leaves a scolloped wavy finish, which can be attractive and provide an appropriate surface on shaped planks at the back of furniture.

Planing end grain is different and here the block plane and bullnose are very useful. Care is needed not to split off the ends of the plank, helped by bevelling or clamping on a piece of wastewood.

The combination plane is used for shaping more than finishing. The blades have to be sharp, but the final finish is often not as important as that left by the smoothing plane. There are several makes of these planes and an explanation as to their use is found with each.

Advice about looking after planes:

(1) Always lay them on their sides when not in use to prevent dobs of glue etc. damaging the edge.
(2) Grease the soles when not in use.
(3) Linseed oil the soles of wooden planes to give a protective shine, which also helps prevent splitting.
(4) Keep sharp.

The finish produced by plane is limited by the grooves and ridges left by the corners. These are removed by scrapers, glasspaper and wire wool.

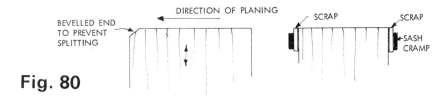

DIRECTION OF PLANING

BEVELLED END
TO PREVENT
SPLITTING

SCRAP

SCRAP

SASH
CRAMP

Fig. 80

6. Glueing

Do-It-Yourself produces pictures in most people's minds of screwing and nailing and attaching patent fitments. Glue is used because the instructions say so. Lap joints, mortise and tenons and dovetails are pinned and screwed, glue being used to fill in the gaps. There is a lingering doubt as to its effectiveness.

In the middle ages, carpenters and joiners relied on the shape of their joints for strength, together with pegs and dowels. Gaps opened as the wood changed shape in response to the weather and stress, often leading to disastrous results. Although the cabinet-maker relies on interlocking pieces of wood and dowels to hold it all together, these days most fixing is achieved by glueing.

Later in the book several pieces of furniture are laminated and veneered. Veneering allows sheets of the most decorative wood to be used where planks of such timber would warp and split. Laminating thin sheets of wood enormously strengthens the resultant thickness of wood because the grains of the individual sheets are glued across each other.

Laminating and veneering depend on reliable glueing. Modern glues bought at D.I.Y. shops when applied correctly are far stronger than the wood on which they are used. To repeat, they are excellent adhesives *WHEN APPLIED CORRECTLY*.

Yet, if you play with pieces of hardened casein adhesive or white cabinet-makers glue, they seem to have no strength. The casein is brittle and snaps while the white glue is soft and pulls out like hardened chewing gum.

It was thought until recently that glue worked by entangling the wood fibres and enmeshing together adjacent pieces of wood in a mass of glue. Modern theories suggest that adhesion is due to an attraction between glue and wood molecules.

If the mechanical theory was correct, then butt joining should be much stronger than it is. The glue would be expected to soak down the holes in the wood cells and produce an unbreakable anchorage. In fact this butt joint is very much weaker than the side grain-side grain joint. An explanation of the paradox lies in understanding the structure of wood and how glue works.

Wood is made up of many spindle-shaped cells, square, hexagonal or polygonal in cross section and about 30-40 times as long as they are wide.

They are composed mostly of cellulose, but also of lignin, hemi-celluloses and small amounts of pectin (the same substance that makes jam set), resins, tannins and volatile oils. Each cell wall is built up of

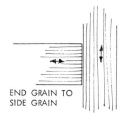

END GRAIN TO SIDE GRAIN

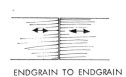

ENDGRAIN TO ENDGRAIN

WOOD CELLS CUT ACROSS AND SEEN UNDER THE MICROSCOPE

Fig. 81

several layers of cellulose fibrils wound around the walls like coils of a spring. The direction of the coils differs from layer to layer. Between the fibrils of cellulose is a crystalline form of cellulose and between the crystals and chains are enmeshed lignin molecules. These are irregular molecular structures of three-dimensional chains. The cell wall is like reinforced concrete, the fibrils acting like steel rods, the crystalline cellulose and lignin the concrete between the rods.

However, the main constituent of wood is cellulose. Each cellulose molecule is made up of 3000 glucose molecules (yes, the same sugar which the adverts tell you gives you more energy).

Freshly cut wood will, like most substances, absorb molecules of air and water into the surface. These will interfere with glueing. Grease and oil, particularly from one's fingers, are soaked up like blotting paper. Dirt is caught up in the tiny crevices and cell cavities. These will prevent the glue coming into intimate contact with the wood molecules.

So, just before glueing, treat the surface of the wood carefully and gently.

(1) Use sharp tools to get the final dimensions and avoid tools which tear, burnish or polish.
(2) Avoid all oil or grease and don't touch the surface to be glued with your sweaty fingers.

SPINDLE-SHAPE OF ONE WOOD CELL

Fig. 82

The commonly used adhesives, Cascamite and Evo-stik cabinet-maker's glue, work by molecular attraction between the glue molecules and the constituents of the cell wall. Nobody understands what adhesion is, but it lies somewhere between chemical combination and electrostatic attraction. The glue molecules want to adhere to the wood molecules. They are avid for each other. The problems encountered by woodworkers with glued joints are due to these molecules not being able to get close enough together, either because of interference by another substance or a wide joint which relies on the mechanical properties of the glue, which as we have seen is very poor indeed.

The world of the exposed wood molecules is a very delicate temporary place. The long chains of glucose molecules are readily destroyed by a variation of trauma. Wood is such a poor conductor of heat that local polishing or rubbing rapidly raises the local temperature to char it to glucose, carbon and other breakdown products. Two pieces of wood vigorously rubbed together will produce the smell of burning. Vigorous planing or scraping will cause the same effect. Local heat in the presence of oxygen will denature wood, rendering it useless for glueing.

Light denatures and changes the surface of wood. Cover half a plank of wood and expose it to sunlight for a few days—see how it fades! Light waves break down the surface molecules of cellulose and lignin.

(3) Just before glueing, sand with sharp medium to fine glasspaper or 'wet and dry' which will not burnish. There is evidence that the closer in time this is carried out to glueing, the better the result.
(4) Brush off all the dust with a clean paint brush.
(5) Apply the glue according to the manufacturer's instructions.
(6) Exclude air bubbles from the glue by not agitating it as it is applied.

Having prepared the surfaces for glueing, the problem of how to get them as close as possible in order to exploit molecular attraction between wood and glue takes up a considerable proportion of the rest of the book.

Two pieces of wood can be mated together accurately by sawing, planing and chiselling. However, wood is constantly changing its shape, with changes in temperature and humidity. In our climate, these can vary from hour to hour. To add to the difficulties these changes vary far more across the grain than they do along it.

Much of this can be overcome by brute force, that is to say heavy pressure clamping. Experts might argue that it puts the wood under considerable stress and distortion and hence weakens it. I would retort by reminding them that another major property of wood is 'creep'. It behaves like plastic whereby if subjected to continuous stress it will accommodate to it by changing its shape and becoming permanently deformed.

MODERN GLUES USED FOR REPAIRING CRICKET BATS

So good are the D.I.Y. glues that they can be used for glueing pieces of willow together to make usable cricket bats. This demonstration should be of great value to those who both do cabinet work and play cricket and also of interest to those who know little of cricket.

Our local cricket club had six broken bats which were cannibalised into three usable ones, which survived three seasons in the nets. A good bat costs around £40.00.

Willow seems rubbery and soft when worked. Planes and chisels have to be very sharp to cut it as the wood 'dents' in front of the cutting edge. Yet it is very tough—the Romans used it for spokes in their wooden wheels. Its toughness and ability to deform under pressure make it an ideal wood to demonstrate how successful is pressure glueing. Even if the surfaces to be glued are not perfectly mated, G-clamps will do the rest. It is like glueing together two pieces of irregularly shaped polyurethane foam with contact adhesive; when the pressure is released, they stay together.

The best bigger pieces of the cricket bats were saved, including those where the gluelines between blade and handle were perfect. One handle was removed, as was part of one blade which was to fit the handle. The waste was carefully removed and hardened glue scraped away. (Fig. 84)

Sloping joints across the grain were limited to 1 in 15.

Where the gradient is more than this, it starts to become a butt joint i.e. endgrain to endgrain. This varies from timber to timber, and willow will glue successfully down to 1:8, though the gradient of the bat splice is much less than this.

The surfaces are mated together with the liberal use of blue chalk and mortise chisels. However, the main trick for glueing pieces of willow together to make a cricket bat is the ability to apply pressure. The handle is glued on to the blade using a sash cramp, G-clamps and two pieces of grooved softwood. Pressure has to be applied in two directions.

The sash cramp stops the wedge-shaped handle being squeezed out like a piece of soap, while five G-clamps apply pressure from blade to handle.

This job is well within the capacity of the D.I.Y. cabinet-maker, given the necessary equipment. Don't be overawed by pictures of elderly bespectacled craftsmen in aprons working in cricket bat factories in darkest Sussex! With careful preparation of the glue surfaces and modern D.I.Y. adhesives you are as good as them.

One blade thus repaired was made up of five separate pieces, another of three pieces. (Fig. 87)

A cradle of softwood has to be made so repairs can be carried out to the face of the blade. Pressure can then be exerted on this surface.

When the glue has set, there is nothing more exciting than reshaping the bats with drawknife, spokeshave and plane. The gluelines are almost invisible. The bat is reborn to its original shape.

A week's raw linseed and gentle beating with an old cricket ball and three remade bats were ready for use in the nets.

Fig. 83-88

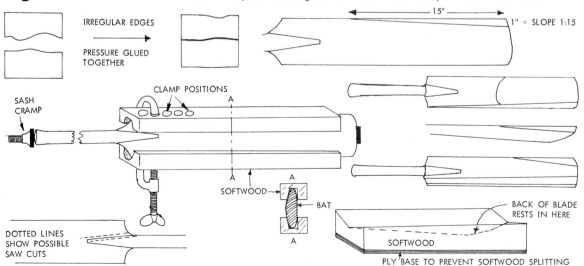

IRREGULAR EDGES

PRESSURE GLUED TOGETHER

15"

1" = SLOPE 1:15

SASH CRAMP

CLAMP POSITIONS

SOFTWOOD

BAT

DOTTED LINES SHOW POSSIBLE SAW CUTS

BACK OF BLADE RESTS IN HERE

SOFTWOOD

PLY BASE TO PREVENT SOFTWOOD SPLITTING

7. The Small Hardwood Bookcase

With sharp tools and a solid stable work cabinet, the D.I.Y. cabinet-maker begins to feel like a craftsman.

This small hardwood bookcase is more complicated than the upholstered box stool and could take nine months to a year to make. Its construction incorporates many cabinet-making techniques.

The correct sequence of assembly is one of the common problems of cabinet-making. Putting this bookcase together with its hidden drawer at the top is a good example of why it is important to take the stages of assembly in the correct order. Often designers do not make this clear.

Individual techniques of cutting and shaping are described as they occur. For example, it seems more realistic to learn about rebates and inlaying as the need arises. However, there are far more extensive accounts in other woodworking books and I hope you will take the opportunity to read them up.

Making the bookcase is an exercise in:
(1) Cutting sliding stopped dovetails.
(2) Cutting a full housing joint for a shelf.
(3) Making cabinet-makers', carpenters' and lap dovetails.
(4) Cutting rebates with gauge, knife, chisel or bullnose plane.
(5) Inlaying and marquetry.
(6) Making beading and chamfering.
(7) Production and use of two $\frac{1}{4}$in veneers.
(8) Producing a fine finish on hardwood.

Apart from the work cabinet, most tools are available from D.I.Y. shops.

A small bookcase is a useful asset to any home. This one can be tucked away in a corner or small alcove, or moved on its castors to a new position. Small bookcases are very difficult to obtain. They are very expensive in antique shops and almost non-existent in modern furniture stores. They have to be made extra strong as books 'en masse' are very heavy. Veneered chipboard bookcases look very nice, but may well disintegrate after a few years. This one is made of hardwood and has two drawers, two shelves and modern castors mounted underneath to allow it to be moved. If made in oak, it can be finished in linseed oil and beeswax.

There is no need to follow the dimensions exactly, although it will be difficult to alter the general layout and arrangements

Fig. 89

Fig. 90

THE BOOKCASE

The visual arrangement took longest to decide on. It has an antique look. The bottom compartment is higher than the top to give visual interest. The architrave is inlaid with maple and laburnum to form a 'flowers and berries' pattern and is emphasised by the beading and overhang of the top.

The lower drawer is similarly emphasised with cock-beading and is set off by brass knobs mounted on etched brass plates, which form a flower petal shape. The shelves and sides are beaded and chamfered to fit in with the richness of the architrave and drawer front.

The inlay in the architrave first catches the eye, followed closely by the brass knobs and beading, chamfering and ogees of the bottom. The beading conveys the eye to the sides, passes on to the thumb-nailing of the shelves and sides, then explores the colour and texture of the wood. The relative proportions of the top and bottom drawer compartments are noted and approved. The perception will then return to the inlay to explore it more carefully, relating it in more detail to the rest of the bookcase.

Three planks of hardwood $10\frac{1}{2}$ in. × 56 in., planed to $\frac{5}{8}$ in., will be needed, together with some odd pieces of $\frac{1}{4}$ in. thick oak for the back, floor of the top, drawer sides and bottoms. Try to select the three hardwood planks so they are the same colour. Better still, find a baulk $10\frac{1}{2}$ in. × $2\frac{1}{2}$ in. × 56 in. and have it sawn and planed to three $\frac{5}{8}$ in. planks. If they are damp or unseasoned, seal the ends with bitumastic paint and clamp together, separated by $\frac{3}{4}$ in. softwood stickers or roofing slats. Leave to dry out slowly at the end of a shed or garage. Pray that they dry out without splitting.

Before starting, carefully inspect the three planks for sapwood, rot, deadknots, splits, shakes and woodworm. Circle faults with a pencil. Note where the most attractive 'graining' is situated and try to arrange so that it is used on the top, the architrave or drawer front at the bottom.

Check and double check all measurements before sawing.

Arrange and cut with as little waste as possible, but allow a little extra on the sides and shelves for the inevitable bruising during making. Preserve all scrap for beading, cock-beading and drawer sides.

There is not enough wood for both drawer front and architrave. They are the same rectangular shape, so cut a piece $\frac{5}{8}$ in.

of the joints. For those who have the curiosity and urge to design their own furniture here is an account of how the bookcase layout was arrived at. A building extension to our sitting room provided an alcove $2\frac{1}{2}$ ft. wide, which could be used only for a bookcase or book-shelves. Fitting bookshelves would be too final, so my wife decided that the space should be occupied by a small bookcase. A search of shops, both antique and modern, was unsuccessful, so I decided to make one.

I browsed through antique magazines, making rough sketches of what I liked. An 'antique' look was preferred. I wanted a drawer at the bottom, beneath the book-shelves, and a small drawer at the back, to hide things away, and to make the task more complicated. The concealed castors were necessary for moving this bookcase away from the alcove.

A small balsawood model was made and placed on the sideboard, where it could be seen several times a day. After several months sketching and remodelling, the final shape was agreed.

It was to be made in English oak, left in its natural colour and finished in the traditional way, that is linseed oil and beeswax.

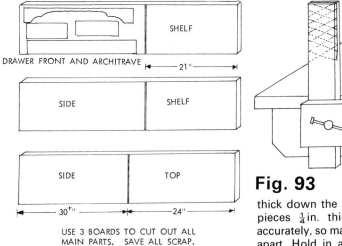

SHELF

DRAWER FRONT AND ARCHITRAVE

←———— 21" ————→

SIDE   SHELF

SIDE   TOP

←———— 30⁺" ————→←——— 24" ———→

Fig. 91

USE 3 BOARDS TO CUT OUT ALL
MAIN PARTS. SAVE ALL SCRAP.

↕ 1/2" DOTTED LINES SHOW
EXTENT OF EACH CUT

Fig. 93

thick down the middle to end up with 2
pieces $\frac{1}{4}$ in. thick. It has to be done
accurately, so mark two lines around $\frac{1}{16}$ in.
apart. Hold in a vice and by constantly
reversing the plant, progress at $\frac{1}{2}$ in. cuts
down the plant, each cut providing a
groove to guide the next cut.

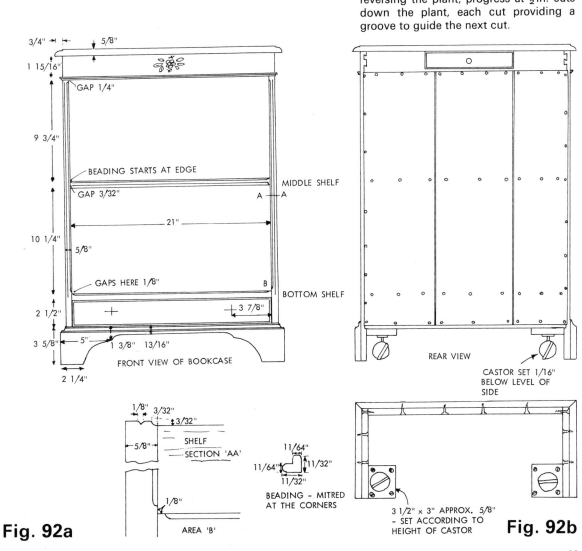

3/4"   5/8"

1 15/16"

GAP 1/4"

9 3/4"

BEADING STARTS AT EDGE

GAP 3/32"

MIDDLE SHELF

A ← A

←———— 21" ————→

10 1/4"

5/8"

GAPS HERE 1/8"

B

BOTTOM SHELF

2 1/2"

3 7/8"

3 5/8"   5"   1 3/8" 13/16"

FRONT VIEW OF BOOKCASE

2 1/4"

REAR VIEW

CASTOR SET 1/16"
BELOW LEVEL OF
SIDE

1/8" 3/32"

↕ 3/32"

5/8"   SHELF

SECTION 'AA'

11/64"

11/64"   11/32"

11/32"

BEADING - MITRED
AT THE CORNERS

1/8"

AREA 'B'

Fig. 92a

3 1/2" x 3" APPROX. 5/8"
- SET ACCORDING TO
HEIGHT OF CASTOR

Fig. 92b

This technique is the precursor of that used later in the book, to produce thin sheets of wood which will be used for veneering and laminating.

THE SIDES OF THE BOOKCASE

Plane and square up the back of each side, and mark the position of each shelf by placing them together in the vice and marking across both.

The two shelves are fitted to the sides by sliding dovetails, which stop $\frac{5}{8}$ in. from the front.

MAKING THE SLIDING STOPPED DOVETAILS

A. Shelf ends:
(1) Mark out as shown with FRONT and REAR clearly written on top and bottom. Allow the shelves to be a little wider than the $9\frac{1}{4}$ in. shown, but stop the dovetail $\frac{1}{2}$ in. from the front. (This can be corrected to $\frac{5}{8}$ in. later). The slope of the dovetail is 10°. The precise angle is not critical as long as it is the same as the slide.
(2) Clamp the shelf to the work cabinet

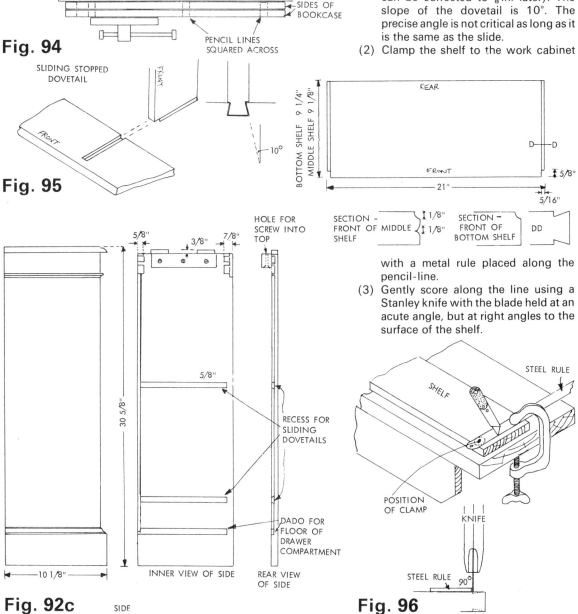

Fig. 94

SIDES OF BOOKCASE

PENCIL LINES SQUARED ACROSS

SLIDING STOPPED DOVETAIL

FRONT

Fig. 95

FRONT

10°

BOTTOM SHELF 9 1/4"
MIDDLE SHELF 9 1/8"

REAR

FRONT

D—D

5/8"

21"

5/16"

SECTION – FRONT OF MIDDLE SHELF   1/8" 1/8"

SECTION – FRONT OF BOTTOM SHELF   DD

with a metal rule placed along the pencil-line.
(3) Gently score along the line using a Stanley knife with the blade held at an acute angle, but at right angles to the surface of the shelf.

STEEL RULE

SHELF

POSITION OF CLAMP

KNIFE

STEEL RULE 90°

Fig. 96

HOLE FOR SCREW INTO TOP

5/8"   3/8"   7/8"

5/8"

30 5/8"

RECESS FOR SLIDING DOVETAILS

DADO FOR FLOOR OF DRAWER COMPARTMENT

10 1/8"

INNER VIEW OF SIDE

REAR VIEW OF SIDE

Fig. 92c   SIDE

(4) Remove the waste wood with a mortise chisel to the bottom of the cut, without clipping the edge of the steel rule.

(5) Repeat until the required depth is achieved, turn the shelf around and repeat the process.

(6) Cut off the dovetail $\frac{1}{2}$ in. from the front.

B. Slides

(1) Mark out, checking that the depth and angle correspond with that on the shelf. Stop the 'slide' $\frac{5}{8}$ in. from the front.

(2) Clamp to the work cabinet, with a piece of wood alongside the pencil line to prevent scoring by the tenon saw if it jumps out of its cut.

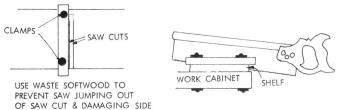

USE WASTE SOFTWOOD TO PREVENT SAW JUMPING OUT OF SAW CUT & DAMAGING SIDE

Fig. 97

(3) Cut with a tenon saw as much as possible, repeat this the other side.

(4) Remove the waste with a mortise chisel, cutting into each sawcut, then removing the lump in the middle.

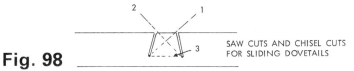

SAW CUTS AND CHISEL CUTS FOR SLIDING DOVETAILS

Fig. 98

(5) Continue the sawcut with the Stanley knife and nibble out the rest of the slide; $\frac{1}{8}$ in, $\frac{1}{4}$ in. and $\frac{3}{8}$ in. mortise chisels will be needed.

When slides and dovetails are complete, test fit and remove any high spots. Err on the side of an easy fit rather than one which

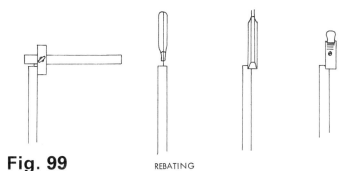

Fig. 99

REBATING

is too perfect, otherwise fitting and glueing will be difficult.

Each night, clamp shelves, sides and top together in the vice as it is inevitable that a $10\frac{1}{2}$ in. wide piece of wood will change its shape as temperature and humidity vary.

Next rebate each bookcase side using knife, marking gauge, mortise chisel and bullnose plane.

(1) Plane and square the corner to be rebated.

(2) Groove with a gauge.

(3) Draw the knife along this gauge line, angling the blade as acutely as possible with light pressure so the blade does not jump out of this gauge line.

(4) Remove the waste with a mortise chisel; repeat scoring with the knife.

(5) Finish off with the bullnose plane.

Leave the moulding, thumbnailing and chamfering till later to avoid bruising or other damage during handling.

Fit the shelves into the sides and plane until their rear edges coincide with the rebate edge.

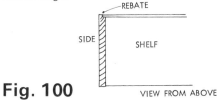

Fig. 100

VIEW FROM ABOVE

Cut the tenons on the top of each bookcase side. Next make the softwood shelf for the front drawer compartment.

Rebating the softwood shelf will be much easier than the hardwood sides.

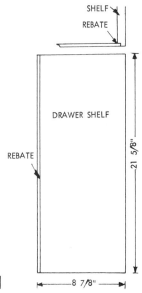

Fig. 101

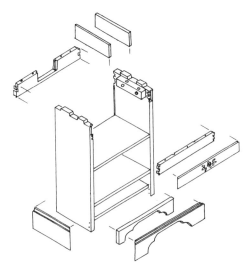

Fig. 102

EXPLODED VIEW TO SHOW GENERAL LAYOUT

The front and rear underframes are the next tasks. Check the widths carefully as the glue joint may add $\frac{1}{64}$ in. each side.

The front underframe is set back $\frac{1}{4}$ in. from the front to allow the inlaid architrave to be glued in afterwards rather like a thick veneer. Cut out the 'carpenters'' dovetails on the underframes and scribe around them on the sides of the bookcase. Rebate the bottom of the rear underframe, both back and front as shown in the detailed layout of the top. Mark across the tops of the underframes to indicate the positions of the rebates which will hold the sides of the drawer compartment. Cut them and make the space for the drawer. Tack a piece of plywood across temporarily to hold it together. Glue them in position together with the hardwood sides of the drawer compartment.

The carcase is now ready for glueing.

Mark the sides and shelves A-A, B-B cut so there is no confusion during glueing. You will need four sets of sash cramps—borrow them if possible, or if not, make the 'frame and wedge' type as described in the chapter on the box stool.

Sand all the joints to remove traces of grease and dirt, then brush away the dust with a paint brush. Use a slow setting glue such as Cascamite. Protect the bookcase from direct cramp pressure by using thin softwood scrap. Before the final tightening of the cramps check the diagonals between opposite corners of the bookcase to ensure squareness. For those unfamiliar with geometry, they should be equal. Remove excess glue with an old chisel rather than a damp rag.

Next make the false hardwood front, screw and glue in position. The screwheads will be hidden by the front and side thickeners.

THICKENERS

These finish off the base and are $\frac{5}{8}$ in. thick. They are made in similar fashion to those of the box stool using gauge, knife, mortise chisel, carving gouge, block plane and a rounded sanding block.

BEADING ON THICKENERS

Fig. 104

They are attached by screwing from the inside of the bottom.

Make the front first, then mitre the sides to it, allowing some waste at the back in case several attempts at mitring have to be made.

Remove and store until the last stages of assembly. The delicate mouldings are easily damaged.

Next fit the castors on the bottom

First make a pair of mortised softwood 'keepers' to protect the top tenons, so the bookcase can be turned upside down.

The blocks to hold the castors should be $3\frac{1}{2}$ in. × 3 in., the exact thickness depending on the height of the castors. Their arrangement is shown in the diagram of the bookcase back and its bottom. The castors should protrude $\frac{1}{16}$ in. below the bottom, so that when the bookcase is tilted back, it rests on the castors and can be moved

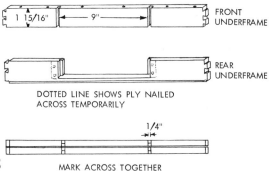

FRONT UNDERFRAME

REAR UNDERFRAME

DOTTED LINE SHOWS PLY NAILED ACROSS TEMPORARILY

1 15/16" 9" 1/4"

Fig. 103

MARK ACROSS TOGETHER

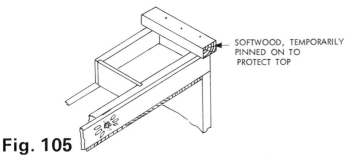

Fig. 105

SOFTWOOD, TEMPORARILY PINNED ON TO PROTECT TOP

across the floor. The slight gap at the rear of the thickness will be hidden by the pile of the carpet.

THE ARCHITRAVE

First mitre the tops of the bookcase sides then fit in the architrave, using blue chalk to find any high spots.

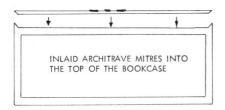

INLAID ARCHITRAVE MITRES INTO THE TOP OF THE BOOKCASE

Fig. 106

Stick masking tape over the sharp mitred ends to prevent their damage. Next inlay:

(1) Cut sheets of laburnum and maple $\frac{1}{8}$ in. thick, planing the side to be glued. Make sure they are dry and seasoned.

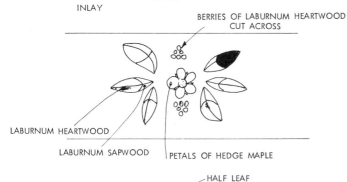

INLAY

BERRIES OF LABURNUM HEARTWOOD CUT ACROSS

LABURNUM HEARTWOOD

LABURNUM SAPWOOD

PETALS OF HEDGE MAPLE

HALF LEAF

Fig. 107

SMALL LOG OF LABURNUM CUT ACROSS OBLIQUELY

(2) Cut out the shapes using a coping or fret saw, supporting the fragile inlays by using a piece of $\frac{1}{8}$ in. ply clamped to the end of the work cabinet. Slope the edges to 80° so they fit more snugly.

(3) Check the central point of the architrave and use it as a reference to place all the pieces.

(4) Mark around and chisel out to a depth of $\frac{3}{32}$ in.

(5) Make some fine hardwood sawdust using a medium grade orbital sander disc. Mix it with hard setting casein glue and set in all the pieces. Clamp in position.

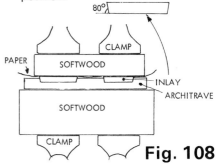

80°

PAPER

CLAMP

SOFTWOOD

INLAY

ARCHITRAVE

SOFTWOOD

CLAMP

Fig. 108

(6) Sand off the excess inlay the following day. It is very exciting to see the inlays emerge from the dust and glue.

(7) Glue the architrave on to the front underframe.

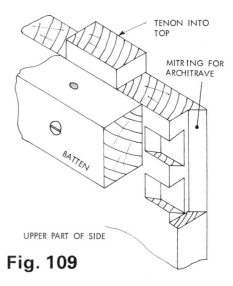

TENON INTO TOP

MITRING FOR ARCHITRAVE

BATTEN

UPPER PART OF SIDE

Fig. 109

MAKING THE TOP

Remove the castors and softwood keepers from the top of the bookcase and place the plank on the exposed tenons. Ensure there is a $\frac{3}{4}$ in. overlay at the front and sides. Draw around the tenons and chisel out the mortises to a depth of $\frac{3}{8}$ in.

Place the top in position and drill through the holes in the underframes and battens to make shallow impressions on its

Fig. 110

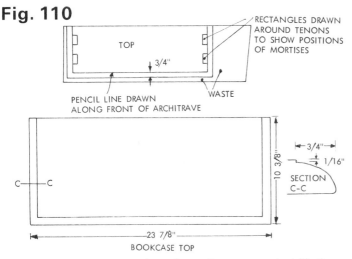

TOP

RECTANGLES DRAWN AROUND TENONS TO SHOW POSITIONS OF MORTISES

3/4"

PENCIL LINE DRAWN ALONG FRONT OF ARCHITRAVE

WASTE

10 3/8"

3/4"

1/16"

SECTION C-C

C — C

23 7/8"

BOOKCASE TOP

undersurface. Remove and drill these impressions to $\frac{3}{8}$ in. using a $\frac{1}{16}$ in. drill. Stick a piece of insulating tape around the drill bit to avoid going too deep.

Draw on the undersurface of the top around the sides and architrave, remove, and draw the final outline $\frac{3}{4}$ in. outside these lines.

Cut the ridge on the top using a 2 ft. steel cabinet-maker's rule clamped in position. Shape this moulded edge with a plane and mortise chisel.

Next bead, thumbnail and chamfer the sides and shelves. This final shaping makes their edges visually very interesting. Only the simplest tools are needed. The thumb-nailing is started with a marking gauge

Fig. 111

cutting lightly at first, then as deep as it will go. Cut a 'Vee' with a Stanley knife and deepen with a mortise chisel used on each side. Repeat the process to a depth of $\frac{1}{8}$ in. At each end of the thumbnail, the groove is narrowed and gradually sloped up the surface over a distance of $\frac{1}{2}$ in. Cut

Fig. 112

LAYOUT OF TOP

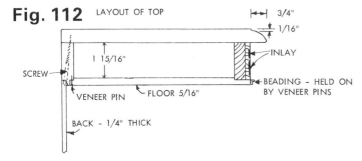

3/4"

1/16"

1 15/16"

INLAY

SCREW

VENEER PIN

FLOOR 5/16"

BEADING - HELD ON BY VENEER PINS

BACK - 1/4" THICK

the curved chamfers by marking $\frac{3}{32}$ in. on each side of the corner and removing the waste with a carving chisel. Stop the ends with a gentle curve. Smooth off the curved bottom with a shaped sanding block.

Professional cabinet-makers would consider these methods too slow and laborious. They would use a piece of steel set in a wooden clamp device called a 'Hag's Tooth', to scrape out these grooves. However, one slip by inexperienced hands would ruin the visual effect.

Screw and glue on the thickeners around the base, and then attach the top. Pin the floor to the front and rear under-frames and 'stop' the holes with a glue/sawdust filler. Plane the end of the floor level with the architrave and use veneer pins to attach beading to it. The beading is made from hardwood scrap from the original planks. It is mitred at the corners.

THE BACK

This is made up of a row of $\frac{1}{4}$ in. thick hardwood planks, placed and rebated as shown in the plan. They are glued and secured to the bookcase with $\frac{3}{4}$ in. screws.

THE DRAWERS

These present a splendid opportunity to practise three different types of dovetail. They are all equally effective, but the cabinet-maker's dovetail always look more elegant.

As an exercise, you could use the carpenter's dovetail on the small drawer and the cabinet-maker's on the bottom drawer. As confidence increases the pins can become smaller.

Make the tops and bottoms of the sides of the drawers extend to the end at the rear. There is less chance of the end pieces splitting off during use.

The dimensions are as shown in the diagrams. Use $\frac{1}{4}$ in. hardwood for the bottoms. There is a description of how to make the dovetails in Chapter 2.

Make sure the dimensions of the drawer correspond with the space available. Don't make the drawer too tight. Some cabinet-makers even taper the drawer towards the back, making it slightly wedge-shaped: it moves more freely and tightens as it is slid home. Don't forget to put a little candle grease on the bottom and sides. Its unobtrusive lubricating effect will last for years.

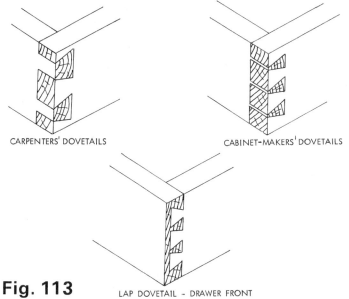

CARPENTERS' DOVETAILS

CABINET-MAKERS' DOVETAILS

Fig. 113

LAP DOVETAIL - DRAWER FRONT

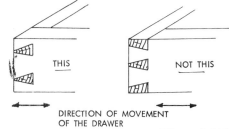

THIS

NOT THIS

DIRECTION OF MOVEMENT
OF THE DRAWER

Fig. 115

COCK BEADING

This is the raised edge around the front of the drawer and emphasises its rectangular shape. It covers the entire thickness of the top and bottom of the drawer but only half or less at the sides, and is mitred at the corners.

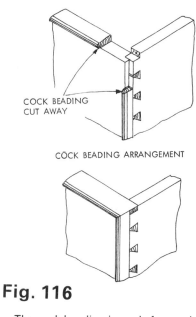

COCK BEADING
CUT AWAY

CÓCK BEADING ARRANGEMENT

Fig. 116

The cock beading is made from strips of scrap so it matches the drawer fronts. Probably you won't have enough clamps to glue/clamp satisfactorily, so use $\frac{1}{8}$ in. plywood squares and veneer pins. These can be removed easily after the glue has set.

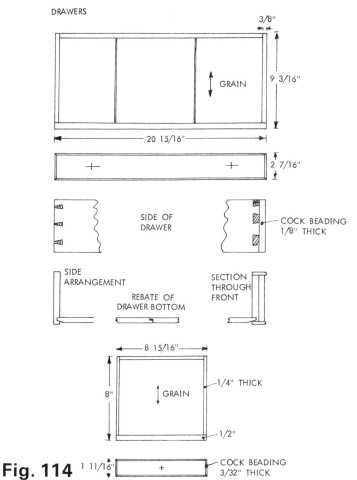

DRAWERS

3/8"

GRAIN

9 3/16"

20 15/16"

2 7/16"

SIDE OF
DRAWER

COCK BEADING
1/8" THICK

SIDE
ARRANGEMENT

SECTION
THROUGH
FRONT

REBATE OF
DRAWER BOTTOM

8 15/16"

8"

GRAIN

1/4" THICK

1/2"

Fig. 114

1 11/16"

COCK BEADING
3/32" THICK

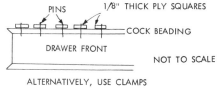

PINS

1/8" THICK PLY SQUARES

COCK BEADING

DRAWER FRONT

NOT TO SCALE

ALTERNATIVELY, USE CLAMPS

Fig. 117

DRAWER HANDLES

Brass fitments always look attractive when set against hardwood. A nice finishing touch is to make back plates out of $\frac{1}{16}$ in. brass sheet rather than use those bought in the hardware store. Make their shape to match the flower on the architrave.

Make a small carving tool out of a nailpunch by bevelling the end and filing it

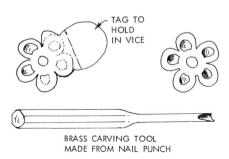

BRASS CARVING TOOL
MADE FROM NAIL PUNCH

Fig. 118

concave with a needle file. Carve out the petals with the punch and light tack hammer. Smooth off the roughness with increasingly fine grades of wire wool and finish with a liquid metal polish such as Brasso. You will have learnt what an accommodating metal brass can be!

Use a very small handle on the top drawer so it doesn't bruise the wall when the bookcase is moved backwards.

FINISHING THE BOOKCASE

Remove the brass handles and sand away the coarser scratches. Finish with wire wool.

Dismissing the finishing in two short sentences represents a gross under-statement of the effort needed. It takes several days or even weeks to achieve a perfect finish. Reflect that because you have spent that extra effort your bookcase may be used and cherished for centuries.

Take the bookcase outside and reflect off it daylight which will emphasise any fine scratches, making them more easily found and removed. Some of the effort of finishing may be saved by using a scraper, as described in a previous chapter. Clean off all the dust with a turps-soaked rag and apply boiled linseed oil liberally. Finally, beeswax many, many times.

Lacquer the brass fitments, then fit. Last of all, put on the castors.

After perhaps nine months it is finished. Light oak will slowly darken and mellow. Use will produce a patina. Hopefully you will be able to pass it on to your children.

8. Finding, getting and seasoning Cabinet-making Woods

Any spare piece or plank of cabinet wood, in whatever condition, is worth sawing up to see if it is suitable for conversion into veneers. Even knots, wormholes and fungal attack may work in the cabinet-maker's favour by improving the appearance of the grain.

Over the years, you will build up a selection of English hardwoods which could supply you with your own veneers during the whole of the time you make furniture. Much of what you come across will be waste, the best trees having been bought by the timber merchants. Occasionally they will turn something down because they suspect it to be rotten or full of nails. Mostly you will have to be content with the battered remains of laburnum or holly bulldozed up from the building sites, or walnut boughs which have blown down in the storm. Don't bother with great baulks of ash or oak—it's easier to buy unseasoned planks from the local sawmills. Look out for the finer cabinet woods such as walnut, yew, fruitwoods, laburnum, box, holly and the like, especially if they are small trees and can be fitted into the back of the car.

So where are you likely to find such trees?
(1) Building sites, especially where gracious old Victorian houses are being knocked down to make way for flats.
(2) People who sell logs get to know them and are likely to accept an offer to buy fruitwoods etc. at more than they would get if they were selling them as logs.
(3) Farmers who are grubbing up orchards or hedgerows. Even pieces of hawthorn or crab apple can be used. Maple is common in hedge-rows, especially those which have been there for hundreds of years.
(4) Occasionally you will hear about such trees in pubs or from a neighbour. Watch out for neighbours grubbing up box or holly hedges.
(5) Councils are always cutting down 'spent' decorative trees, especially cherry or almond. Ask about buying such trees or contact the contractors who clear them for the council.
(6) Keep on good terms with the local timber yard. They will sell you potential cabinetwork wood, planks which commercial firms do not want. Tell them about potentially valuable trees which are about to be cut down or have been blown down in a storm, and of course, are too big for you to tackle. They will often reward you with some boughs.
(7) Practise recognising valuable trees from a distance, and watch them over the years. They often shed boughs during gales.

Many of the smaller trees will fit into the back of your car. If you have a choice, next time you buy a car, acquire an estate or a hatch-back. Check on how much weight they can carry. Shock absorbers are expensive!

If you are given a tree tell the person that you will cut it down and move it all yourself. Don't put them to any trouble or inconvenience. Keep smiling, even if it is rotten and useless; the logs will keep you warm in winter and pay for the hire of the chainsaw. Hollow trees can be converted into geranium tubs and hollow branches into bowls for winter hyacinths or crocuses. Sometimes the lower half of the tree is rotten but the boughs sound. Where the rot meets the healthy wood can be very attractive. Applewood turns pink and mauve, while walnut goes mad with a frenzy of reds, greens, buffs, mauves and blacks.

You will need some equipment to cut down the tree and move it to your car. A chainsaw is best hired as they are always reliable and sharp. A set of pram wheels capable of carrying 2 cwt. can be found at the local council's tip. These are useful for moving the lengths of tree from where you have cut it down to the car. Wedges can be bought from the local junk shop in the form of large blunt cold chisels or discarded axeheads. I have bought large wedges from stalls in markets when the stallholders have purchased these from foundries as 'seconds'. You will need a felling axe, a small chopper and a sledge-hammer. Buy the best, otherwise they will quickly lose their edge, or the heads will come off, or the handles will break. There is no substitute for a hickory handle.

A small bowsaw is useful, as is a five foot two-handed saw. A breaker's yard will supply car jacks for lifting a couple of tons. A 6 ft. $\times 1\frac{1}{4}$ in. bright steel crowbar can be bought from a steel stockholder. I got mine from the old wartime sea defences on the Pembrokeshire coast. Don't buy it all at once, but acquire as the need or opportunity arises. Always keep your axes and saws sharp.

When you have been given or bought a tree make sure you have enough time to deal with it. Remember that summer daylight hours are from 5 a.m. until 10 p.m. and winter from 8 a.m. until 4.30 p.m. Wear your oldest clothes with a cap to keep the dust out of your hair. Wear a crash helmet and goggles when using the chainsaw and put your trousers over your boots to stop them filling with sawdust.

If you are lucky enough to find a walnut tree rejected by the timber merchants, and it has a sound base, be prepared to dig up the roots, as this part has the best grain pattern. It is about 8-10 hours work. You will need to dig around the trunk, severing the roots as you go. There are always one or two roots which burrow vertically, so jack up the trunk and/or use the crowbar to get at them. You will be left with a huge crater 3 ft. deep and 5 ft. across. If you find the stump is too heavy to move, saw it down the middle with the two handed saw.

Saw the trunk into convenient lengths. If a 6 ft. length is too heavy, cut into 4 ft. and 2 ft. pieces. Support the heavy pieces in such a way that the saw does not jam in the cut. Jack up or place branches underneath. If necessary avoid risks to the hired chainsaw by finishing the cut with the two-handed saw. Use wooden wedges in the sawcuts to stop them closing up.

If you have to fell the tree, cut a wedge out of the trunk as near to the ground as possible on the side you intend the tree to fall. If necessary get a friend or helper to pull on a rope to guide its fall. Then cut from the other side at 90° to the trunk to $\frac{1}{4}$ in. above the apex of the wedge.

It may be worth lopping off the higher branches to avoid destroying a greenhouse or asbestos roofed garage. Think it out carefully and avoid damage, as you are liable for cost. On the other hand, if you carry out such difficult tasks successfully, your fame will spread and other people with useful trees will come up and ask you for a favour.

Having felled it, cut off all the small branches and put in a heap ready for burning. Avoid using a chainsaw on the smaller boughs, as it tends to 'kick' uncontrollably. Some of the larger useful boughs will still be attached to the trunk. Undercut first so that as the main sawcut progresses through, a great splinter will not be torn off. Cut boughs up at natural bends so you end up with several straight pieces. The sawmill will find it easier to cut this into planks. If the baulks are still too heavy to move, split them with wedges. Avoid this if possible as they often split 'on the twist', which wastes a lot of useful timber.

Next, use the pramwheels to move it to your car. If the ground is uneven or muddy, use planks or corrugated iron as a trackway. Sometimes the baulks are so heavy it is possible to lift one end only. Kick the pramwheels underneath, lower the log on to them, pull it to the car, lift the log on its end and then tilt over the car tail into the

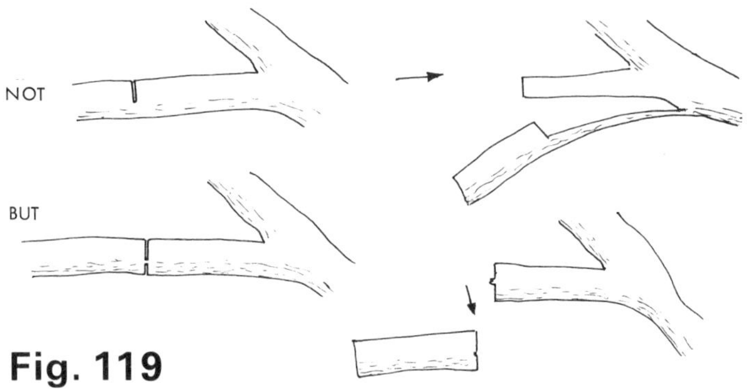

NOT

BUT

Fig. 119

Fig. 120

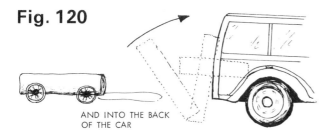

AND INTO THE BACK
OF THE CAR

car. Cushion and line the car with lots of rags or old rugs. If there is a ditch which has to be crossed fill it up with logs or short lengths of cordwood which can be used later as firewood. When you have finished tidy up the mess, moving all the twigs and sawdust into a heap ready for burning.

Before taking it to the sawmill, look it over carefully for nails and hooks etc. Trees from farmers' fields can have staples for barbed wire set in at 9 in., 2 ft. and 3 ft. Fruit trees from gardens may have hooks screwed in at 6 ft. from the ground. Look for blue stains in the cut ends of the baulks, which indicate iron; a metal detector may find them. I have seen 6 in. nails, gatepost hangers, wireless aerial attachments and even half-housebricks and concrete extracted from tree-trunks.

Naturally sawmills hate these things as it is expensive to resharpen the bandsaw blades. If you suspect a baulk of timber is full of nails, saw it up yourself. This is not as difficult or as hard work as you might think.

Number one rule is have your saw sharp and keep it sharp.

Number two rule is to hold the log still while you saw it up.

A saw trestle or two small workbenches are useful to hold it. Stand on the top and saw the log. Alternatively, saw it in half by laying it on the ground and sawing

Fig. 121

SAW STROKES

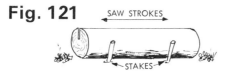

STAKES

lengthways. This is not hard work, as the sawteeth scrape a groove rather than make a sawcut. You will end up with a pile of shredded wood at each end of the 'saw-cut'.

If you intend to take the baulks to the sawmill, coat their ends with old paint or a bitumastic compound. The best is Ruber-oid roofing compound which dries in a

couple of days to a flexible waterproof coat. This will stop the logs from drying out too quickly at the ends, splitting and wasting 3 or 4 in. of the timber. Ring up the sawmill and ask the best time to bring them down. Brush off the sawdust with an old stiff-bristled brush before putting them in your car, and check that none have got lost or overlooked. Have a selection of thicknesses cut—1 in., 2 in. or 3 in. Thinner logs are best ripped down the middle.

Select the planks you wish to season and discard useless sapwood or pieces too discoloured or weakened by fungus. Remove useless sapwood with an axe, as seasoning space in a small garden is valuable. Paint generously with Rentokil if the wood is susceptible to woodworm, especially areas of sapwood or those affected by fungus.

SEASONING TIMBER

Having sweated and slaved to get the timber home and sawn into planks, then discarded the waste and painted the rest with Rentokil, it is worth taking care seasoning it, without losing more through ignorance. Seasoning is a process whereby the moisture content of wood is reduced to that of the surrounding air. There is nothing complex about the principles involved, and there are considerable advantages in carrying it out.
(1) It makes the wood stronger.
(2) It increases its stability.
(3) It makes it 50% lighter.
(4) It helps to make it resistant to bacterial fungal attack.
(5) It enables the wood to be polished.

It is worth understanding the changes taking place in the wood as is seasons, as these explain some of the hazards of the process.

As mentioned in the chapter on glueing, wood is mainly composed of cellulose. This makes up most of the substance of cell walls and consists of chains of cellulose molecules wound around the cell walls like springs. Interposed between these is an amorphous, formless mass of cellulose. 50% of the weight of unseasoned wood is water, of which 75% is in the cavities of the cells and the remainder in the cell walls, bound up with the cellulose molecules.

As the cell dries and the water molecules leave the cell walls the cellulose molecules, no longer separated by the water molecules, are attracted to each other and bind themselves together by electrostatic forces. The overall effect is to strengthen the wood. Because of the loss of moisture, bacteria and fungi cannot break down the cellulose to feed in the resulting glucose.

As much of the cell wall is wound around with helically arranged cellulose chains, the spring will shrink much more across than lengthways, which explains

Fig. 122

HELICAL FIBRES WILL SHRINK
RELATIVELY MORE ACROSS
THE TURNS THAN LENGTHWAYS

why a plank will shrink 8-10% across and only 1% lengthways. There are, of course, considerable variations from timber to timber. There is also much difference in the moisture content of sapwood and heartwood. The upper part of the trunk and branches may contain much more moisture than the lower part of the trunk and roots.

TIME OF YEAR

It used to be accepted practice to fell trees only in the winter when it was thought the moisture content was low, but research has shown that there is no difference. Felling in winter diminishes the likelihood of invasion by pests and fungus. It also avoids the risk of damage by the breaking off of overladen leafy branches as the tree is cut down. The winter months allow the timber to start to dry out more slowly as the temperature is lower and the humidity higher.

There are two experiments that you can carry out to show the process of drying out and seasoning:

(1) Place a small piece of fresh cut unseasoned timber in a kitchen oven and dry it out at such a temperature that does not char (150°C). Weigh before and after and note the difference.

(2) Put a similar piece of wood in a domestic central heating boiler-house and weigh every day for a month. The initial loss is high, but it gradually tails off. It shows the water being readily lost from the cell cavities but more slowly from the cell walls. It is the loss from the cell walls which causes the timber to change its shape and split during seasoning.

SEASONING DEFECTS

Cupping:

Quartersawn timber seasons true, but shrinks more towards the periphery of the trunk:

Fig. 123

Twisting. This happens because of spiral and interlocking grain. It is very common in fruitwoods and elm:

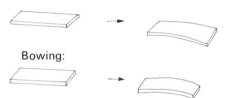

Bowing:

Springing: As the timber is converted into planks at the sawmill, the internal stresses are relieved and the board immediately adopts a different shape.

This happens as yew baulks are sawn up.

Checks: These are surface cracks in timber caused by the outer part drying too quickly and stresses being set up which could not be taken up by a change in the shape of the timber. Checks which go further through the planks are splits.

Shakes: are splits in large baulks of timber.

Case hardening: This happens when the outer surface dries out rapidly without splitting or shrinking, then becomes set. The inner part dries out and shrinks and collapses away from the hard set outer skin. Many small checks arise which cannot be detected by surface examination.

Many other things can happen when seasoning planks cut from a baulk of timber. Wood shrinks much more in a tangential than radial direction. It may shrink diagonally where there is spiral grain. Knots complicate the drying process as the grain around them is much denser and more complex. Knots split and shrink and may become loose and usually stand out above the plank.

The final shape of the plank is the sum of a number of complex factors and it is fortunate the wood can take a considerable amount of abuse during seasoning without actually splitting.

What can be done to minimise losses due to shrinkage and pests? Drying out timber depends on humidity, the circulation of air and the surrounding temperature. Even in this damp country, timber dries out readily, and the main problem is to prevent it drying out too quickly.

The first rule is that it should be stacked as soon as possible after cutting. Fungus and mould can begin to grow and discolour within a few hours in the warm humid conditions of spring and summer.

The second rule is always keep fresh cut timber away from the sun. If exposed, the surface will check within a few days.

So have the site ready to receive your freshly sawn timber. Find a flat piece of ground and build a series of brick or concrete piers several inches high 18 in. apart. Lay across some heavy beams of timber and make sure they are parallel and

Fig. 124

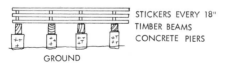

STICKERS EVERY 18"
TIMBER BEAMS
CONCRETE PIERS

GROUND

level by using a spirit level. Have the pile less than 6 ft. wide otherwise the air will not circulate freely and the timber in the centre of the stack will not dry.

Have a pile of dry softwood stickers ready, the most suitable being $1 \text{ in} \times \frac{3}{4} \text{ in}$. roofing slats (tile battens). Make sure the ends of all planks are coated and that fruitwoods have been liberally coated with a woodworm preventative. Every two feet place a softwood sticker, so the ends just protrude beyond the edges of the plank. Make sure that air can circulate freely under the pile. If necessary weight down the planks with concrete slabs, especially if you are seasoning fruitwoods which have the treacherous tendency to twist.

The roof should keep out heavy rain although a little moisture does not matter. It should overhang the edges of the woodpile.

The sides of the pile should be away from the sun, but if this is unavoidable lean some sloping boards under the roof, but away from the timber, to interrupt the sun's rays. Leave gaps between the planks to allow the air to circulate.

Fig. 125

You can often tell whether timber is seasoned by cutting into the centre and feeling it. If you are unsure, cut a small piece, weigh it, bake it in the oven at 150°C overnight and weigh again. If it has lost 20% of its weight then its moisture content was 20%. After seasoning the moisture content will settle at around 20%, varying a little depending on the time of year. Unfortunately, the humidity in most houses is around 12% so that even after seasoning, there is bound to be a little more shrinkage when you finally bring it in as finished furniture.

It is difficult to minimise the movement of wood in response to changes in humidity. It will even change its shape after 200 years. No paint or varnish yet discovered will prevent this moisture exchange, although they will slow it down and allow the wood to stretch without splitting.

TREATMENT OF INDIVIDUAL TIMBERS

Most of the timbers which the amateur cabinet-maker will need are to be found in the gardens and fields around him and a description of individual seasoning is confined to these.

Ash Once sawn into planks, it will dry quickly. Leave the bark on as it slows the drying on the edge of the plank. Weight this pile with concrete slabs.

Blackthorn A very difficult timber to season because of its spiral grain. It twists, splits and checks. Be prepared for much wastage. Coat the ends well. Use $\frac{3}{4}$ in. thick stickers and be prepared for disappointments.

Box A most difficult timber to season and needs special treatment, but it is a cabinet wood 'par excellence'. It checks and splits if left exposed to the air. Saw down the middle to relieve the internal tensions. Dry it *as slowly as possible* by burying it in sawdust. It is possible to season it 'in the round' by this method, although it might take several years. But at the end, what a beautiful smooth pale creamy-yellow wood!

Cherry Has a marked tendency to split and warp. Rentokil well. Pile up the planks and put concrete slabs on the top.

Apple Season and dry as slowly as possible by using sawdust; leave on the bark to slow the drying. Rentokil as the bugs like it. Don't be put off by signs of rot –it adds to the colour.

Pear Stable once seasoned, but tends to warp and twist due to spiral grain. Very dense, so season slowly to prevent surface checks.

Laburnum A beautiful deep brown wood, with a creamy grain sapwood. Season in the round for 'oystering', by burying in sawdust.

Beech Remove the bark, as the insects tend to get under it. Dries quickly so use $\frac{3}{4}$ in. stickers. It shrinks more than many other home-grown timbers.

Holly It has a great tendency to warp and crack, so weight the pile of planks with heavy concrete slabs. It dries to a greenish white colour. If you want it dead white for inlay, cut it into $\frac{1}{8}$ in. thick strips as soon as it is felled. Boil it up for several hours in a large container of water. Dry it as quickly as possible to prevent any mould patches, in a central heating boiler house, if you have one. Don't worry if it has turned black through boiling it in an iron container, this stain is only 'skin deep.'

Yew Dries slowly because it is so dense. It tends to shake, especially down the centre of the log. It can be seasoned in the round in sawdust, but if the logs are too thin to cut into planks, cut down the middle to relieve tensions and avoid unwanted splitting.

Sycamore Tends to stain as it dries out. Convert the log to planks as quickly as possible after felling. It is best to season with as much air circulating around it as possible. It warps and checks. Be prepared for failures. Remove the bark–store in a dry place, and keep off the rain, which tends to stain it.

Oak Dries slowly and tends to warp and check. Use narrow stickers to slow the drying even more. It is best quarter sawn to bring out the silvery medullary rays. Keep away from the sun, which soon 'checks' the surface.

Maple Dry out as quickly as possible; if you leave the planks up against a wall fungus and mould will soon grow on it. Use wide stickers.

Walnut The easiest to season. Keep on the sapwood and paint with Rentokil. Checks and warps the least–the cabinet-maker's dream wood!

Generally speaking wood dries in our climate at 1 in./year so a 1 in. thick piece will be ready to run at the end of a year and a 3 in. thick board after 3 years. The pieces immersed in sawdust may take several years. Don't be discouraged by failures, learn by mistakes. It will take decades to accumulate a treasure house of timbers– but it will have been worth all the sweat and effort.

WATER SEASONING

It is possible to season timber under water. Attach a 'green' plank on the bed of a stream with the root end facing upstream. Come back in a few weeks and you will find strands of sap attached to the 'branches' end. Remove it from the water and you will find it dries out very quickly as it no longer has the cell contents and mineral salts to hold in the water by osmolarity. However, it will not be as strong as air dried timber, because the cells have lost their 'gluey' contents.

9. Veneer Cutting and Veneering

Most cabinet furniture is veneered. A thin layer of wood, the veneer, is glued onto the structural ground work, and this technique has many advantages over using solid wood. The attractive graining of wood can be shown at its best without risk of splitting or breaking. Planks of the wildest, most attractive grain cannot be used in the solid because they would shrink or warp.

Veneering has been used for thousands of years, having been introduced by the Egyptians, used by the wealthy Romans and adopted for everyday furniture in Europe in the 17th Century. The term 'veneer' has been used wrongly to denigrate furniture made in this way. In recent years many beautiful pieces of veneered cabinet-making have been sold for tens of thousands of pounds.

This chapter is how to cut and lay your own veneers.

The D.I.Y. cabinet-maker will be able to select, make and use suitably grained veneers from his own store of hardwood planks, instead of having to search endlessly and buy the left-overs and offcuts of veneer merchants.

Most commercial veneers are knife-cut to about $\frac{1}{32}$ in. thickness. They are peeled off a log by a long knife, rather like sheets of toilet paper off a toilet roll. These do not show a fine picture of the grain. Other commercial veneers are cut across a half or quarter log but are still very thin and fragile.

Sawcut veneers are much thicker and tougher. They can be sanded and planed, in fact, treated like solid wood. They are more durable, being less likely to become split or frayed during handling. Glue does not soak through to the outer surface and spoil the natural colour of the wood. The finish of sawcut veneers is always deeper and more lustrous.

During the making of the hardwood bookcase, a technique was described where a $\frac{5}{8}$ in. plank, 2 in. wide was converted into two sheets of wood $\frac{1}{4}$ in. thick. This same method could be used to cut $\frac{3}{32}$ in. thick sheets of wood from a plank 7 in. wide and 1 ft. long. A sharp, correctly set ripsaw is used. The grain has to be straight and the sawcut has to start at both ends and meet in the middle.

There are limits to the production of veneers by this method. It cannot be used on a plank of this size if it is very hard or if the grain is wild. The sawcut will bow in the middle as more and more force is used. The veneer may be $\frac{3}{32}$ in. around the outside and a $\frac{1}{4}$ in. or more in the middle, or, worse, the saw may break through to the surface of the plank half way across.

The only tool which the amateur can use to cut his own veneers is a frame saw, which will produce sheets of wood of consistent thickness, of any length, from any baulks of timber up to 1 ft. wide. Only patience and stamina are needed. A veneer cut off a plank of hard walnut 10 in. × 36 in. will take 1 hour's sawing. The teeth face

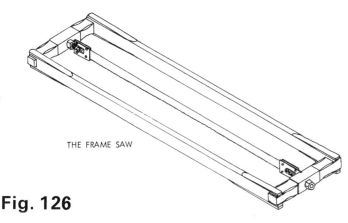

THE FRAME SAW

Fig. 126

towards the handle end, so cutting takes place during the pull stroke. Sheets of any thickness can be produced from any baulk provided the frame will fit over it. Whereas sheets of $\frac{3}{32}$ in. are used for veneers, those of $\frac{1}{8}$ in.-$\frac{1}{4}$ in. can be used for gusseting and laminating, techniques described in later chapters. I have not encountered any modern book on furniture-making which describes the use of this kind of saw in producing veneers. Similar veneers could be cut on a commercial bandsaw, but few amateurs have access to such large, expensive equipment.

It is worth describing how the techniques of veneer cutting took four years to perfect, as I hope it will encourage other amateurs to develop their ideas. Please forgive the extensive use of the first person singular, but it is the easiest way of telling the story.

I needed 16 sheets $7\frac{1}{2}$ in. × 12 in. and $\frac{3}{32}$ in. thick cut from a block of wet walnut. The surface was planed true, a sawcut groove was cut all around $\frac{3}{32}$ in. from the surface and 16 sheets of veneer were obtained using a ripsaw. The grain was straight and the sawcut true, following the pre-cut groove. The smell of wet walnut wood was gorgeous.

Soon after that, I was given the rounded offcut from the outer part of a rotting butt of walnut. It appeared fit only for the fire. However, a sander proved that it was good in parts and rubbing with linseed oil showed a glorious range of colours from black, brown, green and mauve to buff and grey.

The ripsaw was set to work on a block 15 in. × 8 in. I obtained the veneers I needed but their thickness was variable. Some were $\frac{3}{8}$ in. thick in the middle, others $\frac{1}{16}$ in. at the edge. The saw bowed in the sawcuts. It followed the grain, and, because the wood was so hard, the force I had to use made it worse. But the colours and pattern of the grain made the frustration worth suffering. I thought it must be the saw, so I bought the most expensive one I could find. Factory sharpened and set, as yet untried on any wood, I set about a small block of exceedingly hard but beautiful walnut crutch 7 in. × 8 in. × 2 in. The result was a disaster. Deep bowed ridges were left in the veneers, some of which had areas less than $\frac{3}{64}$ in. thick. The veneers were cut in the spring and left stacked on a shelf in the shed with a weight on top, to keep them flat. Within six weeks the sapwood had been invaded by woodworm.

I sulked over the problems of cutting veneers for several months. It occurred to me that if the teeth on the ripsaw were reversed, to enable it to cut on the pull, then the harder the saw is pulled, the straighter the blade. Such a saw was made using an old blade bought for 30p from a local junk shop. I thought I had beaten the problem when, one after another, ten $\frac{1}{8}$ in. thick veneers were sawn off a plank of walnut 30 in. × 10 in. There was a beautiful swirling knot in the middle of each sheet.

I was very proud of my achievement and wrote to a well-known sawmaker asking if they could make me a super one with a tapered blade. They wrote back a very apologetic letter declining the request, but sent a booklet about saw making from the caveman to the present day. A saw manufacturer in East London offered to make one at a reasonable price, using a blade 30/1000 inch thick instead of the usual 40/1000. The teeth were increased to 8 per inch.

It worked well until I tried it on a very hard piece of yew. The sawcut bowed in the middle! A foot wide piece of hard walnut with sloping grain did the same thing. I suspected that the force needed both to pull the saw through and keep the teeth on the bottom of the sawcut was buckling the blade and bowing the sawcut.

How could I keep the blade buckle-free yet maintain sufficient downward pressure to make the teeth cut? A bowsaw blade came to mind and the one my father bought in the last war to cut up logs was converted to a ripsaw. It produced the best cut, but its progress was impeded by the iron frame.

Then the answer came—a frame saw similar to those in pictures of Roman saws —but where could I find a suitable blade? The nearest I had seen was in a wholesale butchers. Then I remembered the bandsaw in the local aluminium foundry. It had a 1 in. wide blade with 6 teeth/inch. Although the tip of each tooth was hardened, the rest of the blade was of a softer steel and could be drilled for fitting to a wooden frame.

I discovered later that not only was it similar to the Roman framesaw, but identical to the futtock saw used to cut the curved ribs of Nelson's ships. Perhaps they copied it from the 18th century cabinet-makers who gave up using it when circular saws were used for veneer cutting around 1800.

The plan of the Framesaw is as follows:

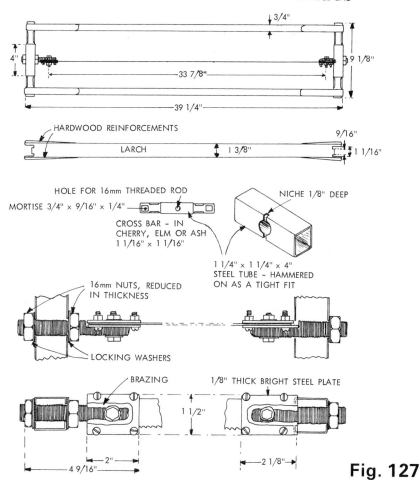

HANDLE END

3/4"

4"

9 1/8"

33 7/8"

39 1/4"

HARDWOOD REINFORCEMENTS

LARCH

1 3/8"

9/16"

1 1/16"

HOLE FOR 16mm THREADED ROD

MORTISE 3/4" × 9/16" × 1/4"

CROSS BAR - IN
CHERRY, ELM OR ASH
1 1/16" × 1 1/16"

NICHE 1/8" DEEP

1 1/4" × 1 1/4" × 4"
STEEL TUBE - HAMMERED
ON AS A TIGHT FIT

16mm NUTS, REDUCED
IN THICKNESS

LOCKING WASHERS

BRAZING

1/8" THICK BRIGHT STEEL PLATE

1 1/2"

2"

4 9/16"

2 1/8"

Fig. 127

Three blades can be cut from a 9ft. 6in. metal cutting bandsaw blade (6 teeth/inch) and work out around £2.50 each, or if cut from 100ft. roll about £1.20, which is not much more than a high speed hacksaw blade. The tips of the teeth are hardened and cannot be sharpened with a triangular file. Carborundum may be used, or better an Arkansas stone. The 'set' of the teeth is reduced by flattening between

Fig. 128

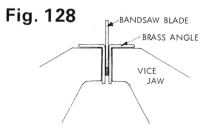

BANDSAW BLADE

BRASS ANGLE

VICE
JAW

pieces of brass arranged in the jaws of a vice. This produces a narrower sawcut,

wastes less wood and is less work. The blade does not bind because the veneer leans away from the sawcut.

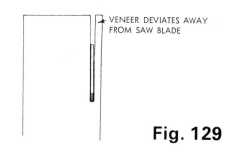

VENEER DEVIATES AWAY
FROM SAW BLADE

Fig. 129

Holes are drilled at $\frac{1}{2}$ in. from each end of the blade. The steel is harder than bright steel but can be drilled by high speed bits, provided the tip is cooled constantly with water. All the teeth up to 2in. from both ends are snapped off. The blade is set up at right angles to the frame and at one end the blade is locked in position with two nuts and their locking washers. At the other, it is tightened by the solitary nut and slackened when not in use to rest the blade and preserve the 'spring' of the larch sides.

The blade is adjusted to and fro between the ends so the holding plate at the handle end just moves into the $\frac{1}{8}$ in. deep niche cut in the square steel tube when the nut is tightened. The larch sides should bow out slightly and the blade give a taut note when strummed.

USE

The surface of the plank to be converted into veneers is planed and trued. A gauge mark is made along each side and the ends joined across the top and bottom with a steel point guided by a steel rule. This ensures that the starting sawcut is straight and true. The cut is started with a panel or crosscut saw to a depth of $\frac{1}{4}$ in. The crisscross method is used, each sawcut providing a guide for the next, and each cut progresses $\frac{3}{4}$ in. Cutting takes place on the pull stroke.

The plank is trued after each cut, although often this is unnecessary.

Fig. 130

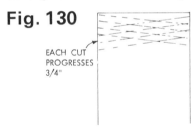

EACH CUT PROGRESSES 3/4"

Sawing veneers is a long boring tedious dusty task. To take short rests, I look out of the shed window. In spring the beech buds elongate, flatten, curl and burst to produce a limp shoot, covered in wispy white hair.

As the shoots harden they become covered with the first flush of aphids which are voraciously collected by the queen wasps for their grubs. It is a signal for me to rush out with my insecticide spray and vent on them all my pent-up aggression. In the autumn they buzz into the shed looking for somewhere to hibernate. My sawing is disturbed and so they are dispatched with a satisfying crunch.

In the late spring and summer the blackbirds and thrushes search tirelessly over the lawn for worms and insects. Their runs are punctuated by sudden immobility as they peer down a wormhole. The hedge sparrows twitch and flit for insects. They are such restless little birds. The cobwebs in the corners of the windows provide further distractions as they enmesh the late summer bluebottles. The spiders emerge, sink in their fangs and the low pitch hum rises to an almost inaudible whine as the venom takes effect.

So time passes and the sawcut reaches as low as it will go before the work cabinet is damaged. The plank is turned around and the cut started from the other end and, as the two cuts meet there is a swish as the sawblade meets no resistance and falls to the bottom. The plank and veneer are laid on their backs and what joy and excitement in seeing the woodgrain patterns that no human eye has ever seen before.

Once the technique of making your own veneers has been mastered the possibilities are vast. All that is needed is to learn how to use them on furniture. The problems are:
(1) How to prepare the veneers before glueing.
(2) How to prepare the groundwork on which the veneers are glued.
(3) How to finish the edge of the furniture.
(4) Curved work.

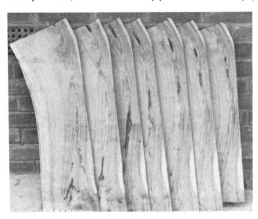
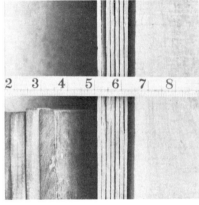

Figs. 131 and 132 show seven veneers cut with the framesaw. Size is approximately 10×30in. and thickness less than $\frac{3}{16}$in. on average.

Fig. 133. Drawer from
walnut chest, 1725.

(5) The use of veneers in laminated
    furniture.

The veneer series from a single plank will
contain sapwood, shakes, fungal stains
and perhaps even a few woodworm holes.

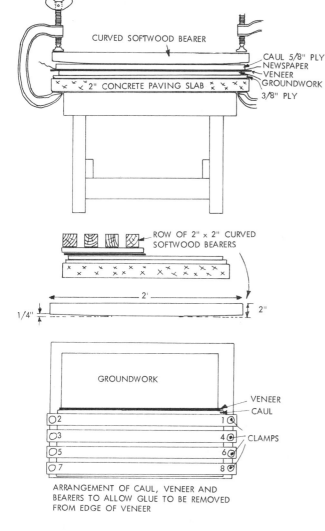

CURVED SOFTWOOD BEARER

CAUL 5/8" PLY
NEWSPAPER
VENEER
GROUNDWORK
3/8" PLY

2" CONCRETE PAVING SLAB

ROW OF 2" x 2" CURVED
SOFTWOOD BEARERS

2'

1/4"   2"

GROUNDWORK

VENEER
CAUL

2   1
3   4   CLAMPS
5   6
7   8

ARRANGEMENT OF CAUL, VENEER AND
BEARERS TO ALLOW GLUE TO BE REMOVED
FROM EDGE OF VENEER

Fig. 134

These faults may be included into the
pattern of grain on the furniture, as in the
photograph on the left, which shows a
drawer from a walnut chest dated 1725.

The maker has incorporated all these
features and somehow he has 'lost' their
significance, emphasising only their
appearance by book matching them.

The surfaces to be glued should be as
level as possible. When a book match is
intended, the veneer with the sawn surface
may have to be planed. Here the bullnose
plane is invaluable. It may be used in one
hand while the other steadies the veneer.
The veneers may be arranged to suit
individual tastes or the pattern of the grain.
They can be bookmatched, quartered,
serialed or left as an individual pattern.
There is much more about this in the
chapters on design.

The veneers are cut to size using a
Stanley knife or a small D.I.Y. bandsaw.
Because of the thickness of the veneers, a
knife is difficult to use. It never cuts at 90°,
tends to run with the grain, especially near
knots, and often splits the wood near the
end of the cut. A D.I.Y. bandsaw is the
ideal tool. They are precise and they cut at
90°. They are rugged little machines and
although they cost around £80 their uses
are legion for anybody keen on D.I.Y.

The edges left by bandsaw or knife on
the sawcut veneer may be planed by
holding the veneer upright in the work
cabinet vice. This is a great advantage over
commercial veneers.

Because of their thickness, they cannot
be glued and ironed on to the groundwork
like commercial knife cut veneers. Sawcut
veneers have to be applied before the
furniture is assembled. Edging and finishing are applied after assembly. The best
material to use for groundwork is good
quality birch ply. It is strong, reliable, glues
well and is free of faults. It should be at
least $\frac{1}{4}$ in. thick.

To avoid veneering on end grain, 'boxed'
cabinet furniture is jointed by concealed
dovetails, those same joints as used on the
upholstered stool. Short cuts in making
these will be described in the next chapter.

The glue of choice for the beginner is
Cascamite. It is slow setting, allowing
correction of the veneer if it slips. The glue
sets hard which allows it to be sanded
without smearing. The veneer has to be
pressed evenly all over its surface on to the
groundwork while the glue sets. However,
the pressure has to be applied in such a
way that the whole job is not buckled. Care

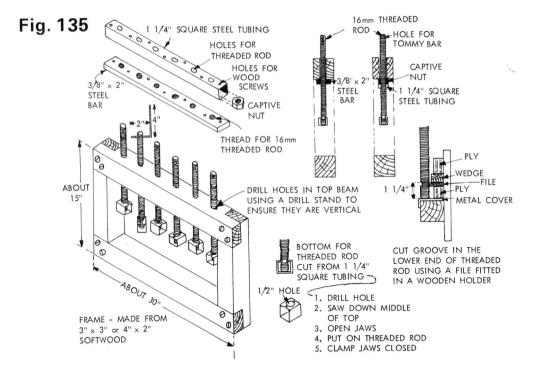

Fig. 135

1 1/4" SQUARE STEEL TUBING

HOLES FOR THREADED ROD

HOLES FOR WOOD SCREWS

3/8" × 2" STEEL BAR

CAPTIVE NUT

2" 4"

THREAD FOR 16mm THREADED ROD

ABOUT 15"

ABOUT 30"

FRAME - MADE FROM 3" × 3" or 4" × 2" SOFTWOOD

16mm THREADED ROD

HOLE FOR TOMMY BAR

CAPTIVE NUT

3/8" × 2" STEEL BAR

1 1/4" SQUARE STEEL TUBING

DRILL HOLES IN TOP BEAM USING A DRILL STAND TO ENSURE THEY ARE VERTICAL

1 1/4"

PLY

WEDGE

FILE

PLY

METAL COVER

CUT GROOVE IN THE LOWER END OF THREADED ROD USING A FILE FITTED IN A WOODEN HOLDER

BOTTOM FOR THREADED ROD CUT FROM 1 1/4" SQUARE TUBING

1/2" HOLE

1. DRILL HOLE
2. SAW DOWN MIDDLE OF TOP
3. OPEN JAWS
4. PUT ON THREADED ROD
5. CLAMP JAWS CLOSED

has to be taken to ensure that the veneer does not slip on the layer of liquid glue.

The classical way described in many books on cabinet-making is to use a caul and curved bearers. It is reliable and, apart from the 6 in. clamps does not need experience or complex equipment. A thick, heavy base is used, such as a 2 in. thick concrete paving slab. It is checked for flatness and finishing. On it is placed a $\frac{3}{8}$ in. lining of plywood and then the groundwork. Glue and veneer are placed on this, followed by a $\frac{5}{8}$ in. caul and finally the 2 in. square sectioned bearers. They are slightly curved, so that the whole length exerts an equal pressure when the G-clamps are tightened. The clamps are tightened in a logical order to squeeze out excess glue.

Because of faults in the grain of the bearers pressure is not evenly distributed along them and a modern D.I.Y. method is to make a series of clamp frames. These are not expensive to make provided you can persuade an engineering acquaintance to cut threads in a $\frac{3}{8}$ in. × 2 in. steel bar and can rescue 4 in. × 2 in. rafters from a house that is being demolished. Another method is to use captive 16 mm nuts in a $1\frac{1}{4}$ in. square steel tube. These are self explanatory in the drawings.

Using a row of veneer frames any length of groundwork can be veneered. 6 in.

clamps set as close together as possible can be used to veneer small jobs. A 2 in. thick hardwood base will prevent buckling.

GLUEING

The secret of glueing veneers is to have everything ready in place where it will be needed. Prepare the surfaces of the veneer and groundwork as described in the chapter on glueing, mark on the groundwork where the veneer is to be laid, and set the clamps to the length at which they will be used and place near their clamping positions.

Put Cascamite on both groundwork and veneer and hold in position with a few G-clamps while the bearers or veneer frames are adjusted in position. Tighten up evenly all over and when the glue has stopped oozing retighten. Scrape off excess glue—old chisels are invaluable for this job. This avoids removing hard blobs of dried glue and hence damage to the veneer.

When veneers are halved and butted, use the same method but force the edges of the veneers together with sash cramps or wedges. It will give a perfect joint. When cauls and bearers are used leave the butt joint exposed so excess glue can squeeze out.

Fig. 136

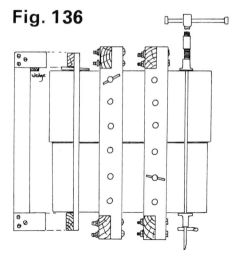

EDGES OF VENEERS SQUEEZED TOGETHER WITH SASH OR MADE-UP WOODEN CLAMPS

There are several different ways of fitting together the veneered groundwork. The corners can be mitred together. Blue chalk may be needed for a perfect joint.

Fig. 137

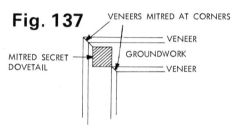

VENEERS MITRED AT CORNERS

VENEER

GROUNDWORK

VENEER

MITRED SECRET DOVETAIL

They can be overlapped in the direction in which the concealed dovetails fit together.

Fig. 138

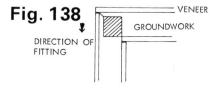

VENEER

GROUNDWORK

DIRECTION OF FITTING

Corners can be left and insets glued in later. These are short strips of wood. The

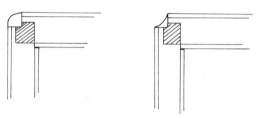

LAST INSET TO BE GLUED

INSETS

Fig. 139

corners are mitred and a piece glued in the middle of a row.

The insets are glued using planks of wood, either side, with a row of nails to hold a web of sisal (i.e. non-stretch) string.

Fig. 140

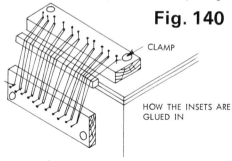

CLAMP

HOW THE INSETS ARE GLUED IN

The insets overlap the veneered edges and are shaped with a chisel, plane or carving gouge. A similar technique is used in edging shelves. Insets are always used in ply groundwork, to avoid glueing an endgrain.

Fig. 141

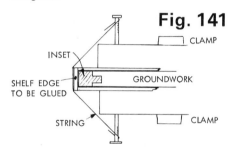

INSET

CLAMP

SHELF EDGE TO BE GLUED

GROUNDWORK

STRING

CLAMP

Veneered internal fitments can be glued as shown:

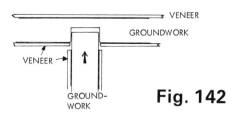

VENEER

GROUNDWORK

VENEER

GROUND-WORK

Fig. 142

Fig. 143 (below). Walnut shelf-end veneered by the method described.

At door or shelf edges, insets made of the same wood as the veneers may be used to avoid the use of a veneer.

Fig. 144

GROUNDWORK — HARDWOOD INSET. SAME AS VENEER — LEFT AS SHELF EDGE

The inset is put into the groundwork before veneering the faces of the door or shelf.

INLAYS

The easiest way is to build up from the centre of the groundwork outwards. Lay the main veneer, being sure to clear away all excess liquid glue.

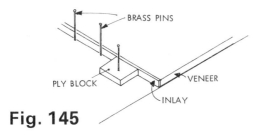

BRASS PINS

PLY BLOCK

VENEER

INLAY

Fig. 145

Hold the strip of wood to be inlaid against the main veneer, using brass veneer tacks or small pieces of ply nailed against the strip. Steel pins will stain the wood. When dry lay the rest of the veneer.

The bandsaw will be invaluable in cutting inlay strips of acacia, box or holly. If this 'building up' is not possible, use a knife sharpened on one side.

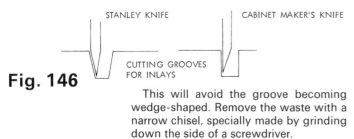

STANLEY KNIFE   CABINET MAKER'S KNIFE

CUTTING GROOVES FOR INLAYS

Fig. 146

This will avoid the groove becoming wedge-shaped. Remove the waste with a narrow chisel, specially made by grinding down the side of a screwdriver.

Fig. 147   SCREWDRIVER MADE INTO CHISEL FOR REMOVING WASTE FROM INLAY GROOVES

CURVED WORK

Types of curved features can be built up from layers of steamed birch ply glued together between a 'male' and a 'female' made out of softwood.

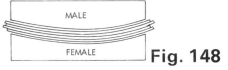

MALE

FEMALE   **Fig. 148**

Arrange so that adjacent layers of grain are at right angles to each other. Glue the layers one at a time, so four layers will take three days. Birch ply of $\frac{1}{8}$ in. or less is easily bent over a steaming kettle or saucepan. Strips should be kept in the bent position by pieces of string while they curl and dry out. Sawcut veneers are treated in a similar way.

More complex curved shapes can be built up out of odd blocks of wood, veneering only the final shaped laminate. An example of this work is shown in the legs of the rotating bookcase.

As well as laminating, thick sawcut veneers can be used as gussets to join

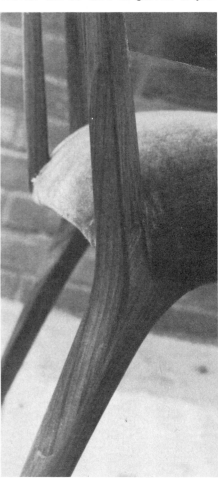

Fig. 149. Use of a thick sawcut veneer to gusset the back joint of a chair.

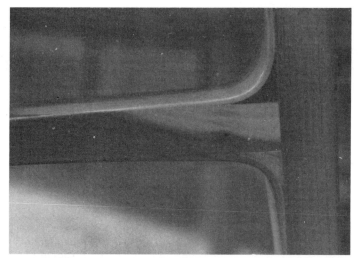

Laminates can make up a mortise and tenon joint, and these will be described in a later chapter.

Fig. 150. Curved gussets with fillet pieces make an attractive joint in this coffee table rail.

together pieces of wood. A curved gusset can be used to form the rail of a coffee table or the back joint of a chair, or a small table can have its leg gusseted on to the top.

Fig. 152. Use of laminates in a mortise and tenon joint for a chairback.

Fig. 151. Gussets used to decorate and strengthen a lightweight table.

FINISHING

There is little risk of damaging a sawcut veneer during finishing, since they are almost impossible to sand or plane through. An orbital or belt sander may be used, sanding along the grain. Use silicon carbide 'wet and dry' followed by various grades of wire wool; linseed oil, wax or French polish may be applied—whatever suits the desired finish.

10. The Dovetail Sewing Box

Fig. 153

The last two chapters described how to cut and lay sawcut veneers. Making this Sewing Box is an opportunity to put these techniques to use.

This piece of furniture does away with the impossible muddle of balls of wool, needles, buttons, half undone cotton reels, hooks and eyes, scraps of materials et. a. which inhabit most workboxes. By carefully selecting and arranging the veneers, it can be made very pretty, its attractive appearance making it respected and looked after by all the family who, hopefully, will keep its contents complete and tidy.

The aim of the cabinet-maker is to show off the quality of the wood in veneer form, at its best. He becomes, if you like, a jeweller in wood.

This chapter also seeks to explain the following techniques:
(1) How to use the small D.I.Y. bandsaw and take advantage of its versatility.
(2) How to in-lay and inset.
(3) How to fit brass piano hinges.
(4) Finish in linseed oil and wax.

The Sewing Box is solidly constructed of $\frac{1}{2}$ in. ply joined together by concealed dovetails of which there are about 100. It contains a dozen mortise and tenons and four stopped sliding dovetails. It is heavy and perhaps contains more ply than is needed. However, it is an excellent exercise in cabinet making and its step by step construction will ensure that it lasts many decades.

It should be contrasted with the laminated sewing box in a later chapter which contains only five tongue and groove joints, a dovetailed drawer and a single piano hinge. The laminates serve as veneers and do away with the need for groundwork. This sewing box, however, is veneered both inside and outside before assembly, the outer covers being finished with insets. The lid is halved, each side opening outwards on a piano hinge. Both halves are lined with padded velvet or dralon to act as needle and pin cushions. The inside slopes to provide a deep compartment at the front for wool and spare pieces of material, and a shallow one for tins of buttons, tape measures and

Fig. 154

Fig. 155

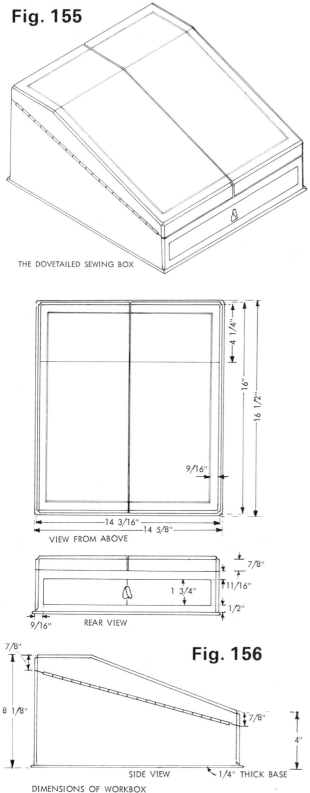

THE DOVETAILED SEWING BOX

scissors. Beneath this compartment is a drawer for cotton reels. It can rest on a table or on the carpet in a corner and will probably take 6-9 months to make. The dimensions are as drawn.

By this time you will have started to accumulate a store of timber: holly and maple from the hedgerows, laburnum, box and fruitwoods from building sites and neighbours' gardens, and fancy hardwoods such as yew, walnut and oak discarded by the timber yards and sawmills.

Select a plank with interesting features and, if necessary, polish with a sander to bring out the grain patterns. You should reckon on at least 5 veneers to the inch. Look for—Colour; Waviness and grain pattern; Large knots or crutches associated with branches; Small pinhead knots; Shakes and splits; Additional colour associated with rot or seasoning in wet conditions; Irregular lines as scars where the tree has been damaged during growth; Burrs.

Try to arrange the most prominent feature, whether knot, stain, split or crutch, to be near the centre of the top. Obviously, if you intend to halve or quarter then start near the edge of the plank which you intend to convert into veneers.

VIEW FROM ABOVE

REAR VIEW

Fig. 156

SIDE VIEW

1/4" THICK BASE

DIMENSIONS OF WORKBOX

PLAN OF COMPARTMENTS

Fig. 157

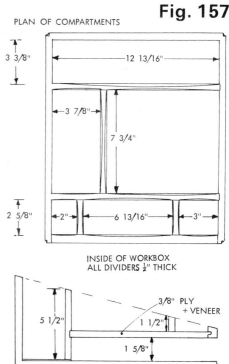

INSIDE OF WORKBOX
ALL DIVIDERS 1/2" THICK

3/8" PLY + VENEER

Fig. 158, crude cut veneers with, right, Fig. 159, similar veneers used on the sewing box.

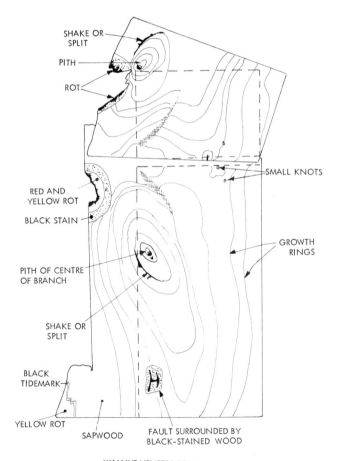

SHAKE OR SPLIT

PITH

ROT

RED AND YELLOW ROT

BLACK STAIN

SMALL KNOTS

GROWTH RINGS

PITH OF CENTRE OF BRANCH

SHAKE OR SPLIT

BLACK TIDEMARK

YELLOW ROT

SAPWOOD

FAULT SURROUNDED BY BLACK-STAINED WOOD

WALNUT VENEERS FOR SEWING BOX

Fig. 160

A photo of crude cut veneers is shown, one plank being wiped with meths to bring out the grain. The final result with similar veneers is also shown. The drawing indicates the most prominent features.

The knots, pith and crutch complex will catch the eye first, and the wavy grain and small pin knots will add general interest. The stiff rectangular shape of the stringing inlay will emphasise the irregularity of the grain.

There may be several weeks between cutting and using the veneers, so put them in order in a pile and place a heavy weight on top to prevent warping. Remember, the more irregular and attractive the grain, the greater the tendency of the veneer to change its shape in response to an ever-changing humidity. If you want to see the eventual colour of the veneer, wipe liberally with methylated spirits. Don't use linseed oil as it will prevent proper glueing later.

The veneer may have large amounts of sapwood on areas which have been subject to fungal attack. These are very prone to invasion by woodworm around spring and early summer, so paint liberally with Cuprinol or Rentokil.

PREPARING THE GROUNDWORK

A small D.I.Y. bandsaw will be of great help in cutting up the ply and in making the many dovetail joints. Here is some advice about its use:

Read the instructions carefully. If treated properly they will give decades of use.

Fig. 161

(1) Adjust the tension of the blade just enough to cut the wood without too much slipping. Too much will stretch and break the blade.

(2) Check the blade is at 90° to the sawing platform. Use a small set-square.

(3) Adjust the top blade guide so it just allows the wood to pass under it.

(4) Lubricate all parts often. The fine sawdust seems to suck out the oil from the moving parts.

(5) Make sure the bottom does not get clogged with sawdust.

(6) Use it gently as excessive force will break the blade.

(7) It will be easier to cut across the grain than down it.

(8) Always keep your eye on the blade when cutting. It is one of the safest power tools to use. The blade stops when it breaks.

(9) They are not very good at cutting steel although they will cut aluminium or brass. However, avoid hard plastics and chipboard which blunt the teeth.

(10) Buy a kind which has been made for years and check the after-sales service. Good manufacturers provide this for blade repairs, rubber driving bands, switches etc. I have found the Burgess Mk II adequate for most cabinet-making needs.

(11) Finally, ALWAYS, repeat ALWAYS slacken off the blade after use, otherwise the blade will snap.

Use the bandsaw to cut out the $\frac{3}{8}$ in. thick ply blanks for the sides, top, front and bottom.

Note the direction of the pins and tails. The sides will be assembled on the centre

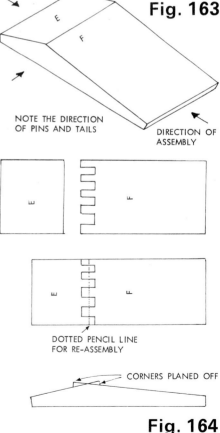

Fig. 163

NOTE THE DIRECTION OF PINS AND TAILS

DIRECTION OF ASSEMBLY

DOTTED PENCIL LINE FOR RE-ASSEMBLY

CORNERS PLANED OFF

Fig. 164

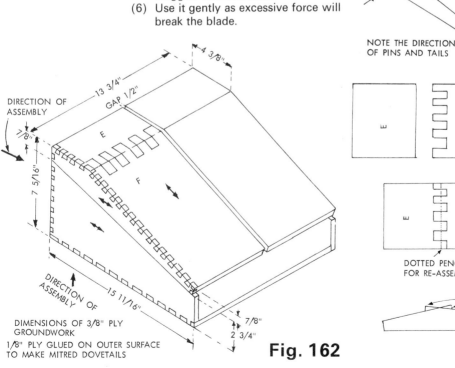

DIRECTION OF ASSEMBLY

4 3/8"

13 3/4"

GAP 1/2"

7/8"

7 5/16"

E

F

DIRECTION OF ASSEMBLY

15 11/16"

DIMENSIONS OF 3/8" PLY GROUNDWORK

1/8" PLY GLUED ON OUTER SURFACE TO MAKE MITRED DOVETAILS

7/8"

2 3/4"

Fig. 162

compartment first, followed by the front and finally the bottom. The back and front of the lid are fitted to the top, then each inner and outer side.

The bend in the top is made first before cutting any of the lid dovetails. Cut the row of tenons in F by placing it on E, and drawing around them. Remove the waste with the bandsaw. The ends are planed off after the lid has been assembled.

Set the bandsaw so the platform is tilted to 10°. Saw one side of all the pins, reverse the bandsaw blade angle and saw the other sides. Cut out the tails completely using the bandsaw. Only minimum use of the mortise chisel is necessary.

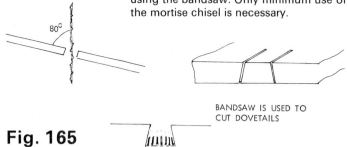

80°

BANDSAW IS USED TO CUT DOVETAILS

Fig. 165

Because of the shape of F, the back of the lid will be at the wrong angle. Glue on a piece of scrapwood and correct the angle. Make all the pins and tails, assemble and check that it all fits.

BACK OF THE LID IS AT THE WRONG ANGLE

PIECE OF SCRAP WOOD GLUED ON

WASTE REMOVED AND ANGLE CORRECTED

Fig. 166

To 'conceal' the dovetails and so avoid veneering on end grain, glue a layer of $\frac{1}{8}$ in. ply on the outside of all parts. 'Pressure glue' with G-clamps, veneer frames or bearer and clamp method. Remove excess glue as it is squeezed out to avoid cleaning up the dovetails later.

Cut off the excess $\frac{1}{8}$ in. ply, leaving an $\frac{1}{8}$ in. overlap. Mitre with a block plane using blue chalk to reveal the high spots. To complete the carcase, insets made of the same hardwood as the veneers are fitted around the lower edge of both lids, the upper edge of the main box and the rear edges of the drawer component. The insets avoid veneering the edges. The tongues

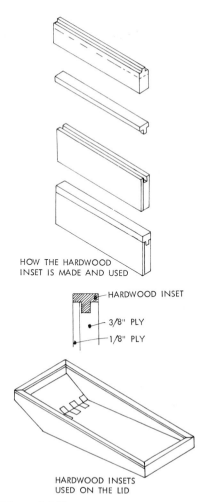

HOW THE HARDWOOD INSET IS MADE AND USED

HARDWOOD INSET

3/8" PLY

1/8" PLY

HARDWOOD INSETS USED ON THE LID

Fig. 167

and grooves of the insets are about $\frac{1}{4}$ in. deep. If possible cut off from the same plank as the veneers.

The corners of the insets are mitred.

The carcase is now complete.

Fig. 168

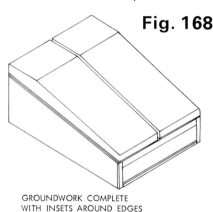

GROUNDWORK COMPLETE WITH INSETS AROUND EDGES

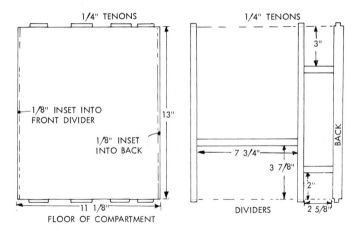

Fig. 169

FLOOR OF COMPARTMENT

1/4" TENONS

1/8" INSET INTO FRONT DIVIDER

1/8" INSET INTO BACK

13"

11 1/8"

1/4" TENONS

3"

BACK

7 3/4"

3 7/8"

2"

2 5/8"

DIVIDERS

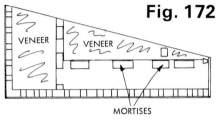

Fig. 172

VENEER   VENEER

MORTISES

ARRANGEMENT OF VENEERS AND MORTISES ON THE SIDES OF THE BOX

Next make the compartments of the box —see also the plan of the components at the beginning of the chapter.

Cut the front divider to $5\frac{1}{2}$ in. height, but plane the slope after fitting. Make the rebate for the floor after veneering.

All dividers are $\frac{1}{2}$ in. thick.

Back Piece

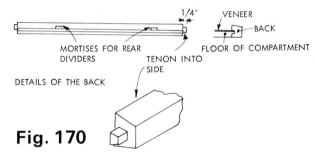

1/4"   VENEER

BACK

MORTISES FOR REAR DIVIDERS

TENON INTO SIDE

FLOOR OF COMPARTMENT

DETAILS OF THE BACK

Fig. 170

Veneer the floor of the compartment; several pieces may be used, provided they join beneath where the dividers rest.

Rebate the back piece to take the floor, and rebate the front divider.

Glue the floor, front divider, compartments and back, using the sides as a jig.

Veneer the sides to leave the mortises exposed.

Trim the veneers on the inner aspect of sides to produce a flush fit with the dividers. Veneer the outer surfaces of the sides, sawing the upper part of the veneer off the sides and front for the lids. Glue on the sides.

Veneer the inner and outer surface of the front, then glue to the box. Arrange the veneers thus:

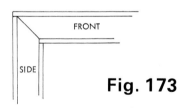

FRONT

SIDE

Fig. 173

Leave the chamfering and finishing until just before the hinges are fitted.

The compartment dividers are fitted together by sliding stopped dovetails, slid in from the bottom. Each divider is higher than necessary and is planed after they have been glued.

Fig. 171

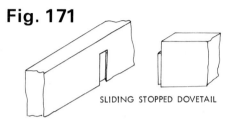

SLIDING STOPPED DOVETAIL

The mortises are cut in the sides to correspond with the tenons of the floor and compartment dividers. The dividers are glued together using the sides and base as jigs. Check for squareness.

Next prepare the bottom. Inset $\frac{3}{4}$ in. wide strips of acacia to take the oak drawer runners. This is a very hard wood which will wear much more slowly than the ply.

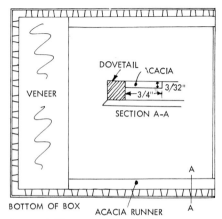

VENEER

DOVETAIL   ACACIA

3/32"

3/4"

SECTION A-A

A

BOTTOM OF BOX   ACACIA RUNNER   A

Fig. 174

Veneer the front part and ensure that its edge will lie beneath the lower edge of the front divider. Check the fit with the sides and glue.

The box is almost complete. All that remains is to chamfer the dividers and veneer the back.

These will be described later.

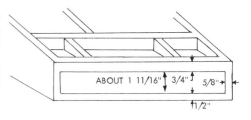

LIDS

Glue together the two parts of each top using the sides as jigs to get a perfect relationship. Remove the sides, then veneer in two stages glueing the larger one first. Plane the front edge and scribe in the second using blue chalk to get a perfect fit.

Fig. 175

LID TOP VENEERED SECTION BY SECTION

Make sure these top veneers will overlap those of the sides by $\frac{3}{16}$ in., particularly those of the inner sides of the lids, where insets are not used on the corners. The relationship of the outer side veneers is not so critical as the edge will be finished by insets.

The front and sides of each lid are veneered, the back being left until later. This is only $\frac{3}{4}$ in. wide and can be veneered after it has been assembled.

VENEERING THE BACK

Make a cardboard template which will fit exactly the entrance to the drawer compartment. Plane the matching pieces of veneer which you intend to use on the drawer and back so they are perfectly butted. Tape together with masking tape. Place on the cardboard template and score around until the pieces for the drawer are detached. Cut off the upper pieces for the lids with the bandsaw.

Veneer the back of the box with two 'square U-shaped' pieces (as 'A' in Fig. 176), holding in place with squares of $\frac{1}{8}$ in. thick ply. Drill $\frac{1}{32}$ in. holes through the veneer to avoid splitting it. The pins and ply are removed after the glue has set and the tiny holes filled with a glue-sawdust mixture.

This was a technique used to glue ply sections on to wooden aircraft in the last

MATCH THE VENEERS AND STICK TOGETHER WITH MASKING TAPE

MARK OUT

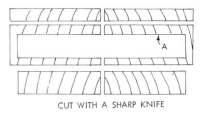

CUT WITH A SHARP KNIFE

Fig. 176

war. Apart from the drawer front, the veneering is finished.

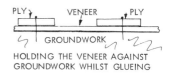

HOLDING THE VENEER AGAINST GROUNDWORK WHILST GLUEING

Fig. 177

FINISHING THE BOX

Plane the edges of the veneers to take the insets. Plane and chisel the tops of the central assembly so they become flush with the sides. Chamfer the divisions with a mortise chisel, working inwards with the grain. (Fig. 178)

HOW TO FIT THE PIANO HINGES

Plane both lids, so they fit each other and the box.

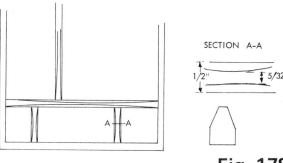

SECTION A-A

1/2" 5/32"

CHAMFERING THE PARTITIONS

Fig. 178

The important dimensions for fitting are:

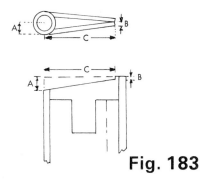

Fig. 183

Take your time with fitting as there is a multitude of mistakes to be made by the

Fig. 179

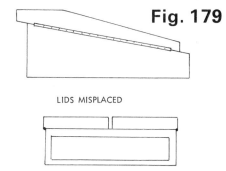

LIDS MISPLACED

Ideally, the hinge should sit:

Fig. 184

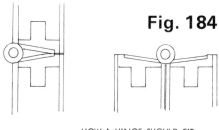

HOW A HINGE SHOULD FIT

unwary. The hinges can be mounted too deep so the lid won't close, or the hinge is bent—the lids become 'hinge-bound.' Or

Fig. 180

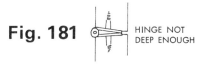

HINGE SET TOO DEEP

the hinges may be mounted too shallow so the lid and box gape when they are closed.

Fig. 181

HINGE NOT DEEP ENOUGH

The screws used to attach the hinge may be too big so as to prevent the hinge closing on itself. The screws should be

Fig. 182

FAULTS ENCOUNTERED WHILE PUTTING IN A HINGE

SCREW NOT COUNTERSUNK

countersunk into the hinges but take care the countersunk hole is not too big as the head of the screw may slip through.

Cut the brass piano hinge so there are screwholes near the ends. The end of each hinge should be $\frac{3}{4}$ in. from the front and back of the sewing box. Clamp the lid to the body, lay on the hinge and mark around it. Fix distance 'a' on the marking

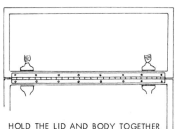

HOLD THE LID AND BODY TOGETHER WITH CLAMPS WHILE THE POSITION OF THE HINGE IS MARKED OUT

Fig. 185

gauge and transfer it on to the sides of box and lid. Establish depth 'c' with a piece of scrap hinge. Remove this waste. If the hinge housing is too shallow dig out more, if it is too deep, plane a little off both lids. Check and adjust, using only two screws on each side of the hinge. When the permanent relationship between lids and box has been established make the rest of the screw holes. The corner insets may now be added to the box.

CORNER INSETS

These can be made from any $\frac{5}{16}$ in. square strip. If the box is veneered in walnut cut these from the end of a plank. Walnut end grain is very decorative.

Fig. 186

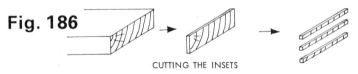

CUTTING THE INSETS

The corners of the box are cut back $\frac{1}{4}$ in. to allow the insets to be glued in. During glueing they are held in position by string

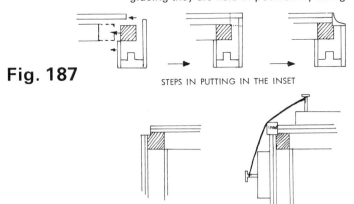

Fig. 187

STEPS IN PUTTING IN THE INSET

as described in a previous chapter. Then they are planed and curved, the curve being finished with glasspaper wrapped around a suitably shaped sanding block. The corners are mitred and a curved stop chamfer cut at the bottom of the box.

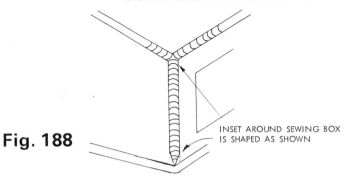

Fig. 188

INSET AROUND SEWING BOX IS SHAPED AS SHOWN

ACACIA OR HARDWOOD INLAY

This can be made from any light coloured wood such as apple, box, holly or maple.

Cut the pieces $\frac{3}{16}$ in. wide and $\frac{3}{64}$ in. thick using the bandsaw. Remove the saw marks using a bullnose plane set fine. Acacia is a horrid wood to plane as the blade 'picks up' splinters, even with the grain.

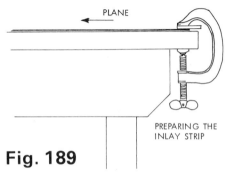

PLANE

PREPARING THE INLAY STRIP

Fig. 189

The groove for the inlay is marked across the lids with the hinges attached as shown. The double line is marked with a Stanley

Fig. 190

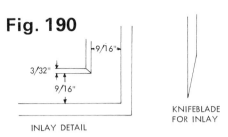

INLAY DETAIL

KNIFEBLADE FOR INLAY

blade sharpened on one side and the waste is removed with a specially shaped screwdriver.

Mitre the corners of the inlay and attach with a mixture of glue and very fine sawdust. Cascamite is preferable to PVA as it does not 'smear' when sanded.

Fig. 191

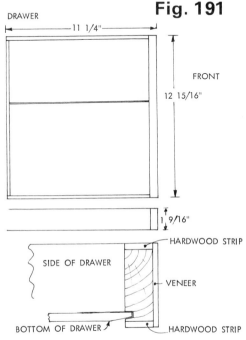

DRAWER — 11 1/4" —

FRONT

12 15/16"

1 9/16"

HARDWOOD STRIP

SIDE OF DRAWER

VENEER

BOTTOM OF DRAWER

HARDWOOD STRIP

THE DRAWER

This is made of oak with veneered softwood front.

First cover the top and bottom of the drawer front with hardwood strip, the same as used to veneer the box and lids. Use the two pieces of veneer removed from the back to cover the drawer. Finally pin and glue $1\frac{1}{2}$ in. $\times \frac{3}{16}$ in. thick strip underneath the box. If you are lucky enough to use walnut expose the endgrain, otherwise have the grain lengthways.

Cover the bottom with green baize after the box has been polished. Use a contact adhesive.

POLISHING

Take off the hinges and sand all parts to a smooth finish by going through all grades of 'wet or dry' paper. Finally, 'blunt' the wet and dry with boiled linseed oil. An evil brown-looking mixture results consisting of oil and fine sawdust. Wipe off excess. The dust will act as a grain filler. Repeat this daily for two weeks, then allow the oil to harden. Wax. A fine finish should result. Polish the hinges and lacquer; they will stay bright for decades.

Line the insides of the lids with padded velvet to make pin and needle cushions.

A small lacquered brass handle is attached to the centre of the drawer. If you wish to 'customise' it, cast one in brass, which is the subject of the next chapter.

Fig. 192

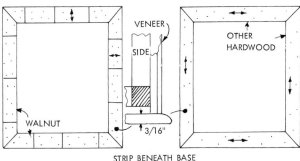

STRIP BENEATH BASE

11. Brass Casting

In the next village there was an aluminium foundry set up in an old cowshed. It nestled beneath a huge horse chestnut tree, covered in ivy and surrounded by heaps of sand, spent mouldings and scrap aluminium. Inside, it was dark except at one end where the crucible stood, where a hole had been cut in the roof and covered with a sheet of warped Perspex.

The walls were hung with pattern boards, patterns, sieves, rakes, watering cans, shovels and tins full of oddments. A pulley and chain hung from one of the oak roof beams and on the floor were fresh castings glistening through the gloom. The business was run from a tiny glass-walled office, with a steel desk covered in piles of papers.

Fig. 193. The rural setting of the foundry where techniques were learnt.

I came to search out the foundry because I wanted a pair of cast aluminium gates. As I arrived, huge ladles of molten silvery metal were being poured down holes in cubes of sand held in wooden boxes, a foot across. It gurgled and hissed amid clouds of steam, which disappeared into the gloom amongst the rafters.

While the metal was setting, the owner came across and chatted, while he nervously eyed the sand mould. Several minutes later he broke the mould and there, shining through the damp sand, was a bright casting.

I mentioned the gates, at which he showed mild interest and suggested I went away and made a wooden blank known technically as a 'pattern'. Many weeks later, after much trial and error and advice and encouragement from the foundry owner, I produced a pattern which we used to cast the gates. I helped to make the sand moulds and pour the aluminium and, eventually, the gates came to hang in our back garden. He still has the pattern, and as far as I know, is producing gates for other people.

While helping, I learnt about brass casting. Why, you may ask, is it worth the amateur cabinet-maker spending time and trouble to learn how to do it? When you have mastered the craft of making furniture and you wish to design your own furniture, the brass fitments must harmonise with the rest of the woodwork and the only way to achieve this is to make them yourself. The photos show what can be done.

There are two ways the amateur can melt brass. One is to use an old bucket set in a pile of earth, the other is to make a small furnace or cupola lined with furnace clay.

First acquire protection from the red hot cinders, molten metal and intense heat.

Fig. 194. Examples of brass casting by the author. Right, a square ferrule, far right a moth-shaped drawer pull and below a specially shaped counter hinge for a desk top.

You will need a cap, a pair of triplex goggles (available from a motor cycle shop), a pair of leather boots and a pair of asbestos gauntlets. Leave your trouser bottoms over your boots to prevent dobs of metal running down into your socks. It is a procedure not without its risks!

Set the furnace up in the open so the zinc oxide and coke fumes are blown away by the wind and not inhaled. Choose a day when your neighbour's washing is not on the line, otherwise it is likely to be peppered with red hot cinders, blown into the air by the forced draught. The principle is to blow air into a coke fire in order to raise the temperature well above the dull red heat of the domestic grate. Temperatures well above the melting point of bright steel are easily reached.

1. THE BUCKET METHOD

Dig a hole in the garden and lay two bricks in the bottom 3 in. apart. Cut a trench from the gap between the bricks and lay an iron pipe or a row of bottomless tins from the bricks to the surface about 4 ft. from the bucket. On the bricks stand an old bucket with holes knocked in the bottom and mound up earth around it, making sure the draught passage is kept free.

Make a small wood fire in the bucket and when well alight add furnacite coke and

blow in a forced draught from the end of a vacuum cleaner. The brass is melted in a crucible or a special porcelain ladle: the 'yellow pages' of a telephone directory will suggest where to obtain these. A pair of tongs will also be needed to lift and pour the molten metal from the crucible, but these can be made.

This is a very simple method of melting brass, but, of course a bucket is destroyed every time the furnace is used. A more professional method is to make a portable, fireclay-lined cupola inside a 6-gallon drum.

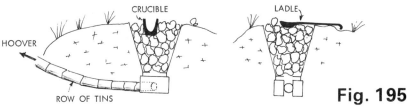

Fig. 195

75

2. THE SMALL CUPOLA

You will need:

A 6-gallon drum 12 in. in diameter and 18 in. high.

1 cwt. of furnace lining clay.

6 ft. of heavy gauge angle iron $1\frac{1}{2}$ in. $\times 1\frac{1}{2}$ in.

1 yard $\frac{5}{8}$ in. diameter steel rod.

$\frac{1}{4}$ in. thick steel plate 12 in. $\times 8\frac{3}{4}$ in.

2 ft. of scrap exhaust pipe, with a flange which has bolt holes.

4 ft. length steel pipe to fit over the end of the exhaust pipe.

2 ft. square concrete paving slab.

6 in. of $\frac{3}{4}$ in. internal diameter gas pipe.

9 in. of 1 in. $\times \frac{1}{4}$ in. steel bar.

Set of pram wheels to move the furnace around the garden.

Build a fire in the garden and bend the draw bars and angle iron by heating to red heat. Rivet on the lugs which are made from the 9 in. length of 1 in. $\times \frac{1}{4}$ in. steel bar. These will prevent the furnace from slipping off the frame. Ask a friendly garage to weld up as shown in the plan.

Assemble and check that the draw bars have plenty of play.

Cut the top out of the 6-gallon drum and attach the exhaust pipe 5 in. from the bottom, knocking a hole in the drum to correspond with the aperture of the exhaust pipe. Cut out a disc from the bottom of the drum leaving a rim 2 in. wide all round. Make a slightly cone-shaped cylinder of wood that will allow a 2-$2\frac{1}{2}$ in. gap all around when it is placed in the 6-

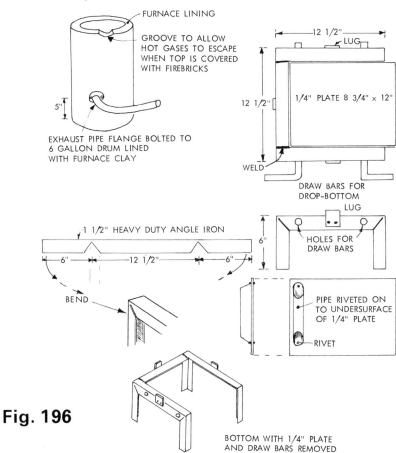

Fig. 196

Cut the $\frac{5}{8}$ in. rod into two lengths of 18 in. for the drawbars. Cut 2 $\times$ 2 ft. $0\frac{1}{2}$ in. lengths of angle iron, and notch as shown. Cut another length of angle iron 9 in. long. Bevel the ends of the 6 in. length of gas pipe and rivet to the undersurface of 12 in. $\times 8\frac{3}{4}$ in. steel plate.

gallon drum. Place the narrowest end in the bottom and ram down the fireclay into the gap. Remove the wooden cone and cut out a hole to the exhaust pipe. Allow the clay to dry a little.

To connect the exhaust pipe to the vacuum cleaner and have control over the

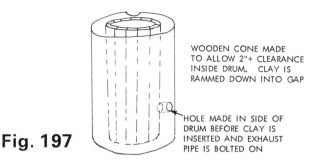

Fig. 197

WOODEN CONE MADE TO ALLOW 2"+ CLEARANCE INSIDE DRUM. CLAY IS RAMMED DOWN INTO GAP

HOLE MADE IN SIDE OF DRUM BEFORE CLAY IS INSERTED AND EXHAUST PIPE IS BOLTED ON

If two old firebricks are used to cover the top, melting temperatures will be reached very quickly. The temperatures reached in this furnace are very high indeed—$\frac{1}{4}$ in. bright steel bar will disappear in a few seconds and, indeed you could use it to melt cast iron, but this is outside the scope of this book.

Further information can be found in a very excellent little book 'Foundrywork for the Amateur' written by B. Terry Aspin and published by Argus Books.

PATTERN MAKING

The real skill in brass casting comes in making the mould in which to pour the molten metal. This is dependent on a good blank or pattern around which a plaster of paris or sand mould is compacted.

Patterns can be made of wood, plastic, metal or resin-based car body filler or a combination of all four. It is an exact copy of the object you want to produce. However, it is not quite that simple, as it has to be made in such a way that it can be removed from the investing material without disturbing or breaking it. The edges need to have a 'draught' or slope. It is the same principle, but in reverse, of getting sand out of a bucket when making sand-castles. A 'lost wax' process could be used for more complex shapes, but it is simpler to use a plaster of paris or foundry sand mould with a reusable pattern. A mould is made around the pattern in two halves. The pattern is removed and two holes are made leading into the impression left in the plaster or sand. One allows the metal to be poured in, the other the waste gases to escape.

A plaster of paris investment gives a casting of a much finer finish than sand; however, there are two major snags. The first is that the pattern sticks to the plaster and can be difficult to remove. The secret is to paint it with a 'slip' of potter's clay. A slip is a mixture of clay and water to the consistency of gloss paint. Nothing else will work. Grease, soap or oil will explode in contact with molten metal. The second is to get rid of the water out of the plaster,

draught cut a window in the 4 ft. pipe and insert a 'butterfly' valve as shown. This is vitally important as you will find out when the furnace is lit and you need to control its temperature.

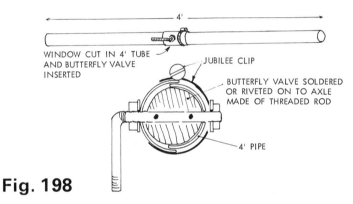

Fig. 198

WINDOW CUT IN 4' TUBE AND BUTTERFLY VALVE INSERTED

JUBILEE CLIP

BUTTERFLY VALVE SOLDERED OR RIVETED ON TO AXLE MADE OF THREADED ROD

4' PIPE

After a few days when the clay has nearly dried, level a 2 ft. square paving slab, so the cupola stands squarely on it. Connect up the 4 ft. length of steel pipe containing the butterfly valve. Place about 2 in. of sand in the bottom, light a wood and coke fire and 'blow' it till it is well alight, then turn off the draught and allow to burn out overnight. This will dry out and partially fuse the clay. Clean out when it has cooled. Don't worry if there are cracks in the fireclay, these will seal when the furnace is well and truly lit, as the clay melts at very high temperatures. Always use 2 in. of sand in the bottom but pull out the draw bars immediately after use and push down most of the slag with a stick, so as to prevent it sticking to the sides.

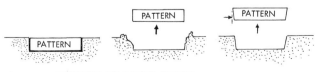

IMPOSSIBLE TO REMOVE PATTERN WITHOUT A DRAUGHT. THE EDGES OF THE SAND ARE PULLED AWAY

PATTERN

PATTERN

PATTERN

Fig. 199

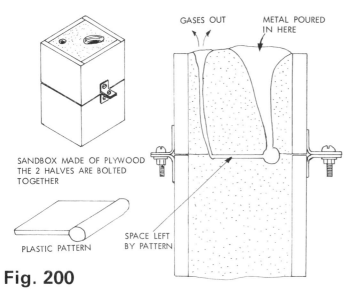

GASES OUT

METAL POURED IN HERE

SANDBOX MADE OF PLYWOOD
THE 2 HALVES ARE BOLTED
TOGETHER

PLASTIC PATTERN

SPACE LEFT
BY PATTERN

Fig. 200

otherwise the steam generated when the metal is poured in will surely cause the mould to explode like a hand grenade. Dry it off in a warm oven over several hours.

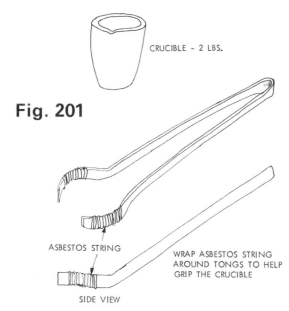

CRUCIBLE - 2 LBS.

Fig. 201

ASBESTOS STRING

WRAP ASBESTOS STRING
AROUND TONGS TO HELP
GRIP THE CRUCIBLE

SIDE VIEW

Bring the two mould halves together and seal any gap with more plaster of paris, drying as before. If necessary support the outside with wire or wire gauze.

THE MELT

Make a pair of tongs from 1 in. $\times \frac{1}{4}$ in. mild steel as shown and wrap asbestos string around the lower end to help grip the crucible. The handle should be raked to the 'holding part' to ease lifting out of the furnace. A pair of coal tongs is useful to adjust and stoke the coke. An old stainless steel spoon is used to scoop off the scum from the top of the melt.

Fill up the crucible with scrap brass and place it on the coke when the fire is going well, placing coke around it to hold it upright. Replenish as it burns away. Be deliberate and don't be alarmed when your goggles steam up or when you smell your cap smouldering.

There is great excitement as the brass starts to melt and the dirty scrap disappears into an ever rising pool of bright yellow molten brass. Remove the scum, turn down the blower and carefully aim the liquid at the downgate. Pour it quickly so that it reaches all parts before it starts to solidify. Leave the metal to cool in the mould and don't be tempted to throw it into cold water. The sudden cooling and differential shrinkage will cause the casting to crack.

FINISHING AND POLISHING

It's lovely metal to work with—warm, yielding and easy to drill and solder. It can be etched or carved with a steel tool. Leave on the 'runners' and use them to clamp in a metal working vice. Clean with a file to remove any 'flash' and sand with wet and dry, finishing with wire wool and finally a metal polish such as Brasso or Duraglit. Before mounting the brass fitment clean and lacquer. It will remain bright and clean for many years.

12. The Rotating Bookcase

In the construction of the sewing box the veneers were arranged to make an interesting visual pattern, which was the dominant feature. Here they are used in a similar fashion, but shape and line are the central ideas.

The basic construction, apart from the bearing and legs, is the same as the sewing box – veneered ply groundwork formed with mitred dovetails, sliding dovetails and mortises and tenons. However, it is much more complex, with a definite sequence of assembly. For those who want both to design and make their own furniture, it is worth considering how the final lay-out came about, for this initial process took nine months.

Motivation is very important and here it was covetousness. I envied a neighbour his Edwardian rotating bookcase and searched London and the Provinces for years, never finding what I wanted. I also envied the memory of a similar bookcase which was in the possession of an uncle who was an M.P. and lived in a castellated house in North London.

The main problem in design was the bearing between the legs and upper part, which was the bookcase. Two discs

Fig. 203

separated by roller bearing was preferred but a bearing supplier looked mystified and said it would be far too expensive.

The shop offered me a free second hand 4 in. car ball bearing and so the design was immediately modified. The outer ring would sit in the legs whilst the inner part would somehow be attached to the top. It was an unorthodox way to use such a bearing, but would probably work as the loading would be insignificant. An engineering friend offered to turn the piece that would sit in the middle when he saw the muddle of bits and pieces which I had intended to use.

As you can see, the central piece is a tight sliding fit into the central ring of the bearing. It is held on to the bookcase by wood screws. Through its centre is screwed a $\frac{3}{4}$ in. threaded rod which is held in place by a nut and washer. A spacer keeps its bevelled edge away from the heads of the gutter bolts which hold the outer bearing ring in the web of the leg.

Fig. 204

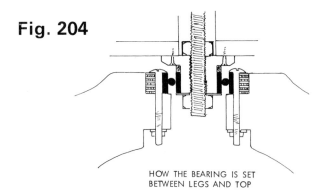

HOW THE BEARING IS SET
BETWEEN LEGS AND TOP

Fig. 205

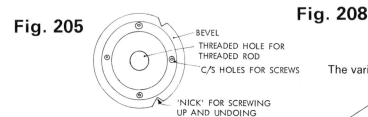

BEVEL

THREADED HOLE FOR
THREADED ROD

C/S HOLES FOR SCREWS

'NICK' FOR SCREWING
UP AND UNDOING

The external appearance took more thought. There was very much more trial and error with hundreds of drawings and diagrams. The untrained amateur had to press on until 'it looked right'.

It is slow patient work which takes months. The temptation is to over-decorate. When the visual design was analysed afterwards it was found that there were three or four simple shapes or visual themes with their variations and different combinations. This principle is universal in painting art and music. Richness is added by the colour and texture of the wood. The struts and sloping edge to the top are reminiscent of the triglyphs around the top of a Greek temple and add to the visual interest.

The themes are:

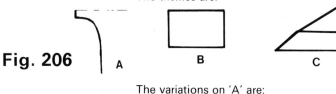

Fig. 206   A   B   C

The variations on 'A' are:

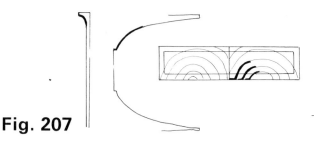

Fig. 207

The variations of 'B' are:

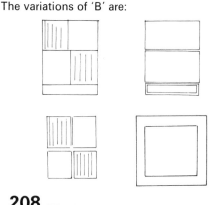

Fig. 208

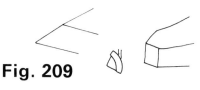

The variations of 'C' are:

Fig. 209

The bottom struts are slightly wider and higher than those on the top shelf.

To emphasise the rotation the veneer on top has a circular pattern and to contrast this it is surrounded by a square inlay.

Fig. 210

This circular, rotational aspect is further emphasised by the arrangement of the compartment dividers. (Fig. 211)

The proportions of the bookcase are roughly 1.6:1, given that it is always looked at isometrically. It looks wrong when drawn as a plan but satisfactory when seen 'in the real'.

Fig. 211

The bookcase consists of: a $\frac{3}{4}$ in. thick ply top with sloping edges, veneered all over and mortised onto a 2 in × 2 in. central column. This column contains the $\frac{3}{4}$ in. threaded rod which is attached to the ball bearing by a piece of turned mild steel. There are four sets of compartment dividers, which are slid over the central column and glued to the top, middle shelf and bottom shelf assembly. The bottom shelf assembly is made of veneered plywood joined by concealed dovetails. The drawer at the bottom is an unusual shape

to utilise as much space as possible, while the legs are a laminated structure made of many glued short lengths of wood so that there is always side grain on the veneered outer surface. Modern castors are attached to the ends of the legs.

It will take at least a year to make and one of the seasons will pass for a second time. The structure appears complex, but it is straightforward to make when taken step by step.

It uses techniques already described, but in addition it shows:
(1) How to mount a ballrace.
(2) How to cut a large veneer off the end of a log using a panel saw.
(3) The use of tin templates to mark out mortise and tenon joints.
(4) The hag's tooth.
(5) How to make curved 'built-up' legs.
(6) How to bend sheets of wood using a warm water bath.
(7) How to glue bent sawcut veneers.

MAKING THE BOOKCASE

First get a fitment made for the ballrace. The exact dimensions will depend on the size of bearing used. These bearings are readily available in bearing shops or the waste boxes of commercial garages. The outer ring of the bearing will be set in a plywood ring which has been glued into

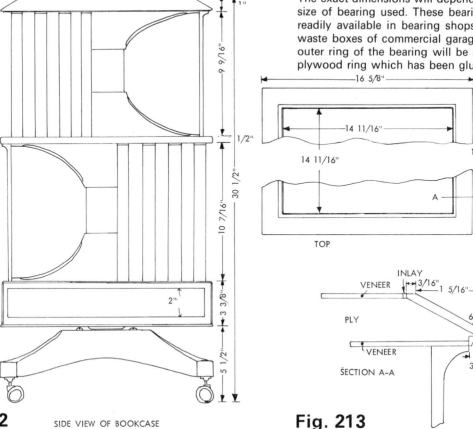

SIDE VIEW OF BOOKCASE

Fig. 212

TOP

SECTION A-A

Fig. 213

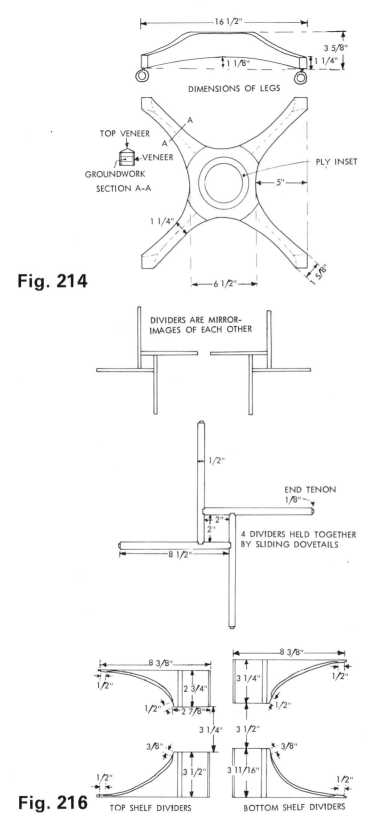

Fig. 214

DIMENSIONS OF LEGS

TOP VENEER
VENEER
GROUNDWORK
SECTION A-A

PLY INSET

DIVIDERS ARE MIRROR-
IMAGES OF EACH OTHER

END TENON

4 DIVIDERS HELD TOGETHER
BY SLIDING DOVETAILS

Fig. 216

TOP SHELF DIVIDERS   BOTTOM SHELF DIVIDERS

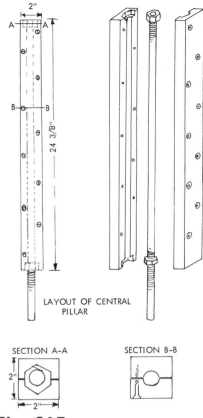

LAYOUT OF CENTRAL
PILLAR

SECTION A-A   SECTION B-B

Fig. 215

the web of the legs and is held firmly in place by the heads of four gutter bolts.

THE CENTRAL PILLAR

This consists of a piece of $\frac{3}{4}$ in. threaded rod 2 ft. 6 in. long with a nut top and bottom as shown in the diagram. It is surrounded by two pieces of 2 in. × 1 in. oak appropriately hollowed out, then glued and screwed around the threaded rod. The bookcase is built round this 2 in. square pillar.

THE COMPONENT DIVIDERS

These are made of $\frac{1}{2}$ in. thick walnut or other suitable hardwood as near to quarter sawn as possible, joined together by sliding dovetails. The channel through the central assembly is 2 in. × 2 in. which slips over the central pillar.

The edges of the dividers are shaped with a carving gouge but finished with a specially shaped piece of metal held in a wooden clamp called a hag's tooth.

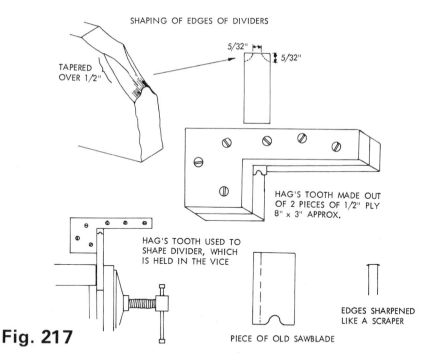

SHAPING OF EDGES OF DIVIDERS

TAPERED OVER 1/2"

5/32"

5/32"

HAG'S TOOTH MADE OUT OF 2 PIECES OF 1/2" PLY 8" × 3" APPROX.

HAG'S TOOTH USED TO SHAPE DIVIDER, WHICH IS HELD IN THE VICE

EDGES SHARPENED LIKE A SCRAPER

PIECE OF OLD SAWBLADE

Fig. 217

The diagram is self-explanatory.

Keep the hag's tooth as close as possible to the divider, which is held in the vice. The wooden surfaces are finished with wet and dry.

When all the dividers are made glue and assemble. Check for squareness.

Fig. 218

LARGE HARDWOOD LOG CUT OBLIQUELY TO PROVIDE LARGE INTERESTING VENEER

MULTIPLE SAWCUTS TO REMOVE VENEER

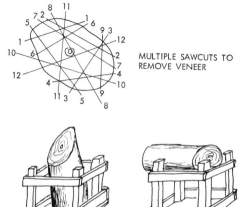

USE THE SMALL WORKBENCH AS A SAW TRESTLE

THE TOP

First cut the veneer 15 in. × 15 in. If possible use one with a large central feature. If it has to be cut from a large log, use the small work table and wedge it in place. A log which might not be quite large enough can be cut on the skew to provide a larger veneer. Plane the end of the log to provide a smooth glueing surface. Repeatedly criss-cross the sawcuts, so each provides a guiding groove for the next. Use a panel saw as you are really crosscutting. It takes a long time and the veneer probably will end up thicker in the middle than at the outside, but this extra planing needed will be worth the trouble.

The groundwork of the top is made from two sheets of $\frac{3}{8}$ in. ply glued together using the veneer presses. Make sure the grains of adjacent glued surfaces are at 90°. Slope the edges to give these dimensions:

Fig. 219

13 3/4"

3/4"

(SQUARE)

16"

DIMENSIONS OF PLY GROUNDWORK FOR TOP

Cut four pieces of hardwood strip 2 in. × $\frac{1}{4}$ in. × $17\frac{1}{4}$ in. mitred at the corners and glued on the slope of the plywood edge by screwing on shaped pieces of softwood waste and using the ledge as a platform for a row of G-clamps.

Fig. 220

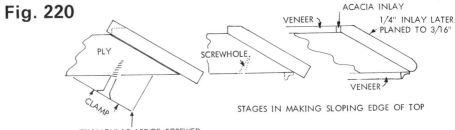

TRIANGULAR LEDGE SCREWED
TO UNDERSURFACE OF TOP
TO ALLOW CLAMPING OF
SLOPING EDGE

STAGES IN MAKING SLOPING EDGE OF TOP

Shape the edges of the four strips as shown and then veneer the top. Cut the veneer to allow a clearance of $\frac{1}{16}$ in. between it and the four hardwood strips. Use small pieces of inlay as spacers. Clear the glue out of the channel as pressure is applied to the veneer. Inlay and mitre the corners. Use a Cascamite/fine sawdust mixture.

Veneer the undersurface of the top, glueing the four veneers on successive days, making sure the veneer joints will lie beneath the dividers. Trim the outer edges of the veneers on the lower surface so as to leave a gap between them and the hard-wood strip. Glue in lengths of inset using a web of string between two rows of nails.

Fig. 222

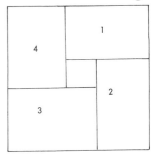

ORDER OF VENEERING UNDERSURFACE OF TOP

THE MIDDLE SHELF

This is made from $\frac{5}{16}$ in. ply, but if this is unavailable, use $\frac{3}{8}$ in. planed down so that the thickness after veneering is $\frac{1}{2}$ in. Inset the edge of the ply. Veneer top and bottom to correspond with the dividers and plane so the shelf is $16\frac{3}{8}$ in. $\times 16\frac{3}{8}$ in.

Fig. 223

SECTION THRO' END OF MIDDLE SHELF

Veneer the edge with vertical grained strips. They will be sanded to give a slightly convex appearance.

THE BOXED DRAWER COMPARTMENT

This is made like the sewing box. The top is veneered so the veneers correspond with the undersurface of the middle shelf. Small insets are glued in the corners. Drawer runners are used inside, and the stringing is inlaid before assembly. A 2 in. square hole is cut in the centre top and bottom to take the central pillar.

The drawer veneers are cut by the same method as the sewing box, and the shaped pieces glued on to the edge of the

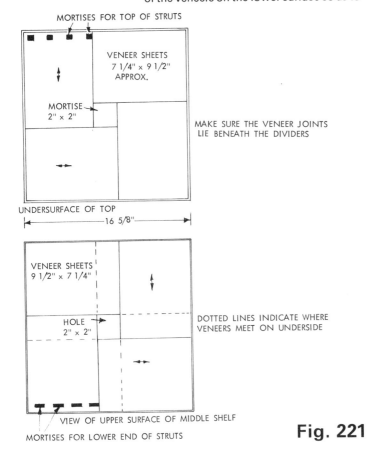

MORTISES FOR TOP OF STRUTS

VENEER SHEETS
7 1/4" x 9 1/2"
APPROX.

MORTISE
2" x 2"

MAKE SURE THE VENEER JOINTS
LIE BENEATH THE DIVIDERS

UNDERSURFACE OF TOP

16 5/8"

VENEER SHEETS
9 1/2" x 7 1/4"

HOLE
2" x 2"

DOTTED LINES INDICATE WHERE
VENEERS MEET ON UNDERSIDE

VIEW OF UPPER SURFACE OF MIDDLE SHELF

MORTISES FOR LOWER END OF STRUTS

Fig. 221

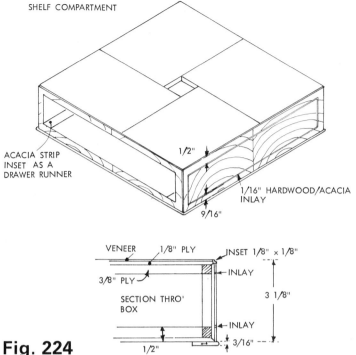

SHELF COMPARTMENT

ACACIA STRIP INSET AS A DRAWER RUNNER

1/2"

1/16" HARDWOOD/ACACIA INLAY

9/16"

THE DRAWER

This is an unusual shape and fits either side of the central pillar. The drawer front is veneered in the same manner as the drawer of the sewing box, but has an acacia inlay set in the corner at 45°. The order and technique are different.

This is repeated at the ends of the drawer front after the drawer has been assembled. A knife and specially shaped screwdriver (see chapter 9) are used to make the groove. The dovetails are hidden by a hardwood strip, the same as those of the top and bottom. A brass handle could be fitted to the drawer front, but I think it would spoil the balance of the four sides. A hole in the bottom of the drawer will allow it to be pulled forward sufficiently for it to be gripped and pulled fully out.

VENEER 1/8" PLY

3/8" PLY

INSET 1/8" × 1/8"

INLAY

SECTION THRO' BOX

3 1/8"

INLAY

1/2"

3/16"

Fig. 224

assembled box are glued by a similar method. Inset all around with $\frac{1}{8}$ in. wide

THE STRUTS

There are 32 to cut—but the work involved in cutting them is much diminished by using the narrow blade on the bandsaw. Cut two tin templates from an old coffee tin—the kind where the coffee is sealed in. The plate is thicker than the usual tin. The holes are cut by sharpening the end of an

VENEER FOR DRAWER-FRONT CUT IN THE SAME WAY AS THE SEWING BOX

Fig. 225

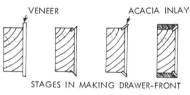

VENEER

ACACIA INLAY

STAGES IN MAKING DRAWER-FRONT

Fig. 227

strip, $\frac{1}{8}$ in. × $\frac{1}{8}$ in. strip and carve as shown. Finally pin and glue 1 in. wide strip, $\frac{1}{8}$ in. thick, all around the bottom of the box, mitring at the corners. However, to prevent damage, the last step may be left until after assembly of the bookcase.

old needle file and repeatedly scoring along the same line. They can be used for checking the size of the tenons top and bottom and marking out the mortises. Also make two templates out of $\frac{1}{8}$ in. ply, one for the top row and one for the bottom. These,

Fig. 226

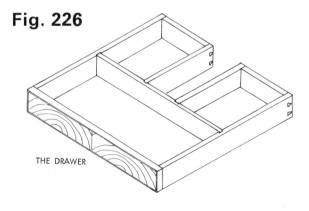

THE DRAWER

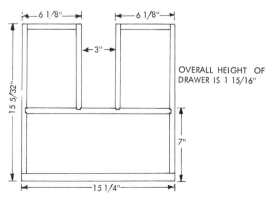

6 1/8"

6 1/8"

3"

15 5/32"

7"

15 1/4"

OVERALL HEIGHT OF DRAWER IS 1 15/16"

Fig. 228

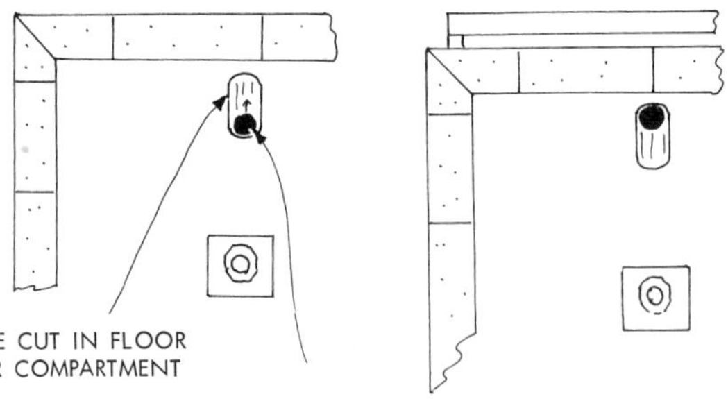

OVAL HOLE CUT IN FLOOR
OF DRAWER COMPARTMENT

ROUND HOLE IN BOTTOM
OF DRAWER TO INSERT
FINGER AND PULL FORWARD

together with the tin templates, will ensure that the 15 in each row are identical.

Next *glue the dividers*. These four assemblies can be used to set the position of the inner strut of each of the 8 sets. Mark the position of the other end strut as shown in the diagram then space the other two so that the three gaps are equal. This is rather imprecise but there are so many variables during assembly, it is the best way of doing it.

Cut the mortises for the tips of the dividers in the top and bottom of each strut.

Fig. 229

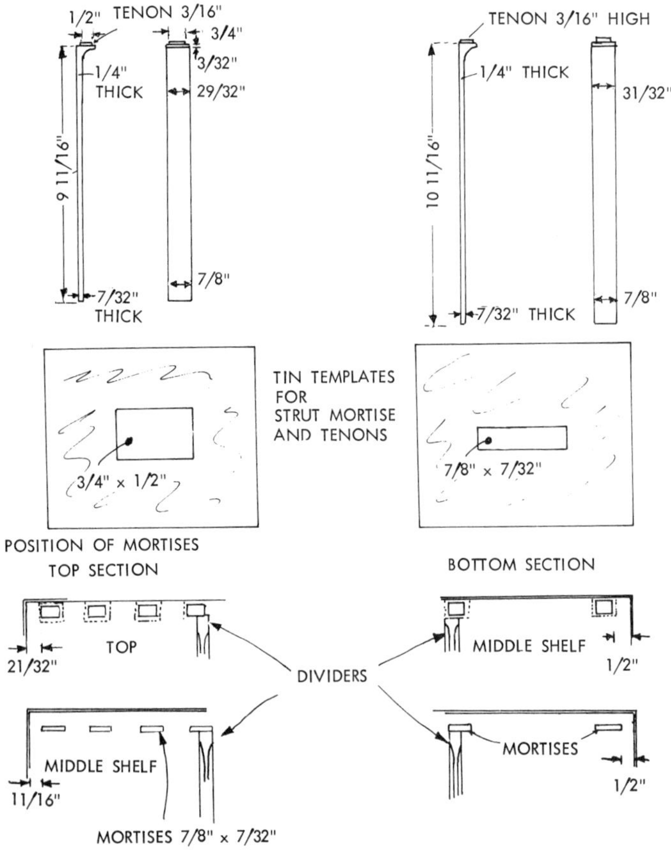

TOP STRUTS
1/2" TENON 3/16"
3/4"
3/32"
1/4" THICK
29/32"
9 11/16"
7/8"
7/32" THICK

BOTTOM STRUTS
TENON 3/16" HIGH
1/4" THICK
31/32"
10 11/16"
7/8"
7/32" THICK

TIN TEMPLATES
FOR
STRUT MORTISE
AND TENONS

3/4" × 1/2"

7/8" × 7/32"

POSITION OF MORTISES

TOP SECTION
TOP
21/32"
DIVIDERS

MIDDLE SHELF
11/16"

MORTISES 7/8" × 7/32"

BOTTOM SECTION
MIDDLE SHELF
1/2"

MORTISES
1/2"

ASSEMBLY

Assemble without glueing, numbering all mortises and tenons with labelled marking tape. Label the relationship of dividers to shelves because there are always small variations. Shorten any struts which are too long, check for squareness and that the top, middle shelf and drawer box are parallel.

Clean up, scrape and sand all surfaces. Now the awesome moment has arrived for glueing. Choose a cool day and use

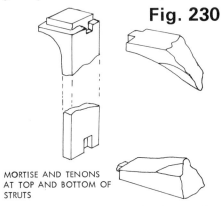

Fig. 230

MORTISE AND TENONS
AT TOP AND BOTTOM OF
STRUTS

Cascamite, which is a fairly slow setting glue and allows time for re-adjustment. Have two ribbon clamps to put around the assembled bookcase at 90°, like string around a parcel.

Use the small workbench, have plenty of space and newspaper on the floor. Have everything set out in sequence of glueing. Remove everybody from earshot as your language is likely to deteriorate.

Place the top upside down on the small workbench. Glue the central pillar into the top tenon. Slide down the top divider, putting glue on its top surface. Glue in the top tenons of all four sets of top shelf struts, catching the tenoned tips of the four dividers. Slide down the next set of dividers and place their tenoned tips into the inner struts of each of the four sets. Follow with the middle shelf, glueing the dividers and all 16 struts. Check for squareness.

Repeat the same with the bottom sets of struts and the drawer compartment. Tighten the ribbon clamp, checking for squareness and that top, middle shelf and drawer box are parallel. Scrape off excess glue with an old chisel before the glue has hardened.

Fill in the gaps between the dividers with blocks of softwood to within $\frac{3}{32}$ in. of their surface.

Fig. 231

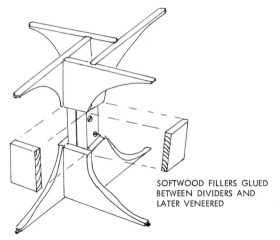

SOFTWOOD FILLERS GLUED
BETWEEN DIVIDERS AND
LATER VENEERED

Finally, fill the gaps between top and bottom dividers with veneers with the grain running vertically.

THE LEG ASSEMBLY

Cut out the shape as shown in the plan in $\frac{3}{8}$ in. ply and to this glue layers of hardwood $\frac{1}{2}$ in. thick or less so that there are at least three layers in the thinnest part of each leg. Plane each layer. Arrange the pieces like a jig saw so that side grain will always be on the surface which will be veneered. The ply base will be discarded. The final dimensions are as shown at the beginning of the chapter. This laminated structure is

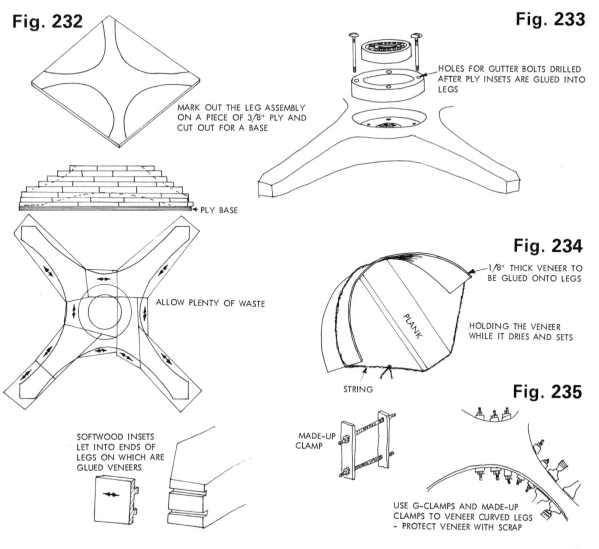

Fig. 232

MARK OUT THE LEG ASSEMBLY ON A PIECE OF 3/8" PLY AND CUT OUT FOR A BASE

← PLY BASE

ALLOW PLENTY OF WASTE

SOFTWOOD INSETS
LET INTO ENDS OF
LEGS ON WHICH ARE
GLUED VENEERS

Fig. 233

HOLES FOR GUTTER BOLTS DRILLED AFTER PLY INSETS ARE GLUED INTO LEGS

Fig. 234

1/8" THICK VENEER TO BE GLUED ONTO LEGS

PLANK

HOLDING THE VENEER WHILE IT DRIES AND SETS

STRING

Fig. 235

MADE-UP CLAMP

USE G-CLAMPS AND MADE-UP CLAMPS TO VENEER CURVED LEGS – PROTECT VENEER WITH SCRAP

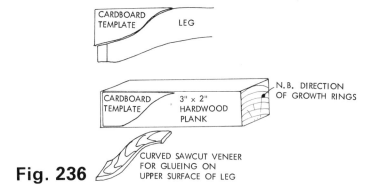

Fig. 236

CARDBOARD TEMPLATE   LEG

CARDBOARD TEMPLATE   3" x 2" HARDWOOD PLANK

N.B. DIRECTION OF GROWTH RINGS

CURVED SAWCUT VENEER FOR GLUEING ON UPPER SURFACE OF LEG

very strong as the grain of each layer has been 'crossed', hence preventing splitting.

Make a circular ply inset to fit tightly around the bearing and glue into the top of the legs. Shape the legs using a Stanley shaping tool and put a softwood inset into the end of each leg to avoid veneering an end grain.

Cut four sheets of walnut veneer 4 in. wide $\frac{1}{8}$ in. thick and 20 in. long. Soak the sheets in a bath of warm water or make a large ply steam-box as described in a later chapter and bend to the curve of the legs, retaining in position with a piece of string and a short length of plank. They will 'set' in position as they dry out.

Glue them one by one using G-clamps and clamps made from strips of steel and threaded rod; protect the veneers and laminated groundwork with wedge-shaped pieces of scrapwood.

Veneer the ends of the legs and shape the upper surface of each leg, making a cardboard template to fit each one. Cut curved veneers $\frac{5}{16}$ in. thick to fit them.

Chamfer the tops of these veneers each side of the centre line to a flat triangular section (see Fig. 214).

Mount the castors, mount the bearing and drill four holes alongside it, through the ply ring, to take the gutter bolts. Clean up, linseed and use the minimum amount of french polish. The technique for application is described in the next chapter.

Congratulations when you have finished it! You can call yourself a cabinet-maker of the old school and should be able to make any small piece of furniture of the reproduction style.

13. Finishing and Polishing

You will have found that however hard you try you can never achieve the perfect finish. Corners are rounded off and a seemingly flat surface is full of hillocks and depressions. Machines will flatten, square and smooth, but seem to provide something that is too perfect. Whatever means we use, and whatever finish we manage, wood will warp and split in central heating and scratch and bruise during use.

Wood was a living growing thing. Every piece is different and deserves to be finished individually. It merits the care and attention which only hands can give, but will be full of small quirks and slips of human failings and imperfections. How lifeless some modern, machine finished furniture looks. It is precise and exact but lacks that life-giving touch of the inexact hand finish.

We are surrounded by dead things, stone, concrete, plastic, metals and wood and bricks. Some things we can give back life, others we can't. Steel, concrete and plastics, particularly the last, need a great deal of contact with live things to show any signs of life. Concrete steps can be worn or grow moss. Steel tools may be rounded with use. Poor plastic—it never looks right! Bricks grow moss, tiles mellow with a multitude of different coloured lichens, limestones weather and mellow to show layers of fossils.

Of all the dead things around us, wood seems most readily to take on the imprint of life around it. Being so recently a living thing it seems to demand to be treated sympathetically. It abhors the tortured finish of a craftsman showing off his obsessional skill, which is so apparent in much Victorian furniture. It resents the soulless and precise line and perfect smooth surface of the machine or the careless hurried shaping of the profiteer. It cries out for the finish of honest endeavour trying to show off its grain pattern and texture, so it will be content with the small irregularities left by the human hand and overlook the small mistakes inherent in the efforts of an earnest being.

But are we content to live with these same small slips and errors? The answer is yes, because we intuitively realise they are in harmony with the material on which they have been made. However, there is a limit to what we will tolerate. The worst faults are black holes where mortises and tenons gape, or dovetails are loose or where veneers fail to meet. Gobs of glue on the visible surfaces are unsightly. Coarse glasspaper scratches or those left by a circular sander are not to be tolerated. Gaping shakes or shrinkage splits are unsightly and should be filled with a glue/fine sawdust mixture. Fine shakes are allowed. Variations in the quality of the surface, where the final sanding has been forgotten, are irritating to the eye. 'Doughiness', that is, smooth hollows, troughs and hillocks left by the circular sander, are unfitted to the final finish. These can always be corrected.

A slightly wavy edge or a variation in the thickness of the edge of a veneer although seen will hardly be noticed. Slips by the inlay knife which have been filled will be ignored by the eye. Pieces of veneer glued in where the tree was not wide enough are common on even the most expensive antiques. A small amount of waviness or judder left by the scraper is acceptable. Variations in the thickness of stringing are inevitable. Hand-finished sanded surfaces are never perfectly level. There is rounding of the veneer towards the edges, depressions where the wood is soft and elevations where it is hard such as around knots. These variations are attractive and add uniqueness to that piece of furniture. This is what hand finish is all about. It is interesting to reflect that the marks left on antiques by everyday use are smiled on by antique dealers, who give it the name of 'patina'.

Thus the amateur cabinet-maker need not be discouraged by the mistakes he thinks he has made. They may seem enormous at the time, but will scarcely be noticed by other people. Generally speaking, they are looking for the good points, the quality of the wood, the overall shape and design, its usefulness, whether they could live with it. This is why thoughtful reasoned design is so important. It will hide a multitude of small mistakes.

Having lovingly sanded and smoothed the wood and accepted that nothing more can be done to improve its finish, preservative or oil or wax or french polish are added to make the wood more acceptable and serviceable. They will:

(1) Make the surface layers of the wood transparent and give the finish 'depth'.
(2) Reveal the pattern, colour and quality of the grain.
(3) Provide a surface that is pleasant to touch.
(4) Provide a sufficiently hard surface to protect it from the bangs and scratches of everyday use, yet make it flexible so that it will not crack or flake.
(5) Seal the surface of the wood to keep out dust and grime.

FILLING AND STAINING

In the past much cheap wood and plywood was filled and stained and sold as 'mahogany', 'oak' or 'walnut'. Even such fine woods as yew or real mahogany were coloured to the fashion of the day. This is not the practice of the modern cabinet-maker, who always wishes to show the natural grain at its best. Each wood has a different colour and texture and people differ in their tastes, so it is as well to know different kinds of polish.

Before starting fill any shakes with a glue/fine sawdust mixture, wash the surface with a meths-soaked rag to remove the last traces of dust. If the particular wood is liable to woodworm paint liberally with Rentokil or Cuprinol and allow to dry.

POLISHES

The oldest is linseed oil, which has been in use for thousands of years. It is still one of the best. It comes either raw or boiled, the latter being a deeper orange-brown colour. The difference is that the 'boiled' has been heated and will dry more quickly, especially if a few drops of terebene are added.

Linseed oil dries by oxidating, that is the oxygen in the air combines with it to form a hard skin. Raw linseed oil dries much more slowly than boiled. It is the best finish to have, although it takes much longer to achieve than french polish. It is harder but more flexible, does not crack or flake and gets deep into the wood to give it a lovely deep glow. Witness the protective effect linseed oil has on the surface of cricket bats.

After the first few layers rub down with the finest wet and dry soaked in linseed oil. Remove the excess but leave a little on, sufficient to give it a greasy feel. Some of the 'sludge' of oil and fine wood dust will sink into the pores of the wood and act as a filler. After a few weeks you will have an unsurpassed finish which will not crack or blister. It appears intimate with the wood and there is no hint of another layer having been added. The disadvantage is that it tends to darken already dark woods, but these may lighten over the years as the ultra violet rays from the sun bleach the wood pigments.

The technique of linseed oil finish was superseded in the 1730s when the Brothers Martin introduced French Polishing, which takes only a few days to apply.

FRENCH POLISHING

The principle is that shellac gum is held in solution by meths and is applied with a pad of wadding enclosed in cotton cloth (a rubber). Most of the alcoholic spirit evaporates rapidly, leaving a concentrated sticky layer of shellac, which is burnished by the rubber to a glossy finish. The remainder of the spirit evaporates as burnishing is carried out. This gives a superb gloss finish but it has little heat or moisture resistance. Drying is by evaporation of the meths. Its great advantage is that, if the process is spoilt, the polish is easily removed with meths and a completely new start can be made.

Four kinds of french polish are available, although you may have to go to a specialist shop to get them. Most D.I.Y. shops sell button polish.

GARNET: Dark greenish brown
BUTTON: A yellow tone
WHITE: Light Creamy colour
ORANGE: A golden yellow shade

The colour depends on how far the shellac has been refined. Try them all out on your piece of furniture to find out which is most suitable. They can easily be removed with meths.

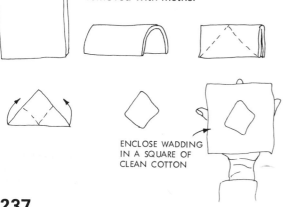

ENCLOSE WADDING
IN A SQUARE OF
CLEAN COTTON

Fig. 237

Here are four pieces of advice for french polishing:

(1) Have the temperature of the room and polish above 65°F. The polish dries by evaporation of the meths. This cools the polish and if it is already cold when it is applied, the polish will cloud.

(2) Work in daylight with the light source in front, so it reflects off your work.

(3) Use clean rags and rubbers. Dust and dirt will spoil the surface.

The best place to french polish is in the lounge when everybody is out. Cover the floor with plenty of newspapers. The polish is applied with a 'rubber'. Building up the layers of shellac is known as 'bodying'. Putting on the final gloss is known as 'spiriting off'.

HOW TO MAKE A RUBBER

This is a pear-shaped blob of unblended cotton wadding as used in upholstery, covered with sheet of fine lint-free cotton.

The wadding can be bought at most drapery shops. Cotton wool cannot be used as a substitute, because it collapses and has no 'body' when soaked in french polish.

Cut a 9 in. square of wadding and fold as shown.

This is placed on a square of cotton material placed on the hand. The pad of wadding is charged with french polish, and the corners of the cloth are twisted in such a way to produce a pear shape.

The twisted end is held in the palm of the hand so it does not 'ridge' the polish as it is applied. The cotton/wadding rubber is squeezed to distribute the polish evenly and is ready for use, but before polishing add just enough linseed oil to the charged rubber to cover the tip of your index finger.

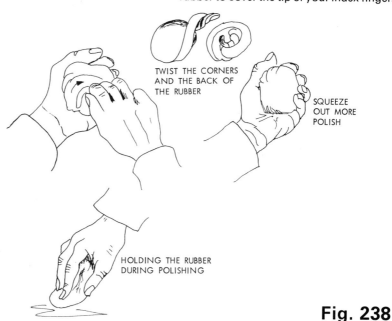

TWIST THE CORNERS
AND THE BACK OF
THE RUBBER

SQUEEZE
OUT MORE
POLISH

HOLDING THE RUBBER
DURING POLISHING

Fig. 238

It helps to lubricate the rubber and the wood.

Recharge as necessary by opening the cotton and pouring the polish directly on to the wadding. Avoid creases on the working surface which will cause ridges of polish. A pear-shaped rubber is best because its shape allows the transference of polish into corners and recesses.

Regulate the amount of polish which gets through the cotton cover by pressure. Cover the surface quickly with a series of spirals or loops. Add enough linseed oil to

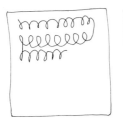 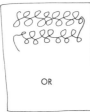 OR 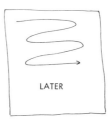 LATER

Fig. 239

cover the top of a finger on to the rubber at each recharge, to act as a lubricant and stop the polish becoming too sticky.

During the application of each layer, gradually increase the pressure of the rubber so the polish keeps coming. Each stroke should overlap the previous one. Recharge the rubber as it gets dry. Wipe over the entire surface both with and across the grain. Allow a few minutes drying between layers. Build up or 'body up' until the surface appears glossy and no more polish seems to be absorbed into the wood. Leave overnight and don't be worried if it appears dull the following day. Rub down ever so gently with the finest

wet and dry and repeat the 'bodying up' process until the gloss you desire is there the following day. The wet and dry clears away any ridges and helps to key the next layer. Don't worry if you make a complete mess of it. Remove all the loose polish with meths and start again.

SPIRITING OFF

Make another rubber and charge with a very small amount of meths. Use figure of eight strokes and gradually change to straight strokes along the grain. As the spirit dries the rubber will act as a burnisher and simultaneously lift the linseed oil off the surface. The cotton cover will become greasy and at the same time the surface will become more highly polished.

Store the rubbers in separate screw-top jars and occasionally add a little meths to keep them soft. Don't use tins, which may rust and stain the rubbers.

Remember, the durability of french polish is proportioned to its thinness. The final coat should be about $1/1000$ in. thick. If it is too thick it will crack and craze.

Finally, wax for that extra sheen. The act of polishing is as important as the wax, for the rag will burnish and gloss the surface.

There are many other finishes. Teak oil can be used instead of linseed oil. It dries faster. Polyurethane is a good finish on such softwoods as larch and pine. It also looks well on yew. However, it is difficult to get a smooth finish and it may be necessary to dilute. It also tends to pick up dust as it dries.

Try all the different methods and try to master all of them. Different finishes suit different woods.

14. The Gusseted Upholstered Stool

Previous chapters have described how to make furniture using dovetails and varieties of the mortise and tenon joint. This one is an exercise in the use of the gusset joint. Because of its initial weakness and instability during construction it has to be assembled on a jig. This chapter concerns both these problems and the contents are:

(1) Construction and use of the gusset joint.
(2) How to make a jig.
(3) How flexibility increases the strength of furniture.
(4) Rounded corners and the avoidance of 'stress concentration.'
(5) Simple upholstery.

This dressing stool or occasional seat stands four square without rails or stretchers. It has a softly curved, upholstered seat and tapered legs, which give it a light appearance. The absence of rails and stretchers together with the ply underseat give it a flexibility which helps it absorb knocks and ill-usage.

The structure relies on the *gusset joint* which was common in wooden aeroplane construction but seldom used in furniture-making. The principle is very simple. The abutment of one piece of wood to another is reinforced with two triangular-shaped gussets which are pressure-glued in place. The angle is reinforced with a prism-shaped fillet to strengthen the joint when it is bent in on itself.

Obviously, this crude joint has to be modified to look more attractive and so be acceptable in the home, as witness the final appearance of the underside of the stool just before upholstery:

You will see from the diagrams that there is a short piece of wood alongside each gusset. This acts as a reinforcement to the gussets as well as allowing the top of the legs to be nicely curved and rounded into the ply fillets which are glued beneath the ply seat. This rounded joint helps to avoid 'stress concentration' and breakage at the joint of the leg and seat. The concept of 'stress concentration' is very simple and most of us are aware of it in everyday life, although it took engineers and designers a long time to realise its importance.

Fig. 240

Fig. 241

THE GUSSET JOINT

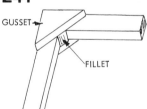

GUSSET

FILLET

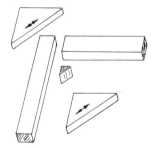

Fig. 242

DIAGRAMMATIC APPEARANCE OF UNDERSIDE OF STOOL BEFORE UPHOLSTERY

thinned towards their middles. This has the triple function of saving weight, improving appearance and making the ply seat slightly flexible. Shocks to the legs can be transmitted and absorbed by both legs and seat. The legs are splayed for both appearance and strength. It allows the fibres of the gussets to be subject mainly to tension forces. Wood is weak in compression but enormously strong in tension, it being comparable, weight for weight, with mild steel.

The legs make a compound angle with the floor, being splayed both forwards and sideways. Knowing the component angles, it might be possible to glue the legs in the appropriate positions on the crosspieces. However, it is much simpler to assemble legs and crosspieces on a jig.

The caveman understood that he only had to make a dent in a piece of wood with his stone axe, to be able to break it at that place. Ships still break their backs, cracks starting in portholes or holes in the decks. The early Comet jet aircraft broke up in mid-air because fatigue cracks started at the corners of square windows. In the same way chairs break at the sharp corners made necessary by the use of the mortise and tenon joint. The photos show the fate of such a joint at the back of a chair, after 10 years' use.

Note that the ply fillets are gradually

Fig. 244

PLAN AND ELEVATION OF JIG

The sides and top are thickened with strips of 2in. wide chipboard. Ply lugs are glued into the lower parts of the sides to fix the slope of the legs. The exact slope can be determined by reference to the plan of the legs. Spaces are cut in the jig to allow the use of G-clamps.

The underframes can now be assembled. Their dimensions when completed are given in Fig. 246.

First cut two pieces of hardwood $1\frac{1}{8}$ in. $\times \frac{7}{8}$ in. $\times 17$ in. for legs and 2in. $\times 1$ in. $\times 17$ in. for the crosspiece. Plane and check for squareness. Clamp the crosspiece centrally on the jig and the legs across it at each end and pencil across. Square around and remove the waste. Provided the ends of the crosspiece and

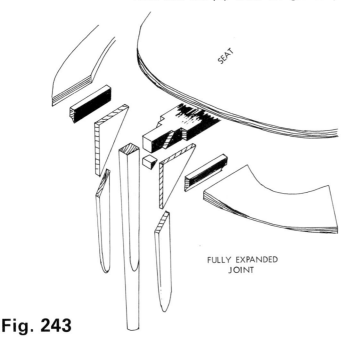

SEAT

FULLY EXPANDED JOINT

Fig. 243

Fig. 245

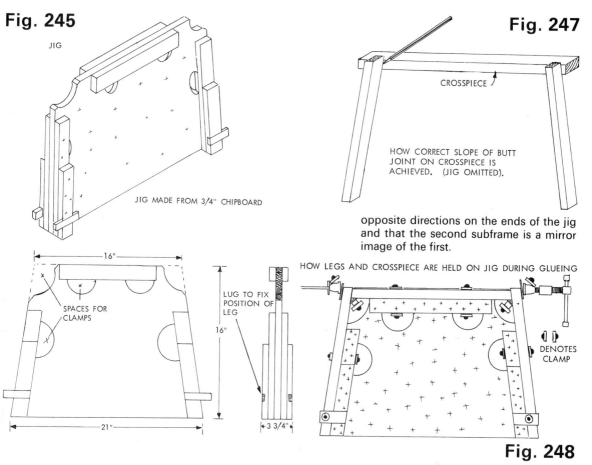

JIG

JIG MADE FROM 3/4" CHIPBOARD

16"

SPACES FOR CLAMPS

21"

16"

LUG TO FIX POSITION OF LEG

3 3/4"

Fig. 247

CROSSPIECE

HOW CORRECT SLOPE OF BUTT JOINT ON CROSSPIECE IS ACHIEVED. (JIG OMITTED).

opposite directions on the ends of the jig and that the second subframe is a mirror image of the first.

HOW LEGS AND CROSSPIECE ARE HELD ON JIG DURING GLUEING

DENOTES CLAMP

Fig. 248

the tops of the legs touch each other, a precise fit is unnecessary.

Cut the fillets for the angles between the crosspiece and legs by first making cardboard templates. Draw around the templates on the endgrain of the fillet so that the glueing surfaces will be side grain to side grain. Make sure that the legs tilt in

The arrangement of sash cramp and clamps is shown diagrammatically. When the glue has set remove sash cramp but wherever possible leave the G-clamp in position, then cut the spaces in the crosspiece for the gussets, also removing excess fillet. Run the saw alongside the leg but try not to scarify it. Cut as far as the lower edge of the fillet.

USE OF TENON SAW TO CUT POSITION FOR GUSSET

Fig. 249

To make the gussets, cut a sheet of hardwood the same as the legs using the veneer saw and plane both sides to achieve a final thickness of $\frac{1}{4}$ in. Then cut out a cardboard template of a gusset large

Fig. 246

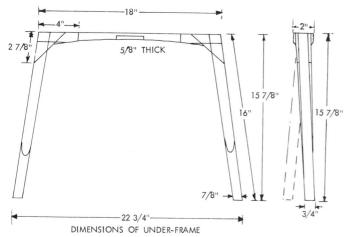

18"

4"

2 7/8"

5/8" THICK

2"

15 7/8"

16"

15 7/8"

7/8"

22 3/4"

3/4"

DIMENSIONS OF UNDER-FRAME

Fig. 250

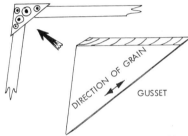

⊙ DENOTES APPROXIMATE POSITION OF LARGE AND SMALL CLAMPS

DIRECTION OF GRAIN

GUSSET

reach to about 3 in. from the bottom of the leg. They are about $1\frac{3}{8}$ in. wide; being slightly wider than the gusset the top clamp will not be impeded. To achieve a thin glueline between gusset and thickener, put on the first clamp two thirds of the way down, then place the second clamp as shown, followed by the rest. Glue both thickeners of each leg at the same time.

enough to overlap the crosspiece and leg. Mark out the gusset on the sheet of hardwood, making sure each lower edge is straight grained and free of knots.

Glue and clamp the four gussets in position and remove the assembly from the jig. Carefully scrape off excess glue and retighten after several minutes.

Make the second subframe in the same way, making sure it is a mirror image of the first one, by using the other pair of lugs.

Fix on the top thickeners by first sawing the crosspiece past the gusset with a panel

When the bottom thickeners are 'set', the frames are ready for rough shaping. Using the bandsaw, remove excess top thickeners, gussets and bottom thickeners. Plane off sawmarks so the legs can be clearly marked with a pencil. Plane off excess wood from the top thickeners to give an overall width of 2 in. Remove waste from the legs using the bandsaw. Begin to round off the legs, but leave the final shaping until the seat and ply fillets have been assembled. Remove excess wood from beneath the crosspieces to give a gentle curve and an overall thickness at the centre of $\frac{5}{8}$ in.

Fig. 251

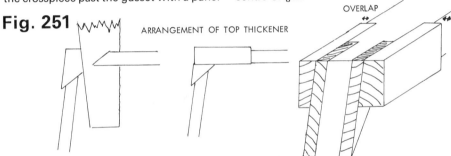

ARRANGEMENT OF TOP THICKENER

OVERLAP

saw to give an overall length of 4 in. Make sure the thickeners overlap the edge of the crosspiece so they can be planed to the same width.

The bottom thickeners are cut from planed $\frac{5}{16}$ in. hardwood sheet and should

ASSEMBLING THE FRAMES

Find the exact centre of each crosspiece, drill $\frac{1}{8}$ in. holes and fit the frames together with an easy-sliding nail. Make sure the legs are splayed and not sloping in towards

Fig. 252

Fig. 253

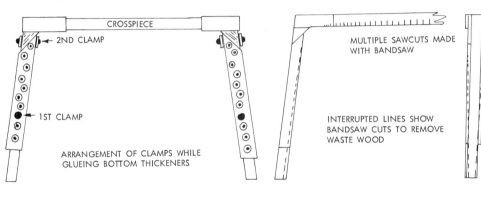

CROSSPIECE

← 2ND CLAMP

← 1ST CLAMP

ARRANGEMENT OF CLAMPS WHILE GLUEING BOTTOM THICKENERS

MULTIPLE SAWCUTS MADE WITH BANDSAW

INTERRUPTED LINES SHOW BANDSAW CUTS TO REMOVE WASTE WOOD

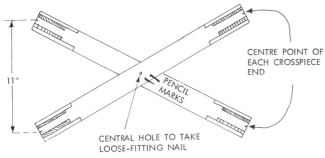

Fig. 254

CENTRE POINT OF EACH CROSSPIECE END

PENCIL MARKS

11"

CENTRAL HOLE TO TAKE LOOSE-FITTING NAIL

the seat, allowing about $\frac{1}{8}$ in. waste all around. Sand and dust. 'Wet' both surfaces with glue if Cascamite is used and scrape off excess glue after clamping. The arrangement of clamps and sash cramps is shown in the diagrams.

When the glue has set, make four cardboard templates to fit into the four spaces between the legs. Trace around each on to scrap $\frac{1}{2}$ in. ply and cut out the rough fillets with the bandsaw. Scribe them into the spaces using a plane and allow an overlap at the edges. Sash cramps can then be used to force them into the spaces, and held, while as many G-clamps can be applied as space will allow.

each other. Clamp the frames together where the centre points of the ends are 11 in. apart.

Mark out and cut a sloppily-fitting lap joint between the two frames and make generous pencil marks so the frames always fit together in the same relationship.

Lay the assembly on a sheet of $\frac{1}{2}$ in. ply and draw around, noting the centre point of each end. Draw an inch grid on the ply and reproduce shape from plan. Cut out

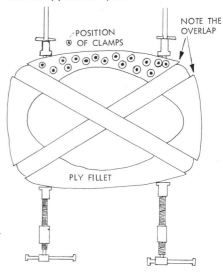

POSITION OF CLAMPS

NOTE THE OVERLAP

PLY FILLET

Fig. 257

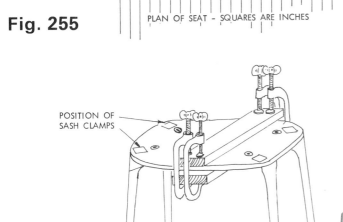

PLAN OF SEAT - SQUARES ARE INCHES

Fig. 255

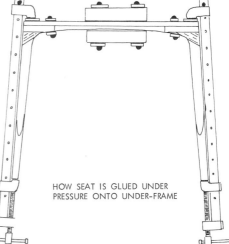

POSITION OF SASH CLAMPS

HOW SEAT IS GLUED UNDER PRESSURE ONTO UNDER-FRAME

Fig. 256

Fig. 258

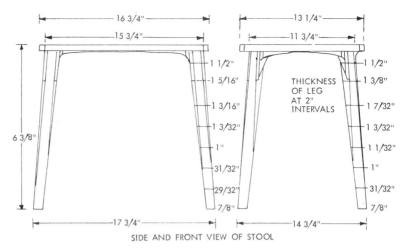

SIDE AND FRONT VIEW OF STOOL

Remove the sash cramps and repeat for the other pair of fillets. When the glue has hardened, shape the stool so that the curves are smooth and run into each other. Use bullnose plane, chairmaker's spokeshave, drawknife, orbital sander, Stanley shaping tool, scraper, glasspaper and wire wool. The dimensions should approximate to those in the diagrams. These are taken every 2 in., horizontally from front and side, and are thus not the narrowest dimensions.

Bring out the grain with a Rentokil/linseed oil mixture and wax or french polish, depending on the hardwood, and the stool is ready to be upholstered.

UPHOLSTERY

This consists of a polyurethane foam pad covered and compressed by a calico lining, and finished with a dralon cover.

Bevel the ply top to allow the 3 in. thick polyurethane foam to wrap neatly over the top edge. Round off the lower edge of the ply so the upholstery materials do not rub on a sharp edge. To mark out the foam, lay

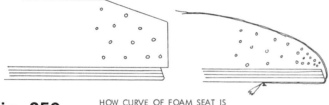

Fig. 259

HOW CURVE OF FOAM SEAT IS
ACHIEVED USING CALICO LINING

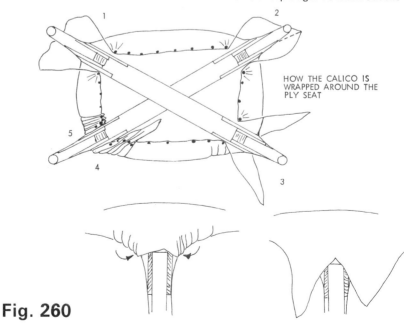

HOW THE CALICO IS
WRAPPED AROUND THE
PLY SEAT

Fig. 260

Fig. 261

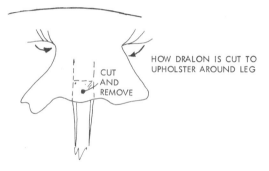

HOW DRALON IS CUT TO
UPHOLSTER AROUND LEG

CUT
AND
REMOVE

Cut a rectangle of calico to overlap the seat by 4 in. Tack between the legs using upholstery tacks (these are wedge-shaped and very sharp, easily hammered in and easily removed.) Pull the calico equally tight all around to compress the foam in a soft curve. The corners are left until last and tackled as drawn.

The dralon cover is tacked down in a similar way, but is more difficult because it is much thicker. Make a double cut at the corner—do a little at a time! Tuck the flap under, pull around one fold, tack, then pull around another. Finally tack around underneath and remove any bulky excess.

Pad the spaces between the ply fillets and the crosspieces with scrap dralon or calico. Finish off with a piece of linen the same colour as the dralon with the appropriately coloured gimp pins.

the seat on it and draw around and cut out on the bandsaw, allowing an overlap of $\frac{1}{4}$ in. Cut off a wedge of foam 1 in. × 3 in., so the calico lining compresses it into a smooth curve.

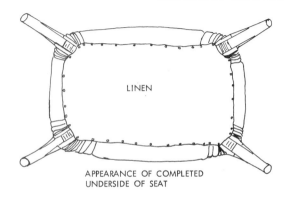

LINEN

APPEARANCE OF COMPLETED
UNDERSIDE OF SEAT

Fig. 262

15. How to make a small table without the use of mortise and tenon joints

Here is a lightweight occasional table for morning coffee or eating off while watching television. There is no back rail, which allows knees and legs to be put under without knocking it over. If this disaster happens its light weight will allow it to bounce rather than break.

Like the stool in the last chapter the top joints depend on gussets. The three rails are attached to the legs by fillets and bent hardwood strips instead of the usual mortise and tenon joints. It is economic in the use of materials and its lightness and slimness fully justify the extra time spent in construction.

It is a lesson in:

(1) Use of fillets and bent hardwood strips instead of mortise and tenon joints.
(2) Use of simple jig during assembly.
(3) How to glue a curved surface.
(4) Economic use of hardwoods.
(5) Use of decorative veneers to relieve the severe simplicity of shape.
(6) Use of the sun to get a flat surface when a belt sander is not available.

A cursory glance at the drawings and plans might suggest that the gussets, strips and fillets would detract from the appearance. However, they do not and are comparable with those of the modern tennis or squash racquet handle and so fit in with the surroundings of the modern house. The big proviso is that the gluelines are invisible at the distance from which we usually look at furniture.

Fig. 264

The table can be made from any hardwood that can be steam bent to a radius of $\frac{1}{2}$ in. when it is $\frac{3}{32}$ in. thick. Larch can also be used (a very underrated softwood), supplies of which can be obtained from any maker of woven fencing. Successive sheets sawn from the same log can be used to veneer the top. If you have the hardwood available, it is best to cut all the pieces from a plank 2 in. × 7 in. × 2 ft. 2 in. using the veneer saw. This gives a unified harmonious appearance and helps to enhance the decorative effect of the paired veneers of the top.

The list of pieces is:

4 legs of $\frac{3}{4}$ in. × $\frac{3}{4}$ in. (at bottom) and $\frac{15}{16}$ in. (at top) and 21 in. long.

Fig. 263

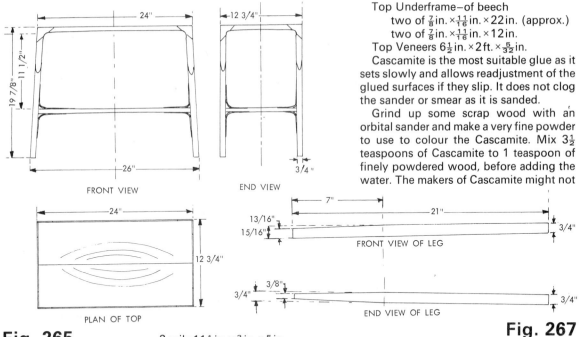

FRONT VIEW

END VIEW

PLAN OF TOP

Fig. 265

FRONT VIEW OF LEG

END VIEW OF LEG

Fig. 267

Top Underframe—of beech

two of $\frac{7}{8}$ in. $\times \frac{11}{16}$ in. $\times 22$ in. (approx.)

two of $\frac{7}{8}$ in. $\times \frac{11}{16}$ in. $\times 12$ in.

Top Veneers $6\frac{1}{2}$ in. $\times 2$ ft. $\times \frac{5}{32}$ in.

Cascamite is the most suitable glue as it sets slowly and allows readjustment of the glued surfaces if they slip. It does not clog the sander or smear as it is sanded.

Grind up some scrap wood with an orbital sander and make a very fine powder to use to colour the Cascamite. Mix $3\frac{1}{2}$ teaspoons of Cascamite to 1 teaspoon of finely powdered wood, before adding the water. The makers of Cascamite might not

2 rails $11\frac{1}{2}$ in. $\times \frac{3}{4}$ in. $\times \frac{5}{8}$ in.

1 rail $23\frac{3}{4}$ in. $\times \frac{3}{4}$ in. $\times \frac{5}{8}$ in.

2 side veneers 22 in. $\times 1\frac{1}{4}$ in. $\times \frac{3}{16}$ in.

2 side veneers $11\frac{1}{2}$ in. $\times 1\frac{1}{4}$ in. $\times \frac{3}{16}$ in.

12 fillers $6\frac{1}{2}$ in. $\times 1$ in. $\times \frac{3}{16}$ in.

12 gussets $\frac{3}{16}$ in. thick $\times 2$ in. $\times 3$ in.

(It is important that the grain of these is as straight, in three dimensions, as possible).

12 bent pieces $1\frac{1}{8}$ in. $\times 7$ in. $\times \frac{3}{32}$ in.

(The grain where each is to be bent should be as straight as possible. The exact thickness depends on how bendable is the wood. This should be found out by trial and error over a steaming kettle spout).

12 fillets (prism shaped) $\frac{5}{8}$ in. $\times$ $\frac{5}{8}$ in. $\times 1\frac{1}{4}$ in.

(Their exact angles depend on where they are fitted).

Ply Top 23 in. $\times 12\frac{1}{2}$ in. $\times \frac{1}{2}$ in. thick.

approve, but it does help make an invisible glueline!

The jig is straightforward and easy to make. Check that the chipboard is not warped.

Before starting to assemble, taper three sides of the tops of the legs to take the gussets and fillets.

NOT TAPERED

WHERE THE WASTE IS REMOVED FROM TOPS OF LEGS

Fig. 268

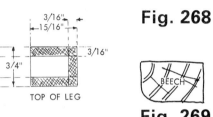

TOP OF LEG

Fig. 269

The inner lower corner of the beech underframe is rounded off.

Cut the beech underframe to fit the top of the legs in a similar way to that used to

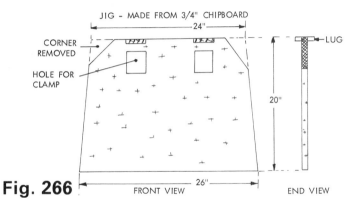

JIG - MADE FROM 3/4" CHIPBOARD

CORNER REMOVED

HOLE FOR CLAMP

LUG

FRONT VIEW

END VIEW

Fig. 266

Fig. 270

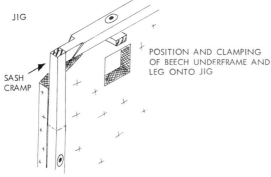

JIG

SASH CRAMP

POSITION AND CLAMPING OF BEECH UNDERFRAME AND LEG ONTO JIG

Fig. 273

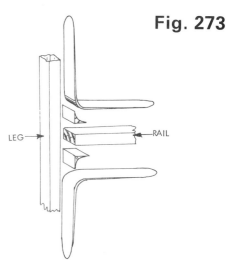

LEG

RAIL

EXPLODED LOWER JOINT TO SHOW HOW THE FILLET AND BENT HARDWOOD STRIPS ARE ARRANGED TO REPLACE THE MORTISE AND TENON JOINT

make the underframe of the stool. The only difference is that here the leg is changed to the face of the jig.

When the glue has set, keep the frame clamped to the jig and cut the beech underframe to receive the gussets in the same way as the stool. When glueing on the outer gussets allow an overlap of at least $\frac{3}{8}$ in. at the top and $\frac{3}{16}$ in. at the side. The gusset must cross below and inside the corner of the leg and beech underframe.

Fig. 271

AT LEAST 3/8"

BEECH UNDERFRAME

FILLET UNNECESSARY

AT LEAST 1/4"

While clamping, protect the gussets with $\frac{1}{8}$ in. thick softwood sheet. Scrap woven fencing is ideal. Remove from the jig and repeat with the other frame and legs.

Scribe and butt joint the long rail $11\frac{1}{2}$ in. down from the underframe. Pressure glue with a sash cramp. Cut hardwood fillets to fit top and bottom at each end of the rail. The quickest way of finding the shape is to cut a cardboard template and draw around

it on the end of the fillet. Glue them in as shown and when the glue has set shape them to a bent quadrant of a circle by using a carving chisel.

Next prepare the hardwood strips. These replace the usual mortise and tenon joint and allow the legs and rails to be thinner and stronger. There is no mortise to weaken the leg. The hardwood strip strengthens the outside of the joint which is the area where bending and breaking stresses first make themselves felt. The resulting joint has an attractive rounded appearance.

Steam the strips over the spout of a kettle and immediately clamp in the hol-

HOW TO CLAMP AND GLUE FILLETS IN THE ANGLE BETWEEN LEG AND RAIL

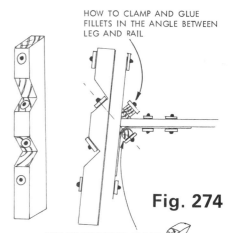

Fig. 274

CURVED SOFTWOOD BLOCK - USED TO BEND AND CLAMP HARDWOOD STRIP INTO CONCAVE FILLET

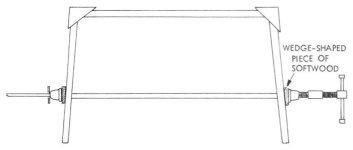

WEDGE-SHAPED PIECE OF SOFTWOOD

Fig. 272

BUTT JOINTING THE RAIL BY USING A SASH CRAMP

lowed fillet using a curved softwood block. If the strip is not snug, remove a little from the fillet; with practice this can be done very quickly. It is a challenge for those who enjoy using their hand and eye.

Leave the bent strip to cool and set while still clamped, then remove and attach the ends by a strip of masking tape, retaining the same relationship they had when between leg and rail. Glue the strips in place using Cascamite and fine wood powder. You will need an assortment of clamps as shown in the photograph.

Fig. 275

Next, glue on the thickeners to cover the sloping surface at the top of each leg. Use the same technique as was used on the

Fig. 276

thickeners of the stool. Leave the four fillers at the ends until later. When the glue has hardened, plane and sand off excess filler, fillet and bent hardwood strip, which will be more difficult later when the frames have been assembled.

Then assemble the frames with the short beech underframes and short rails. All these, to start with, are simple butt joints, the top on to the inner gussets, the bottom on to the legs at the same level as the ends of the long rail. The overall width of the table should be 12¾ in. top and bottom. Use diagonals and steel rulers to check the squareness of the top and sides. Sash cramp across short rails and underframes to pressure glue the butt joints.

Glue on the remaining eight fillets, two at the end of each short rail. Fit and glue the triangular gusset to the end of each

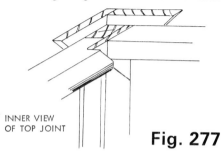

INNER VIEW
OF TOP JOINT

Fig. 277

short underframe, making sure they over-lap upwards by ⅜ in. Use a sash cramp and wedge-shaped softwood packing as G-clamps cannot be used because there is nothing to clamp to.

The resulting top joint may seem complex, but much simpler when broken down in an exploded drawing.

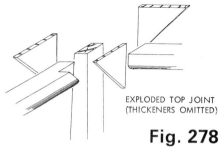

EXPLODED TOP JOINT
(THICKENERS OMITTED)

Fig. 278

Glue the bent hardwood strips to the short rails and then the last four fillers to the outer ends of the legs. This completes the framework.

At this stage remove as much waste as possible, sand down the ends of the bent gussets, plane down the end fillers and round off the legs.

THE TOP

There should be $\frac{3}{8}$ in. overlap of all outer gussets, above the beech underframe. However, because of the tapered tops of the legs and the slope of the legs, the gussets will not be at 90° to the underframe. They will be about 87° at the sides and 84° at the ends. Use a bullnose plane to correct them and remove its front to get right into the corners. Then place the frame upside down on the $\frac{1}{2}$ in. thick ply top, so it rests on the gusset tops. Draw around, cut out and plane to a perfect fit into the space enclosed by the eight gussets. Pencil on the ply top around the inside of the beech underframe. This border will be removed to a depth of $\frac{3}{8}$ in. after veneering. By leaving its removal to a later stage, the veneers can be glued to full pressure around the edges. Conversely, the veneers will support the edge of the ply as the waste is removed.

Fig. 279

HOW THE EDGES OF THE SAWCUT VENEERS ARE FORCED TOGETHER WITH A SASH CLAMP JUST BEFORE THE CLAMPS OF THE VENEER FRAMES ARE TIGHTENED

Draw a line down the centre of the ply top to mark where the veneers will meet. It will offer a gorgeous opportunity to display two matching sheets of sawcut veneer. Arrange any curves so they face inwards towards each other. The resultant pattern and richness will contrast with the severe lines of the rest of the table.

Glue the first sheet of veneer using the veneer frames as described in an earlier chapter. Remove the waste glue before it is set, so that it does not obstruct the butting of the second veneer. Butt the second veneer as closely as possible to the first,

using sash cramps. With these held tightly in position, screw down the clamps of the veneer frames.

Remove the border on the inside of the ply top to a depth of $\frac{3}{8}$ in. Check that it fits. Then plane the veneers to a perfect fit inside the gussets. Use plenty of cramps to get a close glue joint between the ply and the beech underframe.

The last assembly job is to glue the edge veneers around the top of the table. Cut the veneers so that they overlap the top veneer and the lower edge of the beech underframe. Use a mitring plane to get a perfect fit against the gussets. Prepare two curved bearers for pressure glueing the veneer strips; the curve should be $\frac{1}{4}$ in. at each end. Use the same technique for obliterating the glueline between veneer and gusset as was used between the filler and gusset, and leave them in position until after the sash cramps have been applied to the curved bearers. The curved bearers will ensure that the pressure on the veneers is equalled along their full length. Apply sash cramps from the top and some from the bottom. This stops the veneer 'tilting'.

FINISHING

Sand or plane off excess veneer and gusset. Round off and curve the exposed surface of each gusset. Arch the edge veneers and thin the rails at their centres. Smooth off the legs and rails with an orbital sander going down through the grades, continuing with wet and dry and finish with various grades of wire wool.

HOW GLUE JOINT BETWEEN SIDE VENEER AND GUSSET IS OBLITERATED

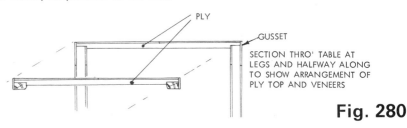

SECTION THRO' TABLE AT LEGS AND HALFWAY ALONG TO SHOW ARRANGEMENT OF PLY TOP AND VENEERS

Fig. 280

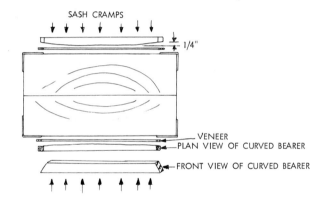

SASH CRAMPS

1/4"

VENEER
PLAN VIEW OF CURVED BEARER
FRONT VIEW OF CURVED BEARER

Fig. 281

The top needs special treatment. Because of the thickness of the veneers, it is possible to over-use the orbital sander and get an uneven surface with a 'moulded doughy' look. This could be avoided with a about 15°-20° below its elevation. The bumps can be ringed with a pencil and sanded away.

Clean away all the dust and iron swarf from the wire wool. Find a piece of waste

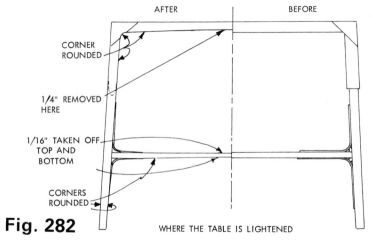

AFTER   BEFORE

CORNER
ROUNDED

1/4" REMOVED
HERE

1/16" TAKEN OFF
TOP AND
BOTTOM

CORNERS
ROUNDED

Fig. 282   WHERE THE TABLE IS LIGHTENED

belt sander but these are expensive to buy. However, by using the sun in the early morning or late evening the 'high spots' can be profiled by holding the table top wood from the original plank and find out which is the best finish, whether linseed oil, wax, french polish or even poly-urethane.

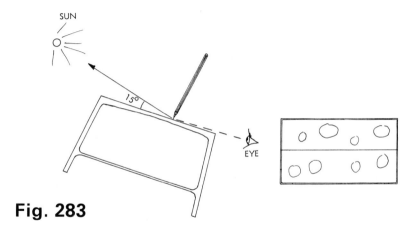

SUN

15°

EYE

Fig. 283

16. The Jointless Upholstered Chair

In the previous two chapters, the gusset, fillet and bent strip were used to join two pieces of wood together, either end to end or side to end. This chapter is an exercise in how to join three ends together at compound angles using two pairs of gussets, one of which has been steam bent. It overcomes the main 'engineering' problem of any chair—the rear joint. This joint has to withstand the continual movements of those who use the chair as well as the loosening effects of changing humidity and temperature. It has to look agreeable and fit in with the surroundings of the home.

Fig. 284

106

The chair described here is lighter than most upholstered chairs, and, as with the stool and coffee table, avoids mortise and tenon joints. This allows the legs to be tapered and hence slightly flexible, enhancing their resilience to insult and stress. The back is laminated from $\frac{5}{32}$ in. sheets cut with the veneer saw. The outer layers are selected for their appearance, hence functioning as both veneers and laminates.

It takes longer to make than the standard mortise and tenoned chair, as it is made from about three times as many pieces of wood. The resulting light weight and slim appearance more than justify this extra effort. Three jigs are used during assembly.

It is an exercise in:
(1) Constructing complex jigs.
(2) Laminating sheets of hardwood.
(3) Using pre-shaped steam-bent gussets to make three-way joints.

Any English hardwood can be used which can be steam-bent to a fairly small radius, e.g. elm, ash, beech, oak, walnut, yew or larch. Cascamite is again the preferred glue as it 'goes off' slowly. About 50 clamps from 2in.-8in. are needed. The seat is made of $\frac{1}{2}$in. cheap plywood upholstered with foam, calico and dralon.

Cutting List:
Crossframe (beech or other hardwood)
(2)   19in. × 1$\frac{1}{4}$in. × 2in.
Ply Seat
(1)   19in. × 19in. × $\frac{1}{2}$in.
Back
(4)   Strips of hardwood—1$\frac{1}{4}$in. × 20in. × $\frac{5}{32}$in.
(2)   Strips of hardwood—1$\frac{1}{4}$in. × 18in. × $\frac{5}{32}$in.
Various shaped pieces which can be cut from two matching sheets 31 × 10 × $\frac{5}{32}$in.

Fig. 285

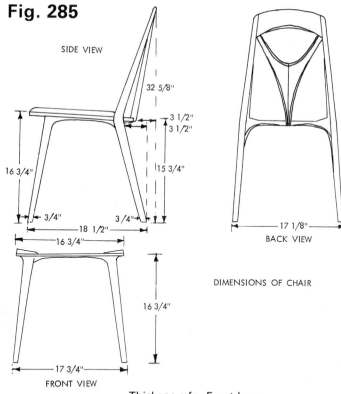

SIDE VIEW

32 5/8"

3 1/2"
3 1/2"

16 3/4"

15 3/4"

3/4"

3/4"

18 1/2"

16 3/4"

17 1/8"

BACK VIEW

DIMENSIONS OF CHAIR

16 3/4"

17 3/4"

FRONT VIEW

Fig. 286

THE CHAIR BEFORE
UPHOLSTERY

Thickeners for Front Legs
(4) $1\frac{1}{4}$ in. $\times \frac{5}{16}$ in. $\times 13$ in.

Gussets for Front Legs
(4) 3 in. $\times 3$ in.:

3"

3"

GUSSETS FOR
FRONT LEGS

Fig. 288

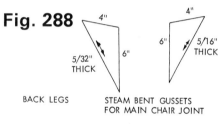

4"

4"

5/32"
THICK

6"

6"

5/16"
THICK

BACK LEGS

STEAM BENT GUSSETS
FOR MAIN CHAIR JOINT

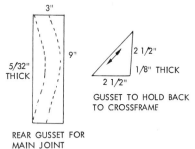

3"

5/32"
THICK

9"

2 1/2"

1/8" THICK

2 1/2"

GUSSET TO HOLD BACK
TO CROSSFRAME

REAR GUSSET FOR
MAIN JOINT

Gussets for Back Legs:
Cut two each of the first three and four of
$2\frac{1}{2}$ in. $\times 2\frac{1}{2}$ in.

Thickeners for Back Legs
(2) of 5 in. $\times 1\frac{1}{2}$ in. $\times \frac{5}{32}$ in.
(2) of 5 in. $\times 1\frac{1}{2}$ in. $\times \frac{5}{16}$ in.

Fillets for top of Back Legs
(2) of $1\frac{1}{4}$ in. $\times \frac{1}{2}$ in. $\times 5$ in. (as diagram)

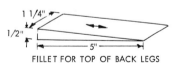

1 1/4"

1/2"

5"

FILLET FOR TOP OF BACK LEGS

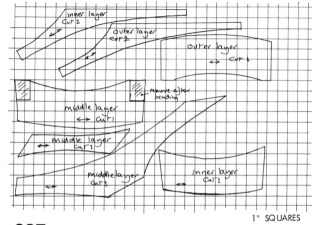

inner layer
cut 2

outer layer
cut 2

outer layer
cut 1

remove after
bending

middle layer
cut 1

middle layer
cut 1

middle layer
cut 1

inner layer
cut 1

1" SQUARES

Fig. 287

COMPONENTS OF LAMINATED BACK

Fig. 289

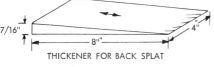

7/16" | 8" | 4"

THICKENER FOR BACK SPLAT

7/16" | 14" | 1 1/4"

THICKENER FOR BOTH SIDES OF
BACK – GLUED BETWEEN LAMINATES

The wedge-shaped thickeners for the back are shown above. The prism-shaped pieces glued on the top of the ply seat are about 15 in. long, 3 in. wide and $\frac{1}{2}$ in. thick.

THE JIG FOR THE BACK OF THE CHAIR

The jig can be made from scrap softwood and scrap ply. Irregularities are filled with car body filler. It is finished in masking tape so that glue will not stick to it. No part should be thicker than $1\frac{1}{4}$ in to allow 2 in clamps to be used. Clearly mark lines x–x and y–y–y as these ensure a symmetrical

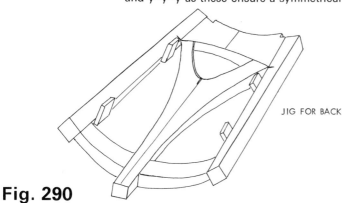

JIG FOR BACK

Fig. 290

Fig. 291

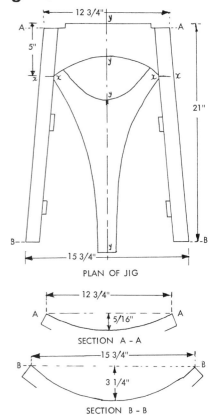

12 3/4"

A — — A

5"

21"

15 3/4"

PLAN OF JIG

12 3/4"

A — A

5/16"

SECTION A - A

15 3/4"

B — B

3 1/4"

SECTION B - B

back, which appears vertical from the front. Extend them over the sides of the jig so they are easily found.

JIG FOR ASSEMBLING BACK TO CROSSFRAME

The base and top are cut from $\frac{1}{2}$ in. ply. The two arms are set at compound angles

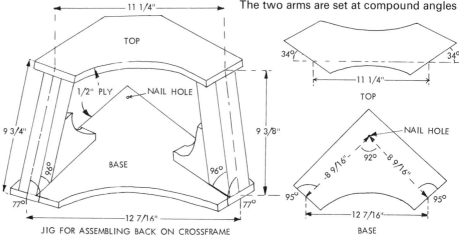

11 1/4"

TOP

1/2" PLY | NAIL HOLE

9 3/4"

9 3/8"

96° | 96°

BASE

77° | 77°

12 7/16"

JIG FOR ASSEMBLING BACK ON CROSSFRAME

Fig. 292

34° | 34°

11 1/4"

TOP

NAIL HOLE

8 9/16" | 92° | 8 9/16"

95° | 95°

12 7/16"

BASE

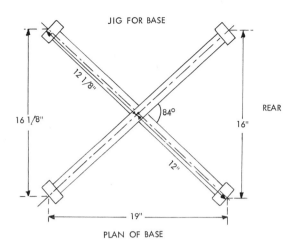

Fig. 293

JIG FOR BASE

12 1/8"

16 1/8"

84°

12"

16"

19"

PLAN OF BASE

REAR

90°

90°

8 1/2"

8 1/2"

96 1/2°

90°

90°

REAR

PLAN OF TOP BEFORE
CORNERS REMOVED

of 77° and 96° as shown. The top is screwed on to the arms so that its edges cross their centre lines. The resulting gap is

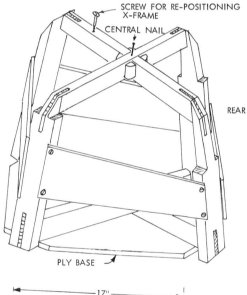

JIG FOR BASE

SCREW FOR RE-POSITIONING X-FRAME

CENTRAL NAIL

REAR

PLY BASE

Fig. 294

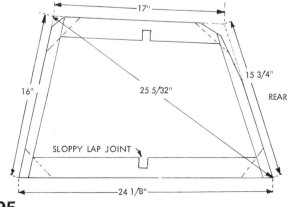

17"

16"

25 5/32"

15 3/4"

REAR

SLOPPY LAP JOINT

24 1/8"

Fig. 295

HALF FRAME

filled with resin filler and the surface of the arm shaped so as to present a slight 'twist' to the back of the chair.

JIG FOR ASSEMBLING LEGS ON CROSS-FRAME

Make the two half frames from 2 in. × 1 in. as drawn and assemble together making sure the lap joints are sloppy. Butt joint each corner with a screw, but do not overtighten.

Fit the two ply formers cut to $84\frac{1}{2}°$ and $96\frac{1}{2}°$ on the ledges, and glue. These set the

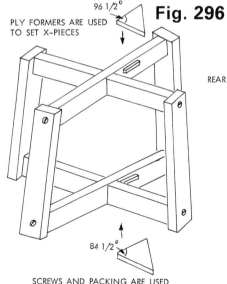

Fig. 296

96 1/2°

PLY FORMERS ARE USED
TO SET X-PIECES

REAR

84 1/2°

SCREWS AND PACKING ARE USED
TO SET ANGLES AT CORNERS

top and bottom of the jig. Use diagonals to true up the trapezium between the pairs of back and front legs.

Screw the four plates of $\frac{3}{8}$ in. ply on the four sides of the jig and replace the screws

Fig. 297

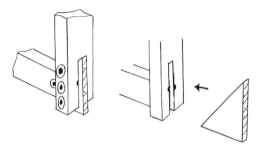

with internal gussets, pressure glueing them in place. This technique of 'internal' gusseting will be used to hold the splat of the chair on to the ply seat.

The top corners of the jig are sawn off to make space for the fillets and top thickeners of the back legs. Fillet the central angles of the jig as shown in the drawing and drill a hole for a 2 in. nail in the centre of the top. Finally mark two parallel ball-pen lines $1\frac{1}{8}$ in. apart down the face of each upright so that the legs can be positioned accurately.

As the jigs are the most important stage in making the chair, their origins deserve a fuller description. The jig for the back was guessed and fortunately turned out to be correct. This fixed the relative positions of the upper part of each leg. The height and slope of the seats of most modern chairs are standard, the front around $16\frac{1}{2}$ in and the back $15\frac{3}{4}$ in. The slope of the back is also fairly standard: the line of the middle of the shoulder blade is above the line of the back of the bottom of the leg.

To make the jig for the legs, a 3 in. wide piece of $\frac{3}{8}$ in. thick plywood is glued and filleted to a base of similar ply 18 in. × 18 in. which is the area covered by the average dining chair.

Another ply sheet, with its corners cut to coincide with those of the back jig, has a slit cut in it, which moves up and down over the upright 3 in. wide piece. It can also move forwards and backwards. Two pieces of $1\frac{1}{2}$ in. square softwood are glued

each side of the slot and when the desired position is reached they are clamped against the upright. The angles and measurements can be read off.

The small jig was a cheat! It was made when a satisfactory angle was achieved between crossframe and back. In other words it was produced *after* the first satisfactory chair was made.

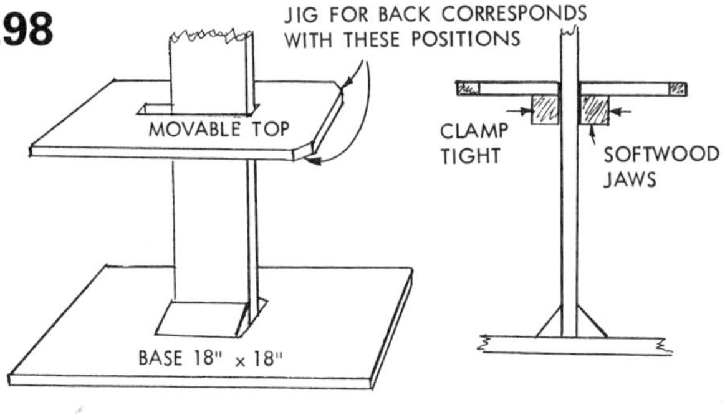

MAKING THE CHAIR

Cut the waste wood from the lower surface of the beech cross-frame to leave 3 in. at each end and $\frac{3}{4}$ in. thickness in the middle. Lap-joint the centre to correspond with the centre of the jig and drill a hole to take the nail in the centre of the jig. Glue the cross-frame and reinforce with a cruciform-shaped piece of $\frac{1}{4}$ in. ply beneath. This can be removed after the seat has been glued to it.

Fig. 299

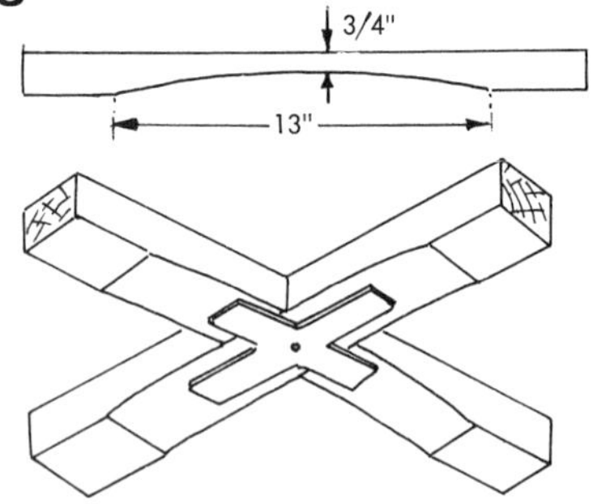

CROSSPIECES GLUED TOGETHER AND TEMPORARILY REINFORCED WITH A CROSS OF 1/4" PLYWOOD

Glue the 5 in. fillets to the tops of the back legs, across the $1\frac{1}{16}$ in. surface.

Fig. 300

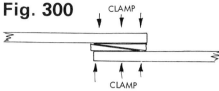

SLOPING FILLETS GLUED ON TOP OF BACK LEGS

Cut out the smaller pieces for the laminated back, then cut out similar but smaller pieces of cheap bendable $\frac{1}{4}$ in. ply. These will be used to clamp the layers of laminate to each other and protect them from damage by the G-clamps.

Boil up the pieces of the laminated back in a metal tray. When they are malleable hold the top pieces in curved positions with rebated pieces of softwood and string.

Fig. 298

JIG FOR BACK CORRESPONDS WITH THESE POSITIONS

MOVABLE TOP

CLAMP TIGHT

SOFTWOOD JAWS

BASE 18" × 18"

Fig. 301

STRING AND REBATED STRIP ARE USED TO HOLD PARTS OF LAMINATED BACK IN A CURVED POSITION WHILE THEY COOL AND DRY

The other pieces are clamped to the jig and allowed to cool. They will flatten when removed but will 'remember' their curved position when clamped for their final glueing. In some ways, wood behaves very much like some modern plastics. When all the pieces have cooled and dried the first layer is clamped and held on the jig with fine veneer pins, hammered in along the edges. Use as few as are necessary. Fit the edges as closely as possible. No glue is needed. Exact fitting of the middle layer is not necessary as little of it is seen. Use glue mixed with fine sawdust.

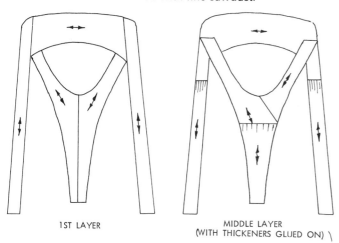

1ST LAYER

MIDDLE LAYER (WITH THICKENERS GLUED ON)

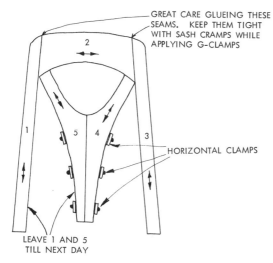

GREAT CARE GLUEING THESE SEAMS. KEEP THEM TIGHT WITH SASH CRAMPS WHILE APPLYING G-CLAMPS

HORIZONTAL CLAMPS

LEAVE 1 AND 5 TILL NEXT DAY

Fig. 302

INNER LAYER

Glueing and fitting the middle layer can be a 'tease'. Use several clamps to fit the pieces in position. Remove and glue one by one, leaving the unglued pieces in situ. The wedge-shaped thickeners are glued later. These will give a visually pleasing taper to the back of the chair, and provide a larger glueing area for the gussets.

Prepare the surface for the inner layer of laminates, initially glueing only three of the five pieces. Plane the long straight inner edge of (4) and make sure it coincides with the central line y−y−y−y of the jig. As (4) is laid, carefully remove all excess glue so there is no difficulty butting (5) to it.

Use horizontally positioned clamps to keep (4) and (5) butted while pressure clamps are applied.

When the glue has set, gently lever the laminate away from the jig making sure the levers do not 'dig' into it. Some veneer pins are left in the jig, some come away with the back. Carefully remove so as not to pull away a chunk of the laminate. Clean up the back and remove excess waste. Square the inside surface to the back and front and make it $1\frac{1}{16}$ in. at the bottom.

SQUARE THE INSIDE TO BACK AND FRONT

Fig. 303

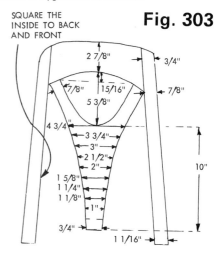

MEASUREMENTS FOR CUTTING OFF WASTE (DRAWING IS NOT TO SCALE)

Then screw the cross-frame to the underside of the small jig. The same screwhole can be used later to locate it on the large jig. The centre is located with the nail. A steel ruler is placed down the arms of the jig and lines drawn across the cross-frame. The waste is sawn off and the back posts glue butt-jointed to the sawn ends of the cross frame, they being held in place with wood screws. Each back post will have to be forced and screwed hard to

Fig. 304

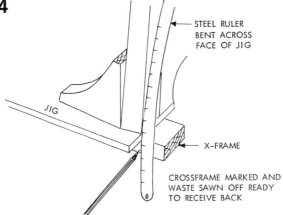

STEEL RULER
BENT ACROSS
FACE OF JIG

JIG

X-FRAME

CROSSFRAME MARKED AND
WASTE SAWN OFF READY
TO RECEIVE BACK

make it mate up with the ends of the frame. This will impart 'twist' and help to make them stiffer. When the glue has set, leave the screws in position and saw off the waste.

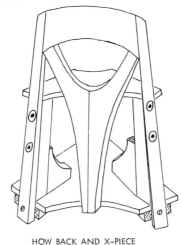

HOW BACK AND X-PIECE
ARE MOUNTED ON JIG

Fig. 305

Saw off part of the ends of the cross-pieces and back posts to receive the gussets.

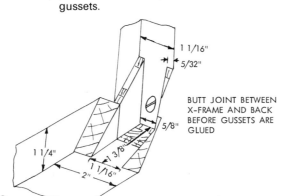

1 1/16"

5/32"

BUTT JOINT BETWEEN
X-FRAME AND BACK
BEFORE GUSSETS ARE
GLUED

5/8"

1 1/4"

1 3/8"

1 1/16"

2"

Fig. 306

The assembly is removed from the jig and the gussets are glued firmly, a temporary fillet being used to force the gussets against the sawcut. Later, remove

Fig. 307

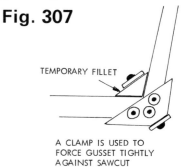

TEMPORARY FILLET

A CLAMP IS USED TO
FORCE GUSSET TIGHTLY
AGAINST SAWCUT

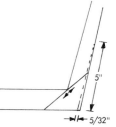

5"

5/32"

WASTE GUSSET IS TRIMMED
BACK IS SLOPED TO ACCOMMODATE
REAR FILLET AND CURVED GUSSET

the screws, saw off excess gusset and then remove a thin triangular piece to slope the back and accommodate the rear fillet and rear curved gusset.

It is worth pausing to study the back joint. It may appear complex but taken step-by-step, assembly is easy.

Fig. 308

EXPLODED BACK JOINT

Mount the back/cross-frame assembly on the large bottom jig, centring it with the nail and positioning it with the wood screw. Identical repositioning is possible if it has to be taken off the jig. Scribe in the top of the leg to butt-joint against the lower part of the back cross-frame assembly. Slope the inner side of the leg 7 in. down and the rear 5 in. down. Leave the outer side until later. Pressure glue the butt joint using a sashclamp and add the small fillet.

Fig. 309

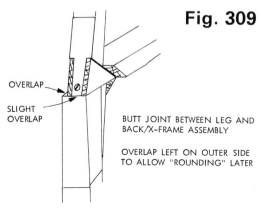

OVERLAP

SLIGHT OVERLAP

BUTT JOINT BETWEEN LEG AND BACK/X-FRAME ASSEMBLY

OVERLAP LEFT ON OUTER SIDE TO ALLOW "ROUNDING" LATER

Glue the fillet on the back of the joint and carve to shape.

Fig. 310

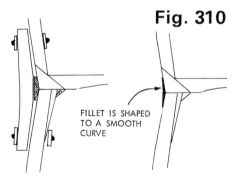

FILLET IS SHAPED TO A SMOOTH CURVE

Do the same on the inner side of the joint. (Fig. 311)

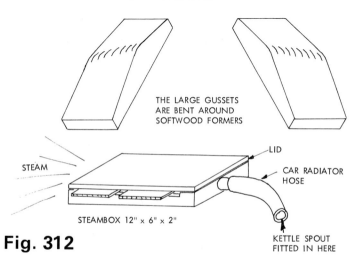

THE LARGE GUSSETS ARE BENT AROUND SOFTWOOD FORMERS

STEAM

LID

CAR RADIATOR HOSE

STEAMBOX 12" x 6" x 2"

Fig. 312

KETTLE SPOUT FITTED IN HERE

Fig. 311

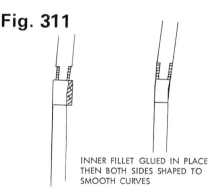

INNER FILLET GLUED IN PLACE THEN BOTH SIDES SHAPED TO SMOOTH CURVES

Make two mirror-imaged softwood formers, which will be used to bend and shape the large gussets and make a small steambox to heat up the gussets. Be sure to protect the gussets from the staining effect of the wet G-clamps.

Remove some of the cross-frame with a panel saw to accommodate the large gussets. Remove the $\frac{1}{32}$ in. overlap above the small gussets, which will allow them to be hidden by the large gussets. Glue the large gussets one at a time, starting with the outer thinner one. Force the thicker inner gusset into its concave 'bed' using a file wrapped in masking tape. Do not worry if the gussets split along the grain as the clamps are tightened.

Fig. 313

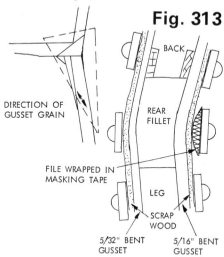

BACK

REAR FILLET

DIRECTION OF GUSSET GRAIN

FILE WRAPPED IN MASKING TAPE

LEG

SCRAP WOOD

5/32" BENT GUSSET

5/16" BENT GUSSET

HOW BENT GUSSETS ARE CLAMPED TO LEG AND BACK

Steam the rear gussets and bend at right angles across the 'hump' of the softwood formers. Glue the four thickeners at the lower edge of each of the four large gussets. Remove excess large gusset from the back of each joint, being careful not to 'round' the surface to be glued.

113

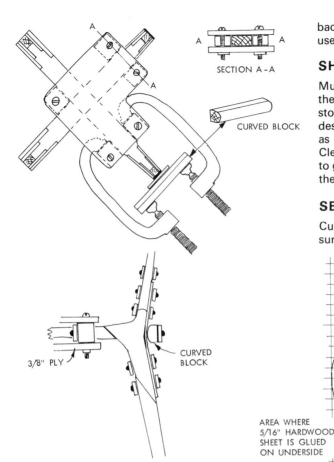

SECTION A - A

CURVED BLOCK

back legs are glued. The same method is used as was carried out on the stool.

SHAPING

Much is done before the ply seat is glued, the same principle being used as with the stool. Round off the legs. Sand to the desired shape, but leave the top of the chair as this tends to get bruised in handling. Clean off excess gusset and top thickener to give a smooth surface on which to glue the seat.

SEAT

Cut out using the 'square' diagram, making sure to leave the ply lugs attached.

3/8" PLY

CURVED BLOCK

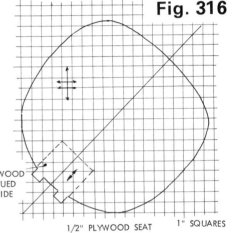

Fig. 316

AREA WHERE
5/16" HARDWOOD
SHEET IS GLUED
ON UNDERSIDE

1/2" PLYWOOD SEAT   1" SQUARES

Fig. 314   HOW THE REAR CURVED GUSSET
IS CLAMPED AND GLUED

In order to apply pressure into the curve of the rear gusset a special ply platform is made.

THE FRONT LEGS

These are jointed simultaneously as the

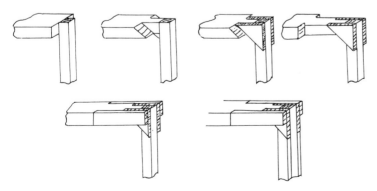

Fig. 315   FRONT LEGS JOINTED USING THE
SAME METHOD AS THE STOOL

Scribe in x–x and y–y to the back of the seat. Glue a small sheet of hardwood underneath the seat to reinforce where the gusset for the splat will be attached. It also provides a larger glueing area. Prepare the bottom of the splat as a simple lap joint over the back of the ply seat. Glue at the same time as the seat is glued on the cross-frame, and scrape off excess glue from the edges of the cross-frame.

The following day glue in the top fillets, made of $\frac{1}{2}$ in. ply scrap. The front one is the long fillet similar to those used on the stool. This helps to stiffen the front of the seat (but not too much). The other shorter fillets need to go in along the cross-frame as far as the clamps will reach.

Cut a slot in the splat and ply seat to take a $\frac{5}{32}$ in. gusset. Glue and clamp using the ply lugs as 'pressure points'.

Next glue the two prism-shaped thickeners on top of the seat. These help to make the seat both comfortable and more rigid.

114

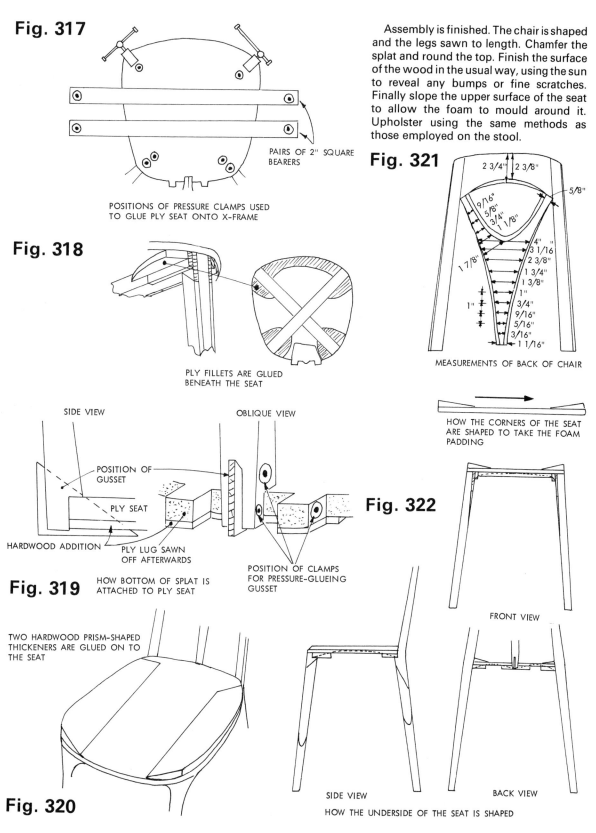

Fig. 317

PAIRS OF 2" SQUARE BEARERS

POSITIONS OF PRESSURE CLAMPS USED TO GLUE PLY SEAT ONTO X-FRAME

Fig. 318

PLY FILLETS ARE GLUED BENEATH THE SEAT

SIDE VIEW

OBLIQUE VIEW

POSITION OF GUSSET

PLY SEAT

HARDWOOD ADDITION

PLY LUG SAWN OFF AFTERWARDS

POSITION OF CLAMPS FOR PRESSURE-GLUEING GUSSET

Fig. 319   HOW BOTTOM OF SPLAT IS ATTACHED TO PLY SEAT

TWO HARDWOOD PRISM-SHAPED THICKENERS ARE GLUED ON TO THE SEAT

Fig. 320

Assembly is finished. The chair is shaped and the legs sawn to length. Chamfer the splat and round the top. Finish the surface of the wood in the usual way, using the sun to reveal any bumps or fine scratches. Finally slope the upper surface of the seat to allow the foam to mould around it. Upholster using the same methods as those employed on the stool.

Fig. 321

2 3/4"   2 3/8"

5/8"

9/16"
5/8"
3/4"   1/8"

4"
3 1/16"
2 3/8"
1 3/4"
1 3/8"
1"
3/4"
9/16"
5/16"
3/16"

1 7/8"

1"

1 1/16"

MEASUREMENTS OF BACK OF CHAIR

HOW THE CORNERS OF THE SEAT ARE SHAPED TO TAKE THE FOAM PADDING

Fig. 322

FRONT VIEW

SIDE VIEW

BACK VIEW

HOW THE UNDERSIDE OF THE SEAT IS SHAPED

17. The Sewing Box and matching Tripod Table

These are an exercise in laminating and avoidance of the mortise and tenon and dovetail joints. The sewing box described earlier in the book contained over 100 mitred dovetails and 12 mortise/tenon joints. It was veneered before assembly and insets had to be used to finish off the corners.

This elliptical sewing box has a padded lid for needles and pins, together with compartments for buttons and pieces of cloth, and a drawer for machine bobbins and cotton reels.

The walls of this box are composed of three layers $\frac{1}{8}$ in. thick, as is the lid. The bottom is $\frac{3}{16}$ in. ply, veneered with one layer up to $\frac{5}{16}$ in. thick. The top is glued

directly on the elliptical body and the angle reinforced with a fillet. The bottom is glued inside the walls and held in place with adhesive and screws.

Fig. 324

TOP - FITS ON THE TOP EDGE OF THE SIDES

BOTTOM - FITS INSIDE THE SIDES

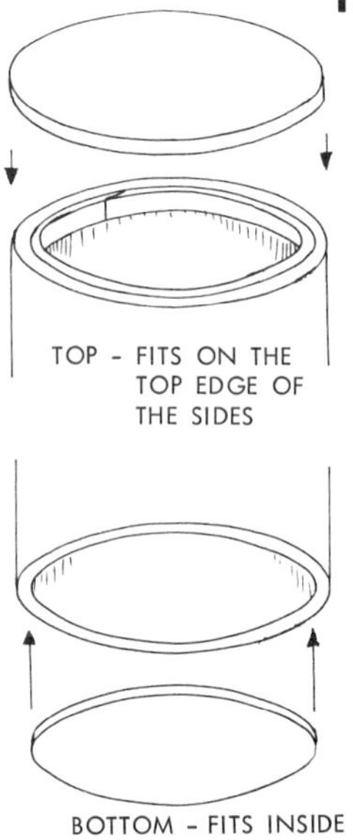

Making depends on the correct order of assembly. The body is built up on a jig which is in two halves, joined by two half inch wide strips of steel which are removable. This allows the two halves of the jig to collapse inwards and be removed from the laminated body. The jig is very strong, having an inner and outer layer of resin impregnated fibreglass ribbon. The multitude of vertical strips of $\frac{1}{8}$ in. ply protect the ribbon from direct steel clamp pressure.

Start making the jig by cutting two ellipses of $\frac{3}{8}$ in. ply. These set the size of the jig and the sewing box.

Fig. 323

Fig. 325

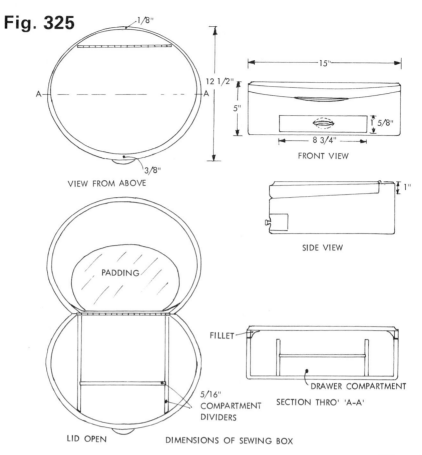

1/8"

12 1/2"

A——————A

VIEW FROM ABOVE

3/8"

15"

5"

1 5/8"

8 3/4"

FRONT VIEW

1"

SIDE VIEW

PADDING

LID OPEN

5/16"
COMPARTMENT
DIVIDERS

FILLET

DRAWER COMPARTMENT

SECTION THRO' 'A-A'

DIMENSIONS OF SEWING BOX

Fig. 327

Also cut two panels (crosspieces) corresponding to the major and minor axes of the ellipse, and saw slots as drawn. Slot together and check that they are at 90°. Screw on the ellipses top and bottom and pin on the $\frac{1}{2}$ in. wide $\frac{1}{8}$ in. ply strips all

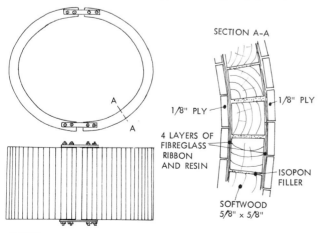

SECTION A-A

1/8" PLY

1/8" PLY

4 LAYERS OF
FIBREGLASS
RIBBON
AND RESIN

ISOPON
FILLER

SOFTWOOD
5/8" x 5/8"

A

A

Fig. 326

JIG

117

Fig. 328

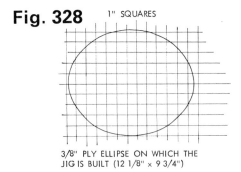

1" SQUARES

3/8" PLY ELLIPSE ON WHICH THE JIG IS BUILT (12 1/8" × 9 3/4")

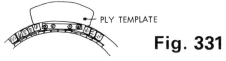

PLY TEMPLATE

Fig. 331

the soft filler. Sand off any proud Isopon or softwood to give a smooth finish. Wrap around the top and bottom four layers of resin impregnated fibreglass. Finally, set in Isopon the outer layer of $\frac{1}{2}$ in. wide plywood strips.

Fig. 329

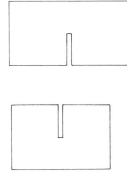

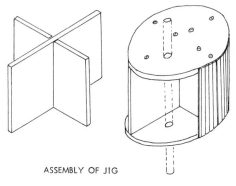

ASSEMBLY OF JIG

around the edges. Drill a $\frac{3}{4}$ in. hole top and bottom so this assembly can be mounted on a thick dowel, which is used as an offset axle on the upturned small workbench. The four layers of 3 in. wide fibreglass ribbon (20 yards in all) can be easily wound around the elliptical 'drum' and the resin stippled in at the same time. Four layers top and bottom will complete the inner skin. Set over this is a layer of $\frac{5}{8}$ in. × $\frac{5}{8}$ in. × 7 in. scrap softwood in Isopon or other car body filler. Leave a 4 in. gap each side, where short lengths of threaded rod with nuts are set in filler, together with

When all is hardened, remove the screws holding on the $\frac{3}{8}$ in. plywood ellipses and remove them piecemeal (with a hammer and chopper). The crosspieces may be salvaged. Remove any veneer pins protruding from the inner ply strips. Then take off the steel strips and saw out a $\frac{1}{2}$ in. wide piece of jig, between the pairs of threaded

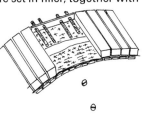

Fig. 330

SAW CUTS

Fig. 332

rods. Replace the steel strips and the jig will resume its original shape. The gap left will enable the jig to collapse away from the laminated body when the steel strips are removed.

Clean up and apply two coats of polyurethane to prevent glue sticking to the jig. Finally make a series of softwood clamping

steel strips $\frac{1}{2}$ in. × $\frac{1}{8}$ in. × 5 in. which will later be removed by undoing the nuts. Note that there is a good 1 in. gap between the pairs of threaded rods. Cover the protruding ends above the nuts with masking tape so the threads do not become clogged with filler.

Make a $\frac{1}{8}$ in. thick ply template (guess the curve) to finish off the curve of the ellipse by smoothing back and forth over

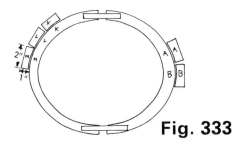

Fig. 333

blocks to fit the curve of the jig (the wider the annular rings, the softer the blocks, the better.) Label their positions. 44 3 in. G-clamps or larger will be needed to hold them in position.

THE SEWING BOX

Cut three sheets of hardwood 47 in. × 7 in. × $\frac{1}{8}$ in. thick, using the veneer saw. Make a steam box out of plywood and scrap and steam the inner sheet. Bend around the jig and join the ends with a 2 in. scarf. Place this at the back of the box. Glue the scarf joint first, making sure the whole sheet is tight against the jig, using the shaped softwood blocks. Apply pressure to the scarf joint in all three positions as shown.

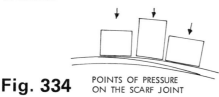

Fig. 334   POINTS OF PRESSURE ON THE SCARF JOINT

Glue on the next layer with the grain set at 90° to the first, then finally the outer layer. Use a slow setting glue such as Cascamite, as it takes $\frac{1}{2}$–$\frac{3}{4}$ hour to apply the glue and clamps.

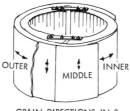

Fig. 335   GRAIN DIRECTIONS IN 3 LAYERS OF ELLIPTICAL BODY

OUTER   MIDDLE   INNER

Collapse the jig and remove the ellipsoid body. Because the outer layer of lamination acts as a veneer and there are no joints, the total time to make the jig and glue the box together is less than that taken to make the dovetailed, veneered sewing box described in an earlier chapter.

Cut a 1 in. wide strip off the bottom and save it as a fillet for the top. Hold it in a vice, or if yours is not wide enough, use the frame of the upturned small worktable. Plane the sawn edge and square it with the side by using a large try-square. This is the base line reference from which all measurements are taken. Cut the height

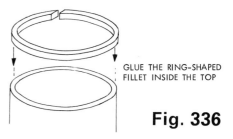

GLUE THE RING-SHAPED FILLET INSIDE THE TOP

Fig. 336

down to 4 $\frac{5}{8}$ in. all around and glue the fillet inside the top. Scarf it at the back.

Plane the fillet and top true.

TOP

Make it from three layers of $\frac{1}{8}$ in. sheet 14 in. × 17 in. cut with the veneer saw. The middle layer is at 90° to the two outer layers.

Carefully select the outer sheet so it has an attractive central feature. (Use a similar sheet off the same plank to veneer the top

Fig. 337

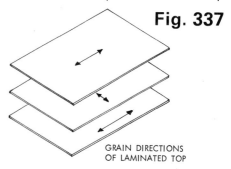

GRAIN DIRECTIONS OF LAMINATED TOP

of the tripod table). Place the elliptical body on the laminated top and mark around, allowing generous waste. Cut off a moon-shaped piece to correspond with the position of the piano hinge.

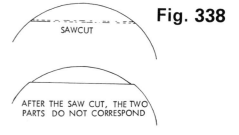

SAWCUT

Fig. 338

AFTER THE SAW CUT, THE TWO PARTS DO NOT CORRESPOND

Glue the larger piece on to the body using as many 5 in. or 6 in. clamps as

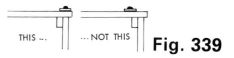

THIS ...   ... NOT THIS

Fig. 339

possible. Make sure they are directly over the body and fillet, otherwise the top will become concave.

Saw off the lid, using the finest gents saw you have.

Fig. 340

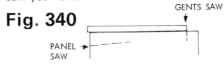

Glue a piece of hardwood between the ends of the fillet.

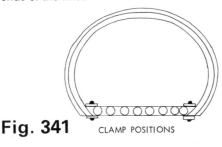

Fig. 341
CLAMP POSITIONS

Remove waste from the inner angle of the fillet with a carving gouge. The structure of the lid is finished.

SHELF AND DIVIDERS

This is the most difficult part of the assembly and depends on 'springing' the shelf and dividers into the elliptical body, which has been slightly flattened with a sash cramp.

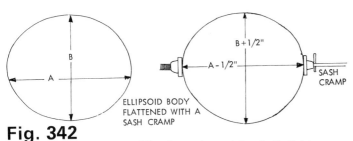

Fig. 342

ELLIPSOID BODY FLATTENED WITH A SASH CRAMP

The dimensions of the shelf-dividers are:

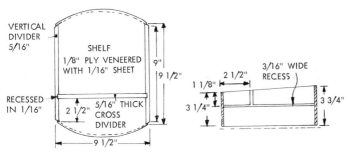

Fig. 343
LAYOUT OF SHELF AND DIVIDERS

Mark out the veneered shelf by laying the elliptical body on it and drawing around inside it with a pencil (dotted line.) Draw a line $\frac{1}{8}$ in. outside this and cut out. Gauge 2 in. from the bottom of the ellip-

Fig. 344

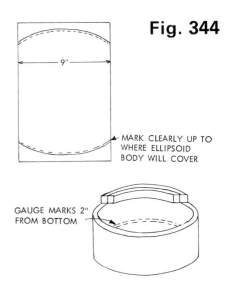

MARK CLEARLY UP TO WHERE ELLIPSOID BODY WILL COVER

GAUGE MARKS 2" FROM BOTTOM

soid body and cut a groove $\frac{1}{8}$ in. deep $\frac{3}{16}$ in. above it to house the $\frac{3}{16}$ in. shelf: use a $\frac{1}{8}$ in. mortise chisel. Test fit the shelf in the groove using a sash cramp to compress the ellipse and carefully plane to fit, as the changes from 'flattening' to 'normal' are complex.

Make the vertical dividers, cutting a groove at the bottom of each for this veneered shelf and a vertical groove in each for the cross divider. Plane the ends of the dividers, test fitting, so the assembly does not permanently distort the elliptical body. Use the completed lid to check the curves.

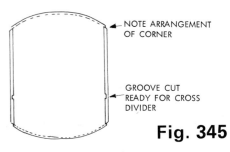

NOTE ARRANGEMENT OF CORNER

GROOVE CUT READY FOR CROSS DIVIDER

Fig. 345

Leave the fitting of the cross divider until after the shelf and vertical dividers are in place. Spring and glue in the shelf and vertical dividers and then fit and glue the cross divider. Later chamfer the top edges of all dividers in a similar fashion to the sewing box described in an earlier chapter.

FLOOR

This is made from $\frac{3}{16}$ in. ply veneered with $\frac{1}{8}$ in. sheet. Make sure the ply and veneer layers alternate in grain direction, but note the direction of the veneer grain.

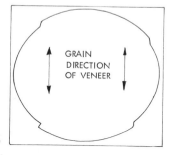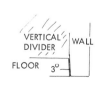

Fig. 346

First chamfer the lower inner side of the body to 3°. Place the chamfered body on the veneered ply floor and draw around inside as far as the dividers will allow. Draw outside the body. Cut and scribe in the bottom using blue chalk. When fitted put to one side. Do not glue yet.

DRAWER END

Cut out, shape and glue in the drawer front thickener as shown:

Fig. 347

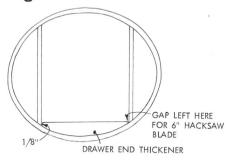

Cut along the top and bottom with a gents saw.

Fig. 348

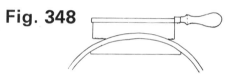

Turn the corner with a fretsaw blade and continue the cut with a 6 in. hacksaw blade, whose teeth have been flattened and a handle made on it with insulating tape.

BRASS DRAWER HANDLE

This is made next and fitted before the drawer is assembled. It can be cut from solid brass using a fine toothed bandsaw blade, or cast in a plaster of paris mould. Make sure the lengths of the threaded rod (brass or steel) are long enough to go through the drawer front, but recess the nuts so they do not damage cotton reels in the drawer.

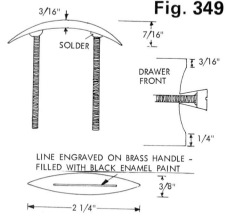

Fig. 349

THE DRAWER

Make sure the drawer is square as it is glued.

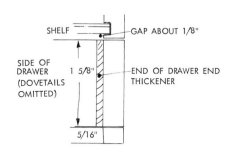

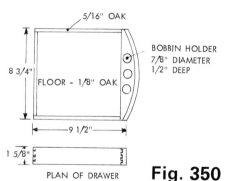

PLAN OF DRAWER

Fig. 350

FITTING THE BOTTOM OF THE BOX

Test fit the bottom. Mark on the floor along the outer side of the dividers and drill holes for $\frac{3}{4}$ in. screws. These will hold it to the lower edges of the dividers. Seven $\frac{3}{4}$ in. screws each side should be enough. Screw and glue on the drawer stop. Then plane it to exact size so the drawer fits sweetly. Fit the bottom.

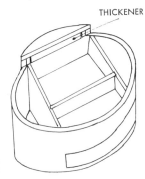

DRAWER STOP

Fig. 351

FINISHING THE TOP

The small moon-shaped piece of top has not been glued yet. Thicken it with a piece of hardwood and glue this assembly on to the top, making sure there is a slight excess to plane down to a perfect fit with the lid.

THICKENER

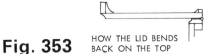

Fig. 352

Then fit a piano hinge so that its ends are $\frac{1}{2}$ in. from each edge of the sewing box. There is no 'stop' or restraining strap to the lid. The light weight of the lid will absorb the shock of the accidentally dropped lid.

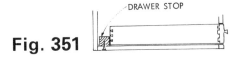

Fig. 353   HOW THE LID BENDS BACK ON THE TOP

The lid fillet has already been gouged out to accommodate the fibreglass liner.

FIBREGLASS LINER

Line the lid with kitchen foil, pushing it well into the corners, then line this with fibreglass mat, holding it in place with veneer pins. Stipple in resin and hardener with a stiff brush. One layer is sufficient to upholster on and sew through.

Fig. 354

ROW OF STITCHES   EVO-STIK CONTACT ADHESIVE TO EDGE

ROW OF STITCHES

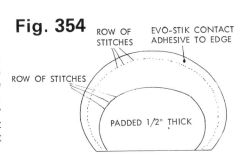

PADDED 1/2" THICK

When the padding and upholstery cloth have been stuck and stitched to it, the whole assembly is held into the lid with coloured gimp pins and the edge hidden with braid.

FINISHING THE LID AND TOP

Plane and sand off a curved compound chamfer as shown, then carve out as shown.

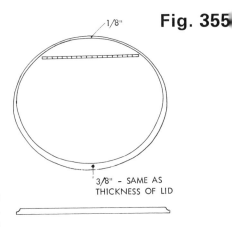

1/8"

Fig. 355

3/8" – SAME AS THICKNESS OF LID

Shape the edges of the lid round, so the finger tips can be inserted to open it. I extends 5 in. around.

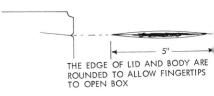

5"

THE EDGE OF LID AND BODY ARE ROUNDED TO ALLOW FINGERTIPS TO OPEN BOX

Fig. 356

Sand, polish, lacquer the brass fitment and piano hinge. Candle grease the bottom of the drawer and glue green felt on the bottom with Evo-Stik contact adhesive.

THE TRIPOD TABLE

This is the support for the sewing box but it can also be used for a coffee table. It has a veneered top to match the sewing box. Its part-laminated construction avoids the splaying of the three sliding dovetail joints which hold on the legs in most orthodox tripod tables. The legs are curved and the 'short grain' strengthened top and bottom with $\frac{1}{8}$ in. strips of hardwood.

The table is made in three sections, each with a short spar (crosspiece) and a leg. The inner part of each section is shaped to 120° and the three glued together. The table top is laminated in four layers, the upper sheet being used as a veneer. The outer curved edge has a $\frac{3}{16}$ in. thick strip of hardwood glued around it and scarfed at the joint.

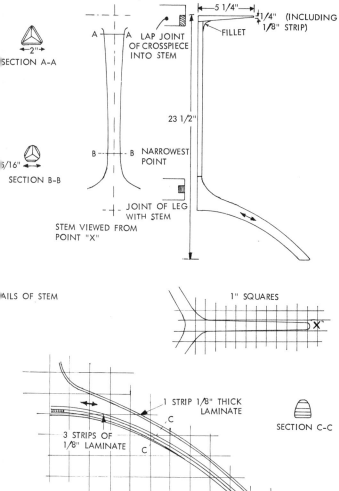

SECTION A-A ← 2" →

SECTION B-B ← 5/16" →

A — A LAP JOINT OF CROSSPIECE INTO STEM

← 5 1/4" →

1/4" (INCLUDING 1/8" STRIP)

FILLET

23 1/2"

B — B NARROWEST POINT

JOINT OF LEG WITH STEM

STEM VIEWED FROM POINT "X"

DETAILS OF STEM

1" SQUARES

"X"

1 STRIP 1/8" THICK LAMINATE

3 STRIPS OF 1/8" LAMINATE

C — C

SECTION C-C

1" SQUARES

Fig. 357

1. MAKING THE LEGS AND STEM

Use a 2 in. thick plank.

    Cut 3 strips of 2 in. wide, 36 in. long, $\frac{1}{8}$ in. thick.

    Cut 3 strips of 2 in. wide, $13\frac{1}{2}$ in. long, $\frac{1}{8}$ in. thick.

    Cut 6 strips of 2 in. wide, 11 in. long, $\frac{1}{8}$ in. thick.

1 strip 48 in. long, $\frac{3}{16}$ in. thick, 1 in. wide for the table edge.

    Cut three pieces as shown for the stem (3 pieces $18\frac{3}{4}$ in. × 2 in. × $\frac{5}{8}$ in.)

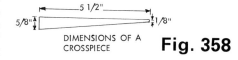

← 5 1/2" →

5/8" ⊥ ⊤ 1/8"

DIMENSIONS OF A CROSSPIECE

Fig. 358

Cut out the legs as shown using a cardboard template, made from the squared diagram.

Make a steel template set at 120° using $\frac{1}{16}$ in. steel plate.

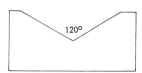

120°

1/16" THICK STEEL TEMPLATE

Fig. 359

Joint the crosspiece at leg on to each stem as shown:

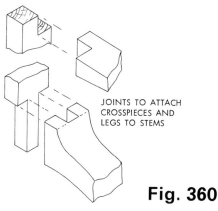

JOINTS TO ATTACH CROSSPIECES AND LEGS TO STEMS

Fig. 360

Scribe in the fillet to the top lap joint and radius in the curve to stem and crosspiece. Similarly, radius the top of the leg so the $\frac{1}{8}$ in. sheet will fit snugly.

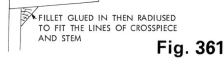

FILLET GLUED IN THEN RADIUSED TO FIT THE LINES OF CROSSPIECE AND STEM

Fig. 361

Make sure all three parts which make up the completed stem are identical.

Steam and bend the three 36 in. × 2 in. strips to fit and the glue and clamp each one.

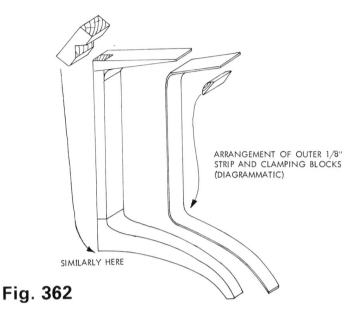

ARRANGEMENT OF OUTER 1/8" STRIP AND CLAMPING BLOCKS (DIAGRAMMATIC)

SIMILARLY HERE

Fig. 362

Use softwood strip to protect the laminate. Note the technique is similar to that used when the coffee table was made in an earlier chapters. Plane off the inner side of each component of the stem to 120° using the steel plate as a template.

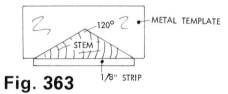

120° — METAL TEMPLATE
STEM
1/8" STRIP

Fig. 363

Mate all three together using blue chalk for a proper fit.

STEM
1/8" STRIP

Fig. 364

Then make 10 softwood clamping blocks from a 1 in. thick plank.

Set all 10 around the stems to equal the pressure when they are glued. Apply more

Fig. 365

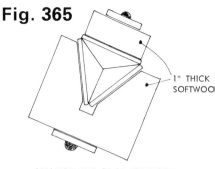

1" THICK SOFTWOO

ARRANGEMENT OF 10 SOFTWOOD CLAMPING BLOCKS TO GLUE 3 STEMS TOGETHER

pressure around the tips of legs an crosspieces using ribbon clamps.

Fig. 366

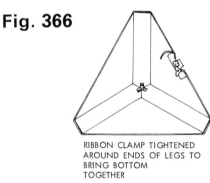

RIBBON CLAMP TIGHTENED AROUND ENDS OF LEGS TO BRING BOTTOM TOGETHER

Then glue the three layers of lamina beneath the legs. The principle is that the is an overlap in each layer, so they all ho each other on.

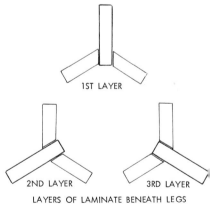

1ST LAYER

2ND LAYER   3RD LAYER

LAYERS OF LAMINATE BENEATH LEGS

Fig. 367

It is impossible for the legs to split awa Use plenty of clamps. Protect the legs wi a shaped piece of softwood above ar scrap $\frac{1}{8}$ in. below.

Apply pressure at the centre with shaped softwood block and a sash cram

Fig. 368

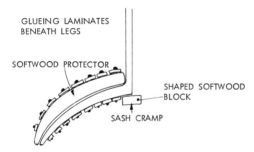

GLUEING LAMINATES BENEATH LEGS

SOFTWOOD PROTECTOR

SHAPED SOFTWOOD BLOCK

SASH CRAMP

running along the long axis of the ellipse. Mark out using 1 in. squares as shown. Scarf the hardwood strip around the outside, then glue using a string network and veneer pins nailed through plywood squares.

Shape the edge of the top as shown and mortise in the top of the stem $\frac{1}{4}$ in. deep. It

It matters not if the laminate strip splits, as it may well because of the compound curve. Shape the legs as shown with drawknife, block plane and Stanley shaping tool. Cut the legs so the top is level.

2. TOP

Cut four thicknesses and glue like plywood. Have the grain of the top layer

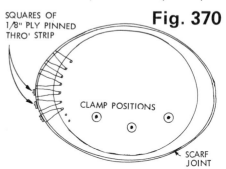

SQUARES OF 1/8" PLY PINNED THRO' STRIP

Fig. 370

CLAMP POSITIONS

SCARF JOINT

HARDWOOD STRIP IS GLUED AROUND EDGE OF TABLE TOP WITH A STRING WEB AND PLYWOOD SQUARES

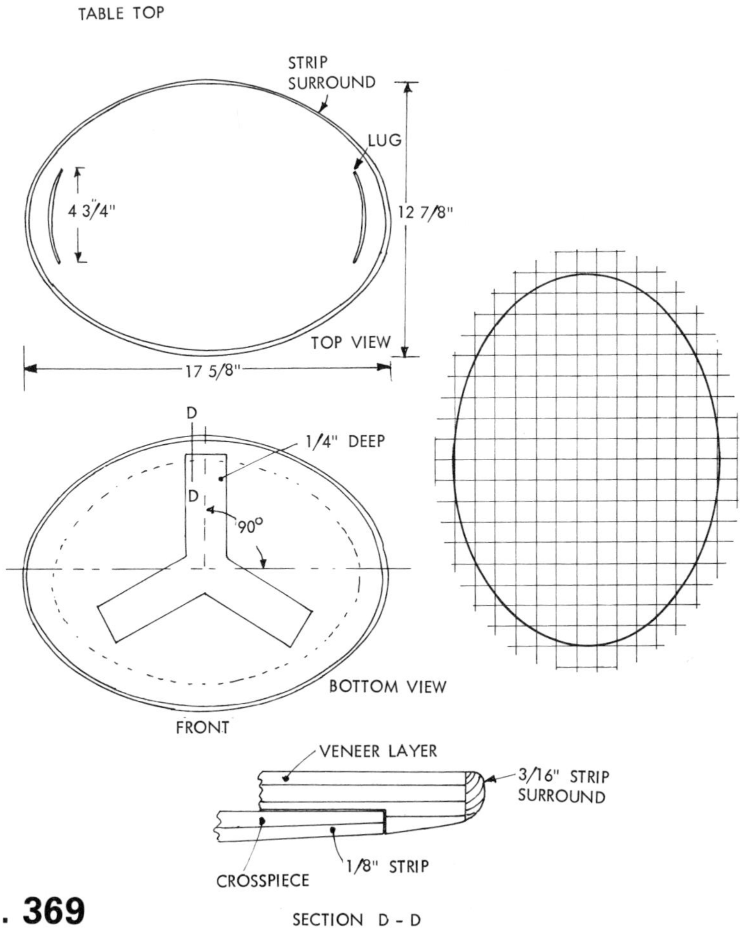

TABLE TOP

STRIP SURROUND

LUG

4 3/4"

12 7/8"

TOP VIEW

17 5/8"

D

1/4" DEEP

D

90°

BOTTOM VIEW

FRONT

VENEER LAYER

3/16" STRIP SURROUND

1/8" STRIP

CROSSPIECE

Fig. 369

SECTION D - D

may seem shallow, but remember there are 30 square inches of side–side grain glueing surfaces. Clean up the top and make lugs as shown from $\frac{1}{4}$ in. strip. Position by centring the workbox on the

Fig. 371

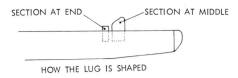

1/8" THICK

1/4" THICK

LUG SHAPE

SECTION AT END   SECTION AT MIDDLE

HOW THE LUG IS SHAPED

top and drawing around its edge. Steam bend the lugs and plane each end to shape.

Score around the lug with a Stanley, checking the position carefully, so that the sewing box sits comfortably between them. Remove waste to a depth of $\frac{3}{16}$ in. Keep the lugs $\frac{5}{8}$ in. high to remove after each 'check fitting'. They will be planed down and shaped after glueing.

Glue on the tripod stem. Linseed oil, french polish and wax.

This basic design can be used for a much larger table or for a three-legged stool, as the method of construction gives a very strong structure.

DISCUSSION OF THE DESIGN

It is a 'play' on the central theme of the ellipse. Both sewing box and table top are elliptical. The curving top rim is between two ellipses, and is itself curved.

Fig. 372

The groove between lid and box is an intersection of two ellipses.

Fig. 373

The drawer handle and its recess are the intersection of four ellipses.

Fig. 374

The straight line on the handle relates to the shape of the drawer and piano hinge.

Fig. 375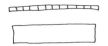

The inside of the box is a part ellipse each side, as is the lid, which is divided by the line of the piano hinge.

Fig. 376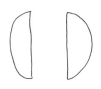

The padded lining of the lid is two part ellipses.

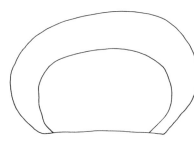

Fig. 377

The table top and sewing box have matching veneers which is another minor theme. The lugs set in the top of the table are ellipsoidal, and the legs are parabolic both in their own shape and the curve subtended by adjacent ones. The parabola is the first cousin to the ellipse.

Design and art in furniture for the house are very important and while we are seldom aware of their exact composition they are an essential part of our surroundings. The following chapter explains more fully.

18. Design and the Amateur Cabinet maker

By now you will have learnt all the techniques of cabinet-making. In doing so, you may have copied the plans in this book or gathered ideas from other sources. However you have acquired your experience, there will come a time when you will want to design your own furniture.

There are few, if any, readily understood books on the subject of design so I have started afresh and written a chapter for the amateur explaining what it is, its significance and how to go about gathering relevant information.

The simple approach to design which most people adopt is that they know what they like or they decide whether or not they could live with it. The keen amateur cabinet-maker will make and re-make a piece of furniture until it looks 'right'. When discussing design with his friends, the conversation becomes awash with such words as beauty, art, workmanship and aesthetics.

A piece of furniture for the home should have three qualities:
(1) Workmanship.
(2) Functional beauty.
(3) Aesthetic appeal (art).

These terms need explaining and elaborating and the reasons why a piece of furniture has to have these qualities will be shown.

1. WORKMANSHIP

This was discussed in the Chapter on 'Finishing and Polishing' but it is well to mention it in relation to the other two. It is the manner in which a piece of furniture is made. Given that it is fit for its purpose, is durable and is not wasteful of material, what should we expect from workmanship?

If the joints don't fit, or the drawers are too tight or the finish detracts from the natural qualities of the wood, then the workmanship is poor. If the joints are not cut perfectly but remain intact in spite of hard wear, the drawers slide smoothly after many years of use, and the finish of the wood has improved with use, then the workmanship is good.

If there is a slight waver of the surface or minor flaws at the edge of the inlay, or corners out of true, but such faults can only be detected by careful close scrutiny, then the workmanship is good. The furniture will have the imprint of conscientious workmanship but with forgivable human failings. It all adds to the appearance.

Sometimes furniture is made with the

Fig. 378

aim of showing off workmanship and technique. There is superfluous inlay, excess curves, and unnecessary fretting and carving. There are swirls and protuberances and even bits of enamel added as on the mid-Victorian chair in Fig. 378.

Workmanship and technique are of the highest standard but have gone mad. The design is dominated by what the craftsman could show off; the craftsman should always be restrained by the designer.

2. FUNCTIONAL BEAUTY

Because furniture has to be functional, its shape will have characteristics in common with the pure forms of nature and the precise lines of the best engineering products of man. These shapes are cold, simple and beautiful. It must be emphasised that such shapes are governed by biological, mathematical and engineering laws and it is coincidental that we find them appealing.

Examples of this kind of beauty are legion. The streamlined shapes of the dolphin and swallow ensure that they travel effortlessly for thousands of miles. The thin wings of the kestrel enable it to hover in the wind or dive at 100 mph. The delicate intricate skeletons of plankton or a dead leaf in winter may be attractive, but they function by supporting or carrying nutrition to the soft tissues.

The elegant clipper ship wasn't designed for the admiration and applause of the Victorian ladies, it was to sail as fast as possible to bring tea first to the London markets. The Spitfire and samurai sword were not evolved for museums or doting collectors. Brunel and Mailliard designed the simplest and cheapest bridges they could conceive. It so happened that these shapes are some of the most elegant ever made by man. The swirls of the galaxies and the rings of Saturn are not made for the admiring eye of the astronomer. Atoms, molecules and electrons and the dynamics of the universe determine their shape.

So what is it about some of the things around us that simply appeals and makes us say 'I could live with that'? It is not functional beauty alone, nor is it added decoration. It is something put there by the designer because he wants to say something through what he makes. This visual communication is known as art. There is, of course, considerable blurring between functional beauty and art, and in practice the functional beauty of an object has to be laid out before the art.

3. AESTHETIC APPEAL (ART)

The visual art component of furniture is the most difficult part to understand. The designer is trying to tell us something new about the way we look at things. His method is the same as in any other art form, whether it be music, ballet, opera, literature or poetry. There is a central idea or theme, with variations on the theme. Some things will be in harmony with the main theme(s), others will contrast with it, to bring it out into relief. There will be lesser themes and variations adding texture and richness. There is usually a symmetry or balance about the whole work.

Where a story is told about people the ideas are readily understood, as they are in plays, opera, ballet and literature. Music seems to be in all of us and we have no difficulty in enjoying tunes and melodies.

But static arts are more remote. There is more about things, less about human relationships. We have difficulty in appreciating even the central idea, which may be a colour, a line, an area of shade, the shape of a tree, the fretting of a chair back, a knot or whirl or even a space between objects.

Most of our contact with the world is through our eyes, yet we receive very little training into how to look at things and interpret what we see. We do not notice sunsets, or the shape of trees or what the colours of our roofs and walls really are. We are not blind to the things around us but that which we notice we make little effort at interpreting or understanding. The painter, sculptor, architect, carpet weaver and cabinet-maker seek to open our eyes and teach us to seek and see new relationships in the things around us.

As nouns and verbs can be made into an infinite number of sentences and spoken in an infinite variety of ways, and notes can be made into a multitude of chords and melodies and played differently by different musicians, so both abstract shapes and familiar objects can be joined and rejoined in an infinite number of acceptable relationships.

Here are a few examples of the visual art made in the last 3000 years, which are in the Victoria and Albert or British Museums and the Tate and National Galleries. They show how the hand and eye can put such shapes together.

Fig. 379

Fig. 382

From the side symmetry is replaced by balance, which passes through the base of the spout and the animal's head. The curves are in perfect harmony. Curiosity asks was the artist aware of all these shapes, or did he, as most of us would, do it instinctively?

This water pourer from around 700 BC made in Iran is the kind of object most of us would like to have on our sideboard. It is attractive because shape and decoration are in harmony. Its long spout and simple, striking decoration catch our eye. Why?

The shape of the spout is the same as the horse's (or is it stag's?) 'eg.

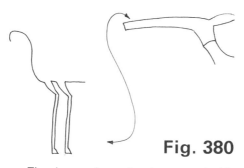

Fig. 380

The zig-zag decoration is repeated with eight variations:

Fig. 381

One wonders if the last shape isn't a representation of an early carpet or rug, as it looks like the Pazyryk rug which dates from 500 BC, the earliest carpet known. However, its pattern fits with the zig-zag and the dots in the squares, and the dots agree with the border around the neck of the jug.

Even the outline of the pot agrees with the shape of the animal.

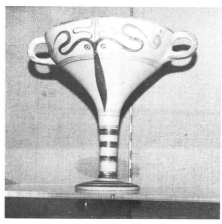

Fig. 383

This is a Mycenian vase from around 1200 BC. Its design is a stylised octopus. It is elegant and stylish, but more formal and remote than the water pourer. The central theme is the head of the octopus where the eyes stare out and the body and tentacles start. There is symmetry, not balance, which passes through the centre of the octopus.

Fig. 384

There are four rings around the base and six around the stem. The handles are emphasised by painting to create another pair of rings. The eyes and ends of the tentacles are variations on the rings. It is a perfect simple example of what design is about.

129

Fig. 385

This Celtic mirror from 1st century AD has an obvious plane of symmetry. The eye starts at the centre and passes outwards to the ever increasing, complex whirls. The curves and shapes are variations of each other, as are the outline of the mirror itself and the handle. These are set off by the zig-zag pattern in the background. It is a mirror fit for a sophisticated lady.

The two delightful sauceboats were made for everyday use in Bristol around 1775. Shape, embossment and floral patterns are all in harmony. The upper one has a bold top edge, a bold large floral pattern and a simple embossment. The lower boat is fussier in floral decoration and embossment. This pair could have been in use in any artisan's house, and his family could have looked at them and enjoyed their appearance without ever realising why.

Fig. 386

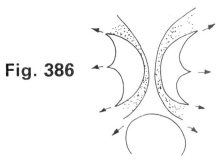

Fig. 387

Fig. 388

This silver water jug of 1765 shows the central idea as the overall shape. The spout balances the handle. The armorial shield catches the eye which then passes to the swirling border around the top and bottom. The swirling outline is reflected in the patterned borders, top and bottom, and the top and bottom borders match, and are variations of each other.

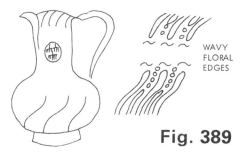

WAVY FLORAL EDGES

Fig. 389

The wavy floral edges to the top and bottom sections are in harmony with the floral decoration around the shield and the pattern is continued on the lid. The balls break up the swirls and are repeated on the lid handle which finally ends in a single knob. One's perception takes it in at one glance to find it pleasing, yet how much more rewarding to ponder why and how the designer worked out the harmony of the decoration.

Fig. 390. Madame Baccelli by Gainsborough.
Reproduced by kind permission of the Tate Gallery.

This is Thomas Gainsborough's Giovanna Baccelli—the elegant mistress of the Duke of Dorset. The lady's half smiling face and neck catch the eye, which then passes down to her low cut bodice, the folds of the blue ribbons on to the dress and finally to the foot. Why do they catch our eye in this sequence?

One normally looks at the face first, and in this painting, we are rewarded with a smile. As if to reinforce the attractiveness of the face, the outline of which is definitely parabolic, the painter has reflected it in the lines of her dress and pointing foot. This is added to by the shape of the tambourine in the brambles. The

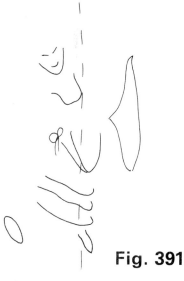

Fig. 391

shape of the lady's face and body is balanced by her outstretched left hand and the drape of her lace pinafore. The background of trees and sky add to the texture and richness. In all a clever, subtle piece of design which seeks to flatter the gentle lady.

Turner's 'Fighting Temeraire' shows an old sailing ship, which fought at the battle of Trafalgar, being towed by a paddle tug. The hard dark shape of the paddle tug with fire and smoke coming out of its chimney is contrasted with the ghostly shapes of the sailing ships behind it. The groups of ships and their reflections in the still sea are balanced by the blaze of colour caused by the setting sun. The colours are the other

Fig. 392. The Fighting Temeraire by Turner
Reproduced by kind permission of the National Gallery.

main theme in the painting. The ships, the sunset and the grey eerie stillness add up to the inferred demise of the sailing ship. The painting is allegorical as well as a wonderful design.

This Ming Rosewood Chair from the 16th century shows how advanced the Chinese were in their refined taste as compared with our heavy Elizabethan furniture. Notice how economical they were with the wood. The back splat has an attractive grained piece to catch the eye. The designer has made the top of the back, the arms and bottom rails variations on the same shape—which is why it is such an attractive chair.

Fig. 393

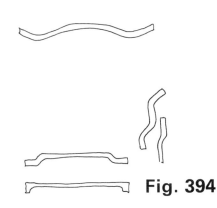

Fig. 394

Fig. 395 Margaretha de Geear (wife of Jacob Tripp) by Rembrandt.
Reproduced by kind permission of the National Gallery.

Finally, this portrait of one of the Tripp family painted by Rembrandt in the 1600's shows how a very simple design conveys a very profound message. The reproduction is a poor representation of the original, which must be seen to be appreciated. The hands and clothes fade into obscurity, while the face stands out. The face is surrounded by a simple hair style and a white ruffled collar.

Fig. 396

To appreciate the picture we have to compare its facial expression with others we know, and then imagine what she is thinking and what sort of person she was. It is an intensely human face. She is neither condescending or remote. It is the face of a woman who has done what *SHE* believed was right, yet has been aware of her own shortcomings. It is the face of individuality.

It is this individuality which art and design seek to bring out in us. We are all similar yet all different. Hence we look at things in different ways. Some of these ideas and relationships we perceive are useful and so we communicate them to our fellows.

Having been given our individuality, we are free to ask 'why?' about anything and everything, making our own observations and drawing our own conclusions. Then these works of art and design encourage us to perceive patterns and meanings sometimes in an abstract way and at a subconscious level. They warm the mind into being uninhibited whilst seeking relationships, and humorous and paradoxical in finding how they fit together.

Who could imagine a horse's leg could be related to a water spout or the arch of a horse's neck remind us of the curve of a jug, or an octopus tentacle the handle of a vase, or the swirls on a Celtic mirror be the same basic shape as its outline and its handle? How humorous to make the size of floral pattern on the two sauce boats reflect the fussiness of their upper edges. The curved row of embossments on the silver water jug could be nothing more than rows of drops of water which have coalesced. How more attractive and dainty does Giovanna Baccelli look because of the ellipse and parabola? I can't help wondering if Rembrandt, when he dreamed up the old lady's portrait, saw such a simple design as a facial expression staring from the centre of a canvas—a simple individual face, as if to emphasise her individuality.

There is no doubt that these objects increase the flexibility of our perception. They help us marry a commercial bandsaw blade to a home-made frame saw and produce a veneer saw so as to widen the amateur's ability to design pretty furniture. The general approach enables the mind to see a wooden aircraft gusset supporting the leg of a chair or making a lightweight coffee table.

As a Doctor, I have to join up together a series of seemingly unrelated meaningless symptoms and clinical signs to make a diagnosis. It is less a problem of a straight memory of facts which equal a disease, but more of having a perceptive mind. So often diagnosis is intuitive and comes before there is an awareness of the reasons.

How important, then, it is to have objects around us which have been well designed and which encourage this intuitive part of our thinking. This is no less true of the furniture we have around our homes, where we spend so much of our time.

Since the war there has been a vast expansion in the design of chairs, using wood, laminated wood, steel, plastics and aluminium. Cold-setting glues have revolutionised methods of assembly. But the designers have concentrated on mass produced forms which look more suitable for the office or factory than the home. They satisfy the requirements of workmanship and functional beauty but fail to please the eye.

Fig. 398

Fig. 397

This picture includes the 'Allegro chair' from the 1951 Festival of Britain and others designed by Charles Eames, Arne Jacobsen, Robin Day, Eiro Saarinen and Alvar Alto. Visually, there is not much to them.

Now look at the chairs by Renee Mackintosh and Neville Neal. By varying the sizes and spacing of the splats, the chair backs are exciting and interesting to look at. Notice in both chairs how the spacing of the stretchers has varied the rectangular spaces between the legs. Mackintosh's dark chair (at the top) has tapered and shaped arms to agree with the varying gaps and sizes of the splats. The 'Allegro' chair was a new concept in 1951. Its legs and arms taper—why didn't the designer vary the gaps between, or the thickness of the vertical splats? How much

more interesting would have been the appearance?

So as amateur cabinet makers and designers, what can we do to improve our own designs? Consider first what the

Fig. 399

Fig. 400. The 'Allegro' chair.

curve has been repeated at the bottom as a kind of pelmet, from which legs are splayed and curved.

The maker could have made all the drawers the same, but how dull and

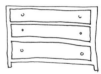

Fig. 402

unattractive. The principle of varying the size of the rectangle applies also where there are vertical divisions. Prominence should be given to the central divisions.

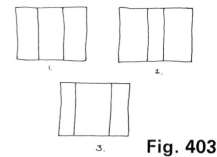

Fig. 403

classical antiques designers did and what is so often repeated in the popular reproduction furniture of today. They used the principle of making a central theme and building variations on it. In most cases it was the rectangle. It has to be a rectangle because this is the shape that comes from using planks joined by mortise and tenon and dovetail joints.

The eye prefers to look at 3.

Fig. 401. Georgian bow-fronted chest.

Fig. 404

This simple, attractive bow-fronted chest of drawers has two themes—the rectangle and the curve. The top drawer section has been cut in half to make two drawers. The shape of the drawers has been emphasised by cock beading, and the height of each drawer has been increased to add further variation. The bow front

The breakfront bookcase has the central section brought forward and emphasised and is more appealing than the one on the next page. (Fig. 405).

135

Fig. 405

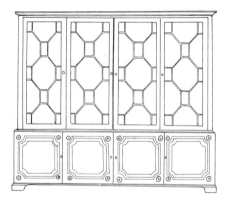

Fig. 406

This breakfront bookcase has only three sections, but how very attractive it is because the central dominant section is wider.

The rectangle may be divided unequally into three with an unexpected visual reward such as a decorated keyboard.

Fig. 407

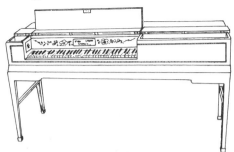

Try to imagine how it would look if the keyboard was in the middle.

Fig. 408

An oval enclosed in a rectangle provides a stark but very attractive contrast.

Fig. 409

The oval encloses a most attractive grained mahogany veneer, which is further emphasised by the direction of the veneer grain outside the oval. The curves of the legs and bottom, together with those on the pediment, further emphasise the curves of the ovals. The rectangles of the drawers contrast with and throw up the curves. Within the limits set by the strength of the grain, curves can be introduced into furniture. The livelier the curve, the more attractive.

Fig. 410

In this Chippendale chair, the central splat is the focus of attention. The upright sides contrast with it, yet compromise as

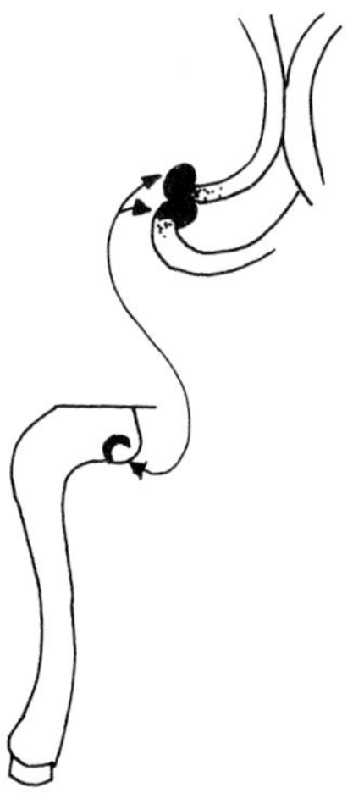

Fig. 411

they curve at the top. The curl at the top of the legs agrees with the knobs on the edge of the splat. The shape of the bottom half of the splat reflects the overall shape of the back of the chair, as does the shape of the seat.

Fig. 412

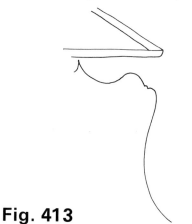

This small oak table is the epitome of curves and elegance. The eye looks at the curves of the legs and can hardly believe

Fig. 413

their delicacy. One's vision carries on up and around the cabriole curves at the top. Their bold curve is reflected in the wide curved pelmet beneath the top. The straight, thinned edge of the rectangular dish top contrasts with these curves. Imagine sitting in the half light watching T.V. each evening and seeing it out of the corner of your eye. How the mind would feast on those lines and curves!

As mentioned in other parts of the book, features of interest can be introduced by using grain patterns. The veneer saw will allow great freedom of choice. Knots, crutches, burrs, areas of fungal colour change, waviness, colour contrasts by mixing dark brown walnut with white holly or including sapwood and boxwood, can all be used. Grain patterns can be further emphasised by book matching or quartering.

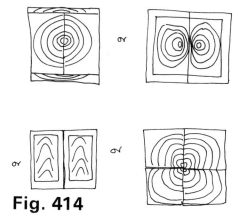

Fig. 414

All illustrations of furniture are in 2-D, but furniture is solid 3-D. The appearance is affected by different light conditions or by our different relative positions as we pass it by. Our temperate climate produces ever-changing light and shadows. We can use this to emphasise the features of our furniture. Recesses become dark, the rectangular shape of drawers can be emphasised by the shadow cast by the cock beading, shelves can be thinned by the shadow lines caused by thumbnailing, legs can be slimmed by rounding, where the shadow thus created is lost in the shadow beneath the chair.

Rectangles change to rhomboids and squares change to rectangles as we change our position relative to our furniture. What we are seeing are a series of variations on the same lines and shapes. Thus all viewpoints must be considered when designing solid structures.

The structure and shape of conventional furniture is greatly affected by the way it is joined together. Since the Egyptians started making furniture thousands of years ago, the basic techniques of dovetail, mortise and tenon and dowel joints have hardly changed. Not only does a hole have to be made for the tenon but there has to be sufficient wood around the joint to leave enough strength to satisfy the function of the part. This makes the furniture unnecessarily heavy and one only has to look at tripod tables and chairs to verify this.

Modern cold setting glues together with improved glueing and laminating techniques have provided the opportunity to make lighter furniture. The strength of such joints was proved by the construction of such wooden aeroplanes as the D.H. 88 Comet, the Mosquito and the Horsa glider. As shown earlier in the book, these techniques can be used to construct chairs, stools, tripod tables, office tables and sewing boxes.

Thus having explained what design is, how the designer expresses his ideas, and why design is so important, why does the amateur cabinet-maker start designing? As with myself, it starts with a need for a certain piece of furniture which cannot be found. He enjoys making it, so he adopts woodwork as a hobby. Then he sees a piece of furniture he would love to have but does not really need. So, through covetousness and envy he decides to make one. He realises he has skill in his hands and eyes so he builds a shed and accumulates a set of tools and pride then urges him on to make other pieces of furniture.

As he searches books and magazines for ideas, he will start to wonder why things are the shape they are. Curiosity will drive him on to read books about design and other kinds of woodwork. The pursuit of design will become a fetish until he finally discovers that it is what life is all about, i.e. making a meaning of the chaos around him. His wife and friends will then find him much more relaxed about his woodwork and the standard of his design will improve enormously.

There are two mental characteristics he will need. One is patience, the other the ability to hold several ideas in his mind at the same time. It will take several months to design a piece of furniture. It will need research, series of drawings, mock-ups of new kinds of joint, balsa wood models, checking and rechecking measurements. Even after all that work, it may be beyond his ability, or the final result may be disappointing. Through any such project there is a mixture of frustration and total dejection, together with success and utter elation. The ups and downs are like a spaghetti Western!

The other ability will depend on many factors. Tiredness seems to limit the number of ideas you can hold at one instant, rest increases it. Ideas may suddenly appear when you are least expecting them. You may wish to use together shapes you have seen in 2-D pictures and 3-D objects, which you have observed years apart, so they will have to be recalled from different parts of your memory. Things people have said to you may be remembered, with no accompanying pictorial memory. Art has to be compromised with function. Together with all this add the techniques you have learnt—glueing, sawing, laminating, jointing, brass casting. All these have to be brought together in the mind's eye at the same instant. Obviously it is easier not to try to remember every relevant fact, but have it stored where you can readily find it.

There are several kinds of information you will need to have:

1. From woodworking books.
2. Notebooks.
3. Photographs.
4. Nature.
5. Man-made objects.
6. Engineering principles.
7. Museums and Art Galleries.
8. Other wooden structures.
9. Scrapbooks.

(1) The literature on woodworking is vast. Start with a simple book on cabinet-making. The Woodworker Annual is a useful book to buy every year. Good sources of books are Stobarts, the publishers, M.A.P. publications and the Bicester Bookshop in the Post Office at Stretton Audley, Oxfordshire.

(2) Keep a spring-backed notebook of plain cartridge paper. Draw your ideas about your projects. Sketch things about you, trees, birds, shells, roofs, leaves, flowers, so as to develop your feel for shape, form and line. If you are poor at drawing buy a simple instruction book which will teach you line and shading. Those written by Adrian Hill are very useful.

(3) A good camera is a useful tool for recording what you see.

(a) It can become a source of material, an image bank; you can record buildings, trees, nature objects in museums.

(b) It can record what you have done, particularly in difficult assembly procedures.

(c) It can freeze movement to give ideas for line and form. These are not seen by the eye. It can be used to study the grace of movement of birds and animals.

(d) It helps in composition. It has been used by many painters. They take a picture and rearrange the images.

Buy a reflex camera, if you can afford it, together with a flash, three close up lenses and a 200mm telephoto lens. The latter is very useful when visiting museums where you are not allowed to get close enough to the exhibits.

Remember that photos are two-dimensional representations of three-dimensional objects and the results are altered by light and position.

(4) Nature: It helps your design if you have been steeped in nature from an early age. You acquire a feel for materials. Fields, woods, hills, mud, stones, clay, fish, green wood, dead wood, dead birds, birds' eggs, foxes, squirrels, clouds, winter, summer, elegant ash trees, solid oaks, dark yew, swallows' flight, rooks' flight all have a quality of their own. Study them with drawings and photographs. All the better if you have a microscope to see the fine structure of bone, feathers, plankton, mosses, seeds. The variation in form is tremendous.

The severe functional beauty will become apparent. It will provide the basic shapes for your furniture before it is given aesthetic approach.

(5) Man-Made useful objects.
Study Malliard, Brunel and Telford. Read about the history of architecture, both style and structure.

Look up the following:
Singer Sewing machine
History of the bicycle
Brunel's S.S. Great Britain
Ford Motor Company (early history)
Anglepoise Lamp (1954– still in use)
Rumford cast iron kitchen range (1780)
Spitfire and the Schneider Trophy
Gordon Russell
Dakota and P51 Mustang
Morphy Richards iron
Willys Jeep
Charles Eames and Robin Day (chair designers)

The history of industrial design is fascinating. Read Lewis Munford's 'Techniques and Civilisation' which gives early background.

(6) Engineering Principles.
Read Professor Gordon's Penguins 'Structures or Why Things Don't Fall Down' and 'The New Science of Strong Materials'. They will provide all the engineering theory you will ever need in the design of furniture. He describes some simple theoretic concepts in engineering. Objects can fail in tension, compression, twisting, bending and abrasion.

Wood is a very strong material when compared weight for weight with other things. In tension it is as strong as aluminium or brass. It is far stronger than cast iron. In compression it is as good as cement, but nowhere as good as most metals. Bending and torsion are more complex because wood can change its shape like plastic, but it is as stiff as steel and aluminium and better than synthetic resins and fibreglass.

Wooden structures fail at joints where there are holes or sharp corners. Professor Gordon is very lucid about concepts such as stress concentration and skin stresses and this explains why chairs break at the main back joint and tripod tables split at the lower joint.

(7) Other wooden structures. Wood was the main building material for most structures and objects of everyday use up to the beginning of the 19th century, and for most aeroplanes up to the start of World War II.

We are fortunate in this country because we have museums and exhibitions full of examples. With the Mary Rose retrieved from the bottom of the sea, the numerous models and illustrations in the Greenwich Maritime Museum, HMS Victory at Portsmouth, HMS Unicorn at Dundee, Cutty Sark at Greenwich and SS Great Britain at Bristol, we have complete examples of sailing ships up to when

Brunel employed both sails and propeller in his steel hull.

The Viking ships in Oslo, the mediaeval boat in Bremen and the 17th century Vasa in Sweden would provide 1000 years of history for the wooden ships. It would take another book to go into the shortcomings of these large structures, but suffice it to say they frequently came apart at seams and joints, particularly where the beams joined the ribs. This latter problem was never solved, even when iron brackets were introduced to reinforce these joints around 1815.

The structure of the farm cart was another fascinating use of wood. Solid wooden axles were used up to 1860 in Gloucestershire and Worcestershire. Wooden-spoked wheels, where the spokes were in compression, were used from Celtic times up to 40 years ago in this country. The Cotswold Country Museum at Northleach is worth visiting and Geraint Jenkins' book on the 'English Farm Wagon' is a classic on the subject.

The wooden aeroplane is a fertile area for study because it covers the transition in the use of scotch glues to water-proof cold setting adhesives. The later aeroplanes could not have been made without the use of the latter adhesives. It also covers the period when engineers came to understand such concepts as stress concentration and stress-skinned structures (1925). Again we are fortunate in this country in having early wooden aeroplanes in the Science Museum, well illustrated Great World War examples at Hendon, the Mosquito at Salisbury Hall, Radlett and the not so well illustrated or explained but still fascinating wooden aeroplanes at the Shuttleworth Collection near Biggleswade.

There are no specific explanatory books about how the mortise and tenon joint demised in the wing ribs of the Bleriot, or the advent of the welded metal fuselage of the 1916 Fokker monoplane, or how the multiple spars of the warped wing of the early monoplane gave way to the flap ailerons of the biplane, the wings of which needed stiffening with twin spars, compression struts and a mass of wires. The twin spars became box spars and together with a reinforced stress-skinned wing surface, became the wings of the De Havilland Comet racing plane and the Mosquito. Without cold setting adhesive, these ultimate developments of the wooden aeroplane would have been impossible.

The other topic worth study in the use of wood is architecture. Two fine books have been written by Cecil Hewlett about historical church carpentry, showing the progress from early Viking churches up to the use of threaded nuts and bolts and metal straps by Sir Christopher Wren in St. Paul's Cathedral in 1675–1710. It is strange that it took another 100 years for this practice to spread to the construction of ships.

The roof of Westminster Hall needs to be seen as it is the greatest mediaeval wooden roof in Europe, spanning 67 ft. You will need to write to your MP for permission as security is very tight. The extension of the Imperial War Museum at Duxford, Cambridgeshire, shows a Belfast Truss with a span of 100 ft. These were made from short lengths of softwood timber nailed together. There are similar trusses in the Hendon Aircraft Museum. However, wooden laminated beams have covered much greater distances, and in the early '60s a hangar with a clear span of 150 ft. was completed at Gatwick.

(8) Museums and Art Galleries.

The Victoria and Albert Museum has a comprehensive collection of furniture and many wooden artifacts from the earliest times. A broken wooden chair (or was it bed) shows the frailty of even the mighty Pharaoh's furniture— it had snapped across a pegged moritse and tenon joint.

The works of art and these artifacts need to be studied and if necessary photographed and drawn. Enough has already been said about the aesthetics of such pieces. The V & A, British Museum, National and Tate Galleries will provide enough design for you to chew over for many years.

(9) Scrapbooks. Collect magazine articles and pictures which interest you. Advertising photography is very good as are the pictures of wildlife in the Sunday magazine supplements.

It will take a decade to visit all the places suggested, collect books and photographs, and absorb the lessons they can teach. Hopefully curiosity will motivate you to want to know and see more, after you have broken the ice of initial shyness.

All that remains is to make time to think up designs and fashion furniture. Here are a few simple guide-lines:

(a) Get up early in the summer months when the mornings are light.

(b) Sketch and doodle projects in the long winter evenings.

(c) Lay out your garden with lawn, shrubs, concrete slabs and fruit trees.

(d) Pay your children to wash up, mow the lawn and clean the car.

(e) Keep off committees, don't waste your time with fools or nattering with neighbours.

(f) Avoid golf, mindless television and children's horses.

(h) Don't waste your time down at the pub, as alcohol rots the brain and liver.

Reflect that it takes half an hour to cut a square foot of veneer, 12 hours for the glue to set, 6 weeks for the woodworm to become rife in a sawcut veneer, 6 months for a deciduous tree to rest each year, 12 months to season a 1 in. thick plank of hardwood, several years to dry out a box log in a bin of sawdust and 150 years to grow a walnut tree. A piece of furniture may take a year   make, but last 200 years. So, what is a couple of hours each day over 10 years to make a competent amateur cabinet-maker/designer?

Index

A
Adhesives 36
Aesthetics 128
Annealing 24
Architrave (bookcase) 45
Arkansas stone 25

B
Back iron 34
Ball bearing 79
Balsa model 14, 40
Bandsaws 56, 59, 67
Bat repairs 38
Beeswax 39
Blanket chest 13
Blue chalk 17
Bookcase, rotating 79
Bookcase, small 39
Box stool 12
Brass carving 48
Brass casting 74
Breaking irons 34
Bucket furnace 75
Button upholstery 19

C
Camera 139
Candle wax 23
Carborundum stone 25
Card mock-up 14
Car filler 108, 118
Casein glue 36
Casting brass 74
Castors 44
Caul, veneer 60
Cementite 24
Chair design 134
Chair, jointless 106
Chair, Ming 132
Chalk, blue 17
Charnley Forest stone 25
Chest hinges 18
Chiselling 31
Chisel protection 25
Cock-beading 40, 47

Cricket bat repair 38
Cupola furnace 76
Curved work 62

D
Design 80, 126, 127
Diagonal checking 44
Drawer handles 48
Drawknife 33

E
Elliptical jig 116
Engineering principles 139
Excess glue removal 44

F
Felling 50
Ferrite 24
Fillets 93
Filling 90
Finishing 89
Firmer chisel 31
Foundry, amateur 75
Frame and wedge 17
French polishing 90
Functional beauty 128
Furnace, bucket 75
Furnace, cupola 76
Furniture design 135

G
Gainsborough 131
Gents saw 31
Glueing 36
Gouge sharpening 26
Groundwork, veneer 59
Grinding 25
Gussets 93

H
Hag's tooth 46, 83
Heat conduction 37
Hinges, chest 18
Hinges, piano 71

I
India stone 25
Information sources 138
Inlays 45, 62
Insets 61
Internal stress, steel 25

J
Jamming, saw 30
Jigs 93, 108, 116
Jointless chair 106

L
Laminating 36, 110
Lap dovetail 15
Linseed oil 39, 90

M
Ming chair 132
Mirror, Celtic 130
Mock-up, card 14
Model, balsa 14, 40
Mortise chisel 31
Moulds (casting) 77

O
Ogee legs 14
Oilstone 25

P
Pattern-making 77
Pearlite 24
Photography 139
Piano hinges 71
Piano stool 13
Plane sharpening 26
Plane types 33
Planing 31
Planing stop 22
Polishing 89
Practice joints 15, 16

Q
Quenching 24

R
Rebating 43
References 139
Rembrandt 133
Rotating bookcase 79
Rubber, polishing 91

S
Sauceboats 130
Sawcut veneers 59
Sawing 30
Sawset 28
Saw setting 28
Saw sharpening 27

Saw teeth 27
Scarf joint 119
Scrapers 26
Screw insertion 11
Seasoning 51
Secret dovetail 16
Sewing box, dovetail 64
Sewing box, laminated 116
Sharpening tools 24
Shaving breaking 34
Sliding stopped dovetails 42
Spiriting off 92
Steambox 113
Steaming 102
Stool, box 12
Stool, gusseted 93
Stress concentration 94
Structure of wood 36

T
Table, small 100
Table, tripod 123
Tempering 24
Tenone 43
Thickeners 18
Through dovetail 16
Thumbnailing 46
Timber defects 52
Timbers, seasoning 53
Tool steels 24
Tree cutting 50
Tree sources 49
Tripod table 123
Turner (painter) 132

U
Upholstered stool 98
Upholstery, button 19

V
Vase, Mycenian 129
Veneer frames 60
Veneering 36
Veneer saw 57
Vice 22

W
Wadding, cotton 91
Water jug, silver 130
Water pourer 129
Water seasoning 54
Wedges and frame 17
White glue 36
Wire edge 25
Wood structure 36
Workbench, small 9
Work cabinet 20
Workmanship 89, 127
Work shed 20